THE PURANA TEXT

OF THE

DYNASTIES OF THE KALI AGE

THE PURANA TEXT

OF THE

DYNASTIES OF THE KALI AGE

WITH INTRODUCTION AND NOTES

EDITED BY

F. E. PARGITER

GYAN

Published by

Gyan Publishing House
5, Ansari Road
Daryaganj, New Delhi-110002
Phone: 011-47034999, 9811692060
E-mail: books@gyanbooks.com

Distribution Network
gyanbooks.com
India, USA, Canada, UK, Australia

ISBN: 978-93-6208-297-8 (HB)
First Published, 1913

2nd Impression 2024

Printed at: Gyan Press, Delhi.

THE PURANA TEXT OF THE DYNASTIES OF THE KALI AGE
Editor: F. E. PARGITER

THE PURANA TEXT

OF THE

DYNASTIES OF THE KALI AGE

WITH INTRODUCTION AND NOTES

EDITED BY

F. E. PARGITER, M.A.

INDIAN CIVIL SERVICE, RETIRED; LATE JUDGE, HIGH COURT, CALCUTTA

HUMPHREY MILFORD

OXFORD UNIVERSITY PRESS

LONDON EDINBURGH GLASGOW NEW YORK TORONTO

MELBOURNE AND BOMBAY

1913

CONTENTS

INTRODUCTION

Authorities.

Accounts of the dynasties that reigned in India during the Kali age are found in the Matsya, Vāyu, Brahmāṇḍa, Viṣṇu, Bhāgavata, Garuḍa, and Bhaviṣya Purāṇas. All these, except the Matsya and Bhāgavata, set out the ancient genealogies down to the time of the great battle between the Pāṇḍavas and Kauravas, and immediately afterwards deal with the dynasties that reigned in North India after that time, of which the three earliest and chief were the Pauravas who reigned at first at Hastināpura and moved in king Nicakṣus' time to Kauśāmbī, the Aikṣvākus who reigned at Ayodhyā, and the Bārhadrathas who reigned in Magadha. But the Matsya and Bhāgavata break these up. The Matsya adds only these later Pauravas to the ancient Paurava line in connexion with the ancient genealogies, and introduces all the rest of the Kali age dynasties separately in some of its latest chapters. The Bhāgavata adds the later Aikṣvākus to the ancient line, and the later Pauravas and Bārhadrathas[1] immediately after the ancient Paurava line in its ninth skandha, and deals with all the subsequent dynasties separately in its twelfth skandha.

2. The editions cited in this Introduction are these :—

Matsya and Vāyu, Ānandāśrama editions of 1907 and 1905 (cited as *A*Mt and *A*Vā).

Brahmāṇḍa, Śrī-Veṅkaṭeśvara edition of 1906 (cited as Bḍ).

Bhāgavata, Gaṇpat Krishṇāji edition of 1889 (cited as *G*Bh)[2].

Viṣṇu and Garuḍa, Jīvānanda Vidyāsāgar's Calcutta editions of 1882 and 1890 (cited as *C*Vṣ and *C*Gr).

The only copy of the Bhaviṣya that I have seen, containing the dynastic matter, is the Śrī-Veṅkaṭeśvara edition.

The passages containing this dynastic matter are these[3]:—

*A*Matsya *50*, 57–89, and *271*, 1 to *273*, 55.

*A*Vāyu *99*, 250–435.

Brahmāṇḍa iii, *74*, 104–248.

[1] The Bārhadratha line was an offshoot from the Paurava line; see JRAS, 1910, pp. 11, 22, 29, 51.

[2] The edition begun by Burnouf cannot be adopted for reference, because it does not contain the Sanskrit text of skandha xii.

[3] The first few kings of the future Pauravas are named in MBh i, *95*, 3835–8 (which agrees with these authorities); and also in Brahma *13*, 123–141, and Harivaṁśa *191*, 11063–81 (which are wholly unlike these authorities and are obviously absurd).

*C*Viṣṇu iv, *20*, 12 to *24*, 44.
*G*Bhāgavata ix, *12*, 9–16; *22*, 34–49; and xii, *1*, 2 to *2*, 36.
*C*Garuḍa *140*, 40 and *141*, 1–12.
Bhaviṣya III, i, *3* and *6*.

The accounts are in verse in the śloka metre in all except the Viṣṇu, which is mainly in prose except in the final portion.

The Versions and their Characters.

3. The versions of the Matsya, Vāyu, and Brahmāṇḍa present a remarkable similarity. The two latter agree so closely that they resemble two recensions of the same text, and the Matsya, though not in such marked agreement, contains a text very similar. There can be no doubt that their versions are based upon one original compilation, and this appears from four facts: *first*, they all declare they are taken from the Bhaviṣya Purāṇa[1]; *secondly*, where the Vāyu and Brahmāṇḍa differ from each other, one of them not seldom agrees with the Matsya[2]; *thirdly*, single MSS of them sometimes vary so as to agree with the reading of the Matsya[3]; and *fourthly*, one Purāṇa occasionally omits a verse which appears in one or both of the two others, yet a single MS (or a very few MSS) of it has at times preserved that verse[4] and so testifies to their original harmony. These three versions therefore grew out of one and the same original text. At the same time the Matsya version has a character of its own which is clearly different from those of the Vāyu and Brahmāṇḍa, and was prior to those two (see § 24). The similarity of the three is however such that, by collating all their MSS, copious material is available for estimating what the original compilation was. The verse is almost epic. One line is generally assigned to each king, and two or more are sometimes given to the more prominent kings; and it is rare that two kings are dealt with in the same line, except in the early portions of the Paurava, Aikṣvāku, and Bārhadratha dynasties for which the chroniclers' materials were necessarily scanty, and in the latest dynasties which are treated succinctly.

4. The Viṣṇu and Bhāgavata have very much in common and their versions are generally alike, with the differences that the latter is in verse and the former in prose, and that the latter by the exigencies of its metre has less freedom and is often cramped. Both are distinguished from the Matsya, Vāyu, and Brahmāṇḍa in being much condensed, so that their accounts are often little more than a string of names fitted in with connecting words and occasional terms of relationship; yet they vary at times in important names and particulars so far as to indicate some independence. The Viṣṇu has ślokas at the end of the Paurava and Aikṣvāku dynasties, and the

[1] See § 7.
[2] Thus the Vāyu agrees with the Matsya in p. 17, l. 32; and the Brahmāṇḍa with the Matsya in p. 22, l. 13. Other instances will be found in the notes.
[3] Especially *e*Vā; as to which see *List of Authorities*: *Vāyu*.
[4] Thus p. 28, ll. 3, 4 of the Matsya version do not occur in any copy of the Vāyu or Brahmāṇḍa except *e*Vā.

whole of its final chronological and astronomical portion is in verse; and it cites all these as pre-existing ślokas. The Bhāgavata has at times fuller verses which resemble those of the three Purāṇas, and its final portion agrees largely with that of the Viṣṇu. Wherever the Viṣṇu and Bhāgavata have the fuller form of verse, they agree with or approximate to the version of those three Purāṇas, and so testify that they have been derived from an original which was the same as or closely like the original of those Purāṇas. These peculiarities show that these two are condensed redactions. They are also later, for the Viṣṇu elaborates its prose at times in the ornate classical style especially when referring to Kṛṣṇa-Viṣṇu [1], and the age of the Bhāgavata will be considered further on [2].

5. The Garuḍa stands by itself, for it gives only the Paurava, Aikṣvāku, and Bārhadratha dynasties, and its account of them is merely a string of bare names put into ślokas, more condensed than the Bhāgavata. It is evidently a late version; see Appendix I, § x.

6. The only copy of the Bhaviṣya which contains this dynastic matter is the Veṅkaṭeśvara edition, but its account is altogether vitiated and worthless. It says each Paurava king reigned at least 1000 years, and Kṣemaka's son was Pradyota (III, i, *3*, 82–96); and it declares that Gautama founded Buddhism in Mahānanda's time, that Gautama reigned ten years, and that his successors were Śākyamuni, Śuddhodana, Śākyasiṁha, his son Buddhasiṁha, and his son Candragupta (ibid. *6*, 35–43). It dilates, however, on more recent 'history' with elaborate details, and with a great quantity of new matter boldly fabricated brings its prophecies down to the nineteenth century [3]. In other copies the ancient matter has dropped out, and some very modern events have been particularized [4].

The Bhaviṣya the Original Authority.

7. The Bhaviṣya is declared to have been the original authority for these dynasties. Both the Matsya and the Vāyu expressly state that their accounts are based upon it. Thus in the Preface the Sūta says he will declare all the future kings—

tān sarvān kīrtayiṣyāmi Bhaviṣye kathitān nṛpān.

This is the Matsya version, and the Vāyu, agreeing, makes it more precise by reading *Bhaviṣye paṭhitān* [5]. Here *Bhaviṣye* cannot mean simply 'in the future', but must mean 'in the Bhaviṣya Purāṇa'. Again, when mentioning the Paurava kings after Adhisīmakṛṣṇa's reign, the Sūta introduces them with a verse, of which the second line runs thus according to the Matsya:—

tasyânvavāye vakṣyāmi Bhaviṣye kathitān nṛpān.

[1] It alludes to Kṛṣṇa thus:—Bhagavataḥ sakala-surâsura-vandita-caraṇa-yugalasyât-mêcchā-karaṇa-mānuṣa-rūpa-dhāriṇo 'nubhāvāt (iv, *20*, 12).

[2] See Appendix I, § viii, and Appendix II.

[3] See ZDMG, lvii, 276.

[4] See *List of Authorities*: *Bhaviṣya, infra.*

[5] See p. 2, l. 7 and notes thereto. The Brahmāṇḍa no doubt had the same line, but it has a large lacuna (see p. 1) and the line has been lost. On the importance of these words see § 23.

The Vāyu agrees, except that it reads *Bhaviṣye tāvato*[1]. The Matsya words can mean nothing but 'in the Bhaviṣya Purāṇa', and this is the best rendering of the Vāyu's words also, even if *tāvato* be not a misreading[2].

8. Again, when citing the genealogical śloka at the end of the Aikṣvāku dynasty, the Vāyu says it was *bhaviṣya-jñair udāhṛtaḥ*, and the Brahmāṇḍa *bhaviṣyaj-jñair udāhṛtaḥ*, but the Matsya says truthfully *viprair gītaḥ purātanaiḥ*. Here *bhaviṣya* and *bhaviṣyat* can hardly mean 'future' because the plural is used. Vyāsa alone was supposed to be gifted with foreknowledge, and those men could only repeat what they received from him; but, as the Sūta says he got his knowledge from Vyāsa directly (p. 2), it was futile for him to refer to them as authorities. The best interpretation therefore is that *bhaviṣya* means the Bhaviṣya Purāṇa, and that *bhaviṣyat* is a perversion of it. Lastly, in the concluding portion of this account of the Kali age the Matsya, Vāyu, and Brahmāṇḍa have this line generally :—

Bhaviṣye te prasaṅkhyātāḥ purāṇa-jñaiḥ śrutarṣibhiḥ.

Here also *Bhaviṣye* can only mean 'in the Bhaviṣya Purāṇa'; and that this was the meaning is testified to by two MSS of the Matsya which read the second half line, *purāṇe śruti-sarpibhiḥ*[3]. These passages therefore prove that the versions of the Matsya, Vāyu, and Brahmāṇḍa were borrowed from the Bhaviṣya or were at least based on it; and the accounts in the Viṣṇu and Bhāgavata must also have been derived therefrom, because they were later redactions as shown above.

9. The Bhaviṣya therefore as the source of all these accounts should be invaluable in elucidating them; but the copies of it, which I have seen or obtained information about, either do not contain this matter or present it in a wholly corrupted form. It is therefore, as it exists now, of no value for the present purpose and has been left out of consideration. An explanation, how it came to be tampered with, will be offered in connexion with the age of these versions (§ 28).

Prophetic Form of the Account.

10. All these accounts profess to be prophetic, yet the standpoints from which these Purāṇas view these genealogies differ somewhat. The Viṣṇu professes to have been narrated by Parāśara to Maitreya, and sets out the Paurava genealogy from the standpoint of the reign of Abhimanyu's son Parīkṣit, and the Aikṣvāku and Bārhadratha genealogies from the time of the great battle between the Pāṇḍavas and Kauravas[4]. This is absurd, because Parāśara was Vyāsa's father and was dead long before that battle and Parīkṣit's birth. All the other Purāṇas profess to have been recited by the Sūta to the ṛishis in Naimiṣa forest and (except in the Garuḍa) at their twelve-year sacrifice[5]. The Vāyu fixes the time of that sacrifice as the

[1] Not cited in the Preface (see p. 1).
[2] See also p. 3, note [45].
[3] See p. 59, l. 10, and note thereto.
[4] *C*Vṣ iv, *20*, 12–13, and *21*, 1: also *22*, 1 and *23*, 1.
[5] *A*Mt *1*, 4; *A*Vā *1*, 13–15; Bḍ i, *1*, 17, 18, 35, 36; *G*Bh i, *1*, 4–6; *C*Gr *1*, 3–11 They differ in the Sūta's name.

reign of the Paurava king Asīmakṛṣṇa [1], who is more often called Adhisīmakṛṣṇa [2], and who was fourth in descent from Parīkṣit; and the Matsya and Vāyu say the same in nearly the same words when mentioning that king in this account of the Kali age [3]. These two Purāṇas thus deal with these genealogies from the standpoint of his reign, and the Brahmāṇḍa, Bhāgavata, and Garuḍa constructively profess to do the same.

11. The Matsya and Vāyu carry out that view. They bring the Paurava genealogy from Abhimanyu and his son Parīkṣit down to Adhisīmakṛṣṇa as already past, and name Adhisīmakṛṣṇa as the reigning king [4]; the ṛishis then inquire about the Kali age, and the Sūta, declaring his intention to set out all the future kings, begins the list of future Pauravas from that monarch. Similarly, in the contemporary Aikṣvāku and Bārhadratha genealogies, these two Purāṇas name Divākara as reigning then in Ayodhyā and Senājit in Magadha [5], and mention their predecessors as past and their successors as future. Hence they virtually declare that these three kings were contemporary [6]. The position taken in the Brahmāṇḍa is the same, though it is obscured by a large lacuna in which all the Paurava and Aikṣvāku kings are lost, and its account begins with line 23 on page 12. Thenceforward it agrees with the Matsya and Vāyu and mentions Senājit as the reigning Bārhadratha king. The Bhāgavata and Garuḍa, though professing to have been recited in Adhisīmakṛṣṇa's reign, take the former the standpoint of Parīkṣit's reign [7], and the latter that of his son Janamejaya [8]; and both treat all the successors and also all the Aikṣvāku and Bārhadratha kings after the great battle as future. The Viṣṇu agrees with the Bhāgavata in this attitude, as already mentioned.

12. Accordingly the texts are framed for the most part in prophetic shape, but this character is not maintained completely because past expressions occur here and there, such as *abhavat* [9], *smṛta* [10], &c. Some MSS have tried to be more consistent by modifying such words [11]. One line found in three MSS frankly states that the whole Aikṣvāku dynasty was ancient, and naturally does not appear in any of the other MSS [12]. There can be no doubt therefore that the accounts have been steadily though slowly revised in details, so as to improve their prophetic character.

[1] In its verse, *1*, 12—
Asīmakṛṣṇe vikrānte rājany an-upama-tviṣi
praśāsatīmāṁ dharmeṇa bhūmiṁ bhūmipa-sattame.

[2] See p. 4, note [10].

[3] *A*Mt *50*, 66, 67; *A*Vā *99*, 258, 259.

[4] See p. 4, l. 6.

[5] See p. 10, l. 5, and p. 15, l. 13.

[6] In equating these kings some 20 years must be prefixed to the Paurava list on account of Yudhiṣṭhira's reign after the great battle, before Parīkṣit came to the throne, see § 14.

[7] *G*Bh ix, *1*, 6.

[8] *C*Gr *140*, 40.

[9] *E.g.* p. 10, note [23]; p. 11, l. 18.

[10] *E.g.* p. 5, l. 11; p. 11, ll. 14, 21.

[11] *E.g.* *bhavet* for *abhavat*, p. 10, note [23]; p. 11, note [61].

[12] P. 12, l. 26. It is no doubt genuine, for no one would be likely to fabricate and interpolate it to mar the prophecy.

13. Though the account is said to have been narrated to Paurava kings or to ṛishis in Naimiṣa forest, yet the ground from which the historic changes are viewed is Magadha. The Paurava and Aikṣvāku dynasties are dealt with briefly, with two kings generally to a line and with no mention of the lengths of the reigns, but the Bārhadratha dynasty of Magadha is set out with one line to each king and the length of his reign is stated[1]. After those three ancient kingdoms disappeared, the dynasties treated of are those which reigned in or dominated Magadha. All other dynasties in North India are noticed only in the aggregate, with the exception of the dynasty of Vidiśā, and even that is described but cursorily (p. 49).

14. The beginning of the Kali age has been discussed by Dr. Fleet, and he has pointed out that it began on the day on which Kṛṣṇa died, which the chronology of the Mahābhārata places, as he shows, some twenty years after the great battle, and that it was then that Yudhiṣṭhira abdicated and Parīkṣit began to reign[2]. But, as shown above, these Purāṇas virtually begin the Kali age dynasties immediately after the battle, and that position is the most convenient to adopt for the present purpose. The text of the Matsya and Vāyu[3] can be brought into harmony therewith by merely altering the order of a few verses without tampering with them, namely, by transposing the four verses containing the ṛishis' questions and the prefatory verses of the Sūta's reply from their position in Adhisīmakṛṣṇa's reign to the commencement of the account; and, so treated, those verses form a fitting preface to the whole: but it is unnecessary to print the questions here, and those prefatory verses are alone introduced as a sufficient preface (see p. 1).

Original Language of the Account.

15. There are clear indications that the Sanskrit account as it exists in the Matsya, Vāyu, and Brahmāṇḍa was originally in Prakrit, or, more accurately, that it is a Sanskritized version of older Prakrit ślokas. The indications are these: *first*, certain passages as they stand now in Sanskrit violate the śloka metre, whereas in Prakrit form they would comply with the metre; *secondly*, certain Prakrit words actually occur, especially where they are required by the metre, which the corresponding Sanskrit forms would violate; *thirdly*, Sanskrit words occur at times in defiance of syntax, whereas the corresponding Prakrit forms would make the construction correct; *fourthly*, mistaken Sanskritizations of names; *fifthly*, the copious use of expletive particles; and *sixthly*, irregular sandhi.

16. A full examination of these peculiarities would overload this Introduction, and the proof of them has therefore been set out in Appendix I. The above conclusion holds good for the whole of the text of the Matsya, Vāyu, and Brahmāṇḍa;

[1] The *Early Contemporary Dynasties* summarize all except the Māgadhas (p. 23).

[2] JRAS, 1911, pp. 479, 675, 686; and p. 62, l. 37 *infra*. Hence in equating the Paurava kings with the Aikṣvāku and Bārhadratha kings, some 20 years must be prefixed to the former.

[3] This portion in the Brahmāṇḍa is lost in the lacuna, as already mentioned.

their verses are older Prakrit ślokas Sanskritized. It also holds good for such portions of the Viṣṇu and Bhāgavata as have preserved the old verses; but the main portions of these two Purāṇas are condensed redactions composed directly in Sanskrit. The Garuḍa version is a more concise condensation composed directly in Sanskrit apparently. These conclusions are explained in Appendix I.

17. Judging from such specimens of old ślokas and Prakritisms as have survived, it would appear that the Prakrit used in the original ślokas was a literary language not far removed from Sanskrit [1]. The art of writing was introduced into India some seven centuries B.C., and there can be no doubt that it must have been adopted early in the Courts because of its manifest administrative usefulness. Records must have been kept by secretaries and chroniclers in the royal offices, and as those men would not always have been Sanskrit scholars, the language they used would presumably have been as elegant a Prakrit as their courtly surroundings and predilections required. There must have been ample written material concerning the dynasties from the 7th century B.C. from which metrical chronicles could have been composed by bards, minstrels, and reciters [2] in the same kind of language, to entertain not only their royal and noble patrons but also all those who found an interest in hearing of former times [3]. As Magadha was a great, if not the chief, centre of political activity during those ages, we can perceive how it was that the account grew up with Magadha as its centre (§ 13). The Māgadhas were celebrated as minstrels, and since traditions are most easily remembered, are best handed down, and confer the greatest pleasure, when cast into poetical form, it is easy to understand how this metrical account of the dynasties in literary Prakrit could have developed among them. Hence we may infer that the original ślokas were composed in Māgadhī; or, since the account, much as we have it now, was compiled and edited apparently in North India [4], and one verse that the Bhāgavata has preserved is in Pali [5], they may have been in Pali, either originally or perhaps more probably by conversion.

[1] Pali is such a language, and other specimens are found in the early inscriptions.

[2] Sūtas, māgadhas, and vandins; and other professional singers.

[3] Such men have existed in India from early times, and a graphic account of them, their methods, popularity, and influence, will be found in Babu Dinesh Chandra Sen's excellent 'History of Bengali Language and Literature', pp. 162–7, 584–5, 588–90. Since the brahmans could and did transmit the Vedic hymns with verbal accuracy for many hundreds of years, there is no improbability in supposing that bards and minstrels could hand down metrical accounts of dynasties with substantial though not with verbal accuracy. As these bards and minstrels existed in all parts of North India, they were a check on one another in the transmission of tradition, and there are indications that the Purāṇic traditions of the dynastic genealogies were compiled with some attempt to ascertain the truth. Moreover there was no objection to the accounts being written down, as soon as writing came into general use; and that would have been also a check on variation.

[4] See § 27.

[5] See Appendix I, § ii. Certain other words mentioned in Appendix I appear to be Pali.

Age of the Compilation of the Account.

18. The account supplies two kinds of internal evidence to fix the time when it was compiled, namely, *first*, the subject matter, and *secondly*, textual peculiarities; and both are important. The latter are dealt with in § 26, and the former is discussed first. The subject matter consists of two parts, the earlier setting out the dynastic details, and the later part describing the unhappy conditions that should prevail and stating certain chronological and astronomical particulars[1]. These are treated here separately.

19. The dynastic portion shows two stages of termination. The earlier of these stages is the period following the downfall of the Andhras and the local kingdoms that survived them a while. The Matsya account ends here with the mere mention of the Kilakila kings[2], and no MS of the Matsya contains anything later. The Andhra kingdom fell about A.D. 236, and it may be said that the Matsya account brings the historical narrative down to about the middle of the third century A.D. and no further.

20. The Vāyu, Brahmāṇḍa, Viṣṇu, and Bhāgavata all carry the narrative on to the rise of the Guptas, which is the later stage. The Guptas are mentioned as reigning over the country comprised within Prayāga, Sāketa (Ayodhyā), and Magadha, that is, exactly the territory which was possessed at his death by Candragupta I who founded the Gupta dynasty in A.D. 319-20 and reigned till 326 or 330 (or even till 335 perhaps), before it was extended by the conquests of his son and successor Samudragupta. With the Guptas are mentioned Nāgas, Maṇidhānyas, and others as reigning contemporaneously over the countries which surrounded the Gupta territory[3] and which were subjugated afterwards by Samudragupta[4]. The account takes no notice of his conquests nor of the Gupta empire. These particulars show clearly that this account was closed during the interval which elapsed between the time when Candragupta I established his kingdom from Magadha over Tirhut, Bihar, and Oudh as far as Allahabad[5], and the beginning of Samudragupta's reign, for he began his conquests immediately after his accession. That interval is approximately A.D. 320-330 or perhaps 335. It is hardly credible that, if this account was compiled later, it would have omitted to notice Samudragupta's conquests, or would have mentioned the foregoing kingdoms (which he subdued) in the same terms as his kingdom. The Gupta era was established in A.D. 320, and it may be concluded that this account was closed soon after the commencement of that era, or, if we allow some margin for delay, by the year A.D. 335.

21. Hence it appears that the versified chronicles were first collected about or

[1] The earlier part pp. 1-55, and the later pp. 55 ff.

[2] That is l. 15 on p. 48. The Vṣ says they were Yavanas, see note [82] thereto.

[3] See pp. 53-5.

[4] V. Smith's *History*, 2nd edn. pp. 267-9; and JRAS, 1909, p. 342.

[5] V. Smith's *History*, p. 266.

Errors, omissions, and rare verses.

30. Though there was originally one text common (but qualified by the revisions suggested in § 23) to the Matsya, Vāyu, and Brahmāṇḍa down to the end of the Andhras, yet present MSS show many errors and omissions and some misplacements. Such defects easily occurred through the carelessness of copyists[1], damage to[2] or loss of[3] leaves, or disarrangement of leaves[4]. The blemishes in the text appear to have been generally accidental. The brahmans who compiled the Sanskrit account could and did fabricate passages portraying the evils of the Kali age, but had neither inclination nor incentive to invent particular dynasties or kings of foreign or base origin. The chief changes that can be placed under the head of fabrications are various attempts by later readers to improve the text in details in which it appeared to be corrupt or inelegant[5], or to remove inconsistencies[6]. Among the latter some alterations, though made apparently in good faith, involved tampering with the text, as in the Śiśunāga dynasty, where the Matsya, by mistakenly introducing the first two Kāṇvāyana kings, names twelve kings instead of ten as all the other authorities declare; so that some copies of the Matsya have boldly altered the total to twelve, while others more cautiously have made the passage indefinite[7]. Misreadings have also produced incorrect statements and there are many errors in names and numbers[8]; but of deliberate falsification I have found no instance except in the story of the dispute between Janamejaya and the brahmans[9].

31. It is reasonably certain, then, that in the main these versions have suffered from nothing but carelessness and accident, and considering what little interest this account could have for educated readers, especially those brahmanically-minded, the text has been fairly well preserved. Much may have been lost altogether, for some passages have almost disappeared. One Purāṇa, or even one MS only, has preserved a passage or verse sometimes which is wanting in all the rest: thus *e*Vāyu, alone of all the Matsya, Vāyu, and Brahmāṇḍa MSS,

[1] As for instance the mistaken introduction of the first two Kāṇvāyana kings among the Śiśunāgas in the Matsya (see p. 21 and note [24]).

[2] Damage probably explains the frequent loss of verses here and there in different MSS.

[3] Hence no doubt the absence of all the first part in the Brahmāṇḍa (see pp. 1, 3, 8).

[4] As for instance the displacement in *e*Vāyu of the last half of the Early Contemporary Dynasties, all the Nandas, Mauryas, Śuṅgas, and Kāṇvāyanas and the first twelve lines of the Andhras after Viśvasphāṇi (see pp. 23, 24, 27, 30, 33, 35, 50).

[5] See p. 26, note [42]; p. 33, note [53]; p. 52, notes [37, 38, 47].

[6] As in p. 29, note [33].

[7] See p. 22, note [43].

[8] As where the Bh misread *trayodaśa* as *bhūyo daśa*, p. 46, note [23]. As regards the readings *Tuṣāra* and *Tukhāra* in pp. 45, 47, it may be noted that *ṣ* has often been pronounced *kh* for centuries in North India, and that the letter *ṣ* was used at times for *kh*; hence these two letters are often confused: cf. p. 6, notes [32, 43]; p. 19, note [28]; p. 41, note [80]; p. 51, note [24]; &c.

[9] See Appendix III.

contains the verse about Śāliśūka, and his existence might be doubted if it depended on that alone, but it is testified to by the Viṣṇu and Bhāgavata[1]. Again in the Bhāgavata only one copy has preserved the verse about Suśarman[2]. Such being the conditions, no verse should be discarded even if it is found in only one MS. Thus line 26 of the Aikṣvākus appears only in three MSS, and lines 12–14 of the Preface only in *e*Vāyu; yet it is not credible that they were fabricated, and they might easily have been regarded as valueless in the other MSS, for the former contradicts the alleged prophetic standpoint, and the latter merely name sundry and some unknown dynasties. Such rare passages appear to be relics of genuine tradition; and it is possible that lines 30, 31 of the Bārhadrathas found only in *j*Matsya, and line 28 of the Andhras found only in *e*Vāyu, may be genuine. Other peculiar verses will be found in the notes[3].

Formation of this Text.

32. The Bhaviṣya account having been the common source of the Matsya, Vāyu, and Brahmāṇḍa versions, the various readings are often equivalent or not materially different, so that real divergencies are far fewer than the places where the readings vary. The text now offered has been prepared according to the printed editions and the MSS collated. The Matsya and Vāyu versions are of far greater value than the Brahmāṇḍa, because they have been printed at Calcutta and in the Ānandāśrama series from a number of MSS, and I have collated besides 13 MSS of the Matsya and 11 of the Vāyu; whereas of the Brahmāṇḍa only the Veṅkaṭeśvara edition has been available[4], and I have seen no MSS containing this account. Where variations occur I have endeavoured to choose the most weighty, it being remembered (1) that the Matsya gives us the oldest version, *e*Vāyu the next, and all other copies of the Vāyu and the Brahmāṇḍa the third recension; and (2) that the Matsya is at times a somewhat crude Sanskritization of the old Prakrit ślokas, and the later versions may be more accurate. Their general agreement must be understood, but variations and omissions are always noticed, so that where no notes are given, the copies all agree.

33. The Viṣṇu and Bhāgavata cannot elucidate that common version except in the occasional passages where they adhere to it; and there they have been used to frame the text. Otherwise they can only help towards determining the correct names of the kings and the duration of the dynasties, and are so utilized in the notes. The Bhāgavata is also useful in determining the order of the kings, because, while the single lines devoted to individual kings might be and have been displaced at times in the Matsya, Vāyu, and Brahmāṇḍa, its versified lists preclude the

[1] P. 29, l. 10. He is also mentioned in the *Gārgīsaṁhitā* according to Max Müller in 'India: what can it teach us?' (ed. 1883) p. 298; but the passage is spurious, see JRAS, 1912, pp. 792–3.

[2] See p. 34, note [19].

[3] As p. 40, l. 13; p. 42, note [8].

[4] See *List of Authorities, Brahmāṇḍa Purāṇa.*

25. The second portion of the account referred to in § 18 consists of (1) an exposition of the evils of the Kali age, and (2) a chronological-astronomical summary of the age, and is found in the Matsya, Vāyu, and Brahmāṇḍa. This second portion therefore existed in the earliest version compiled soon after the middle of the 3rd century, yet with a difference. While the Matsya has a good deal of the exposition, the Vāyu and Brahmāṇḍa version contains some 32 more lines and is nearly twice as long as the Matsya; so that a large addition was made at the revision, and it was made mostly at the first revision, because the account in *e*Vāyu has the full description with the exception of a few verses which may have been omitted by oversight. As regards the chronological-astronomical summary however, all three Purāṇas practically agree, the Matsya wanting only two lines. These particulars therefore were complete in the first compilation and were not added to in the revisions; and this conclusion is corroborated by the fact that this summary in all three Purāṇas brings the reckoning down definitely only to the end of the Andhras, and uses the vague term *Andhr-ânt-âdyās* in referring to future kings [1]. No addition was therefore made to it at the revisions to bring it down to the Gupta era. It belongs then to the middle of the 3rd century and must be interpreted accordingly; and it shows that the *Saptarṣi* cycle of 2700 years was known and was in use in India at that time, that is, about three centuries earlier than has been supposed [2]. The treatment of these two subjects, the evils of the Kali age and the chronological-astronomical particulars, affords an excellent illustration of what the revisers did and did not do. They had no knowledge with which to augment or alter those particulars and so left them unmodified; but the deterioration of the Kali age was a subject congenial to pessimistic brahmanic views and they freely availed themselves of the opportunity of dilating upon it.

26. I come now to the subject of textual peculiarities mentioned in § 18. Further information may be discovered by examining the divergent readings of the same passage and especially the corruptions in names. A study of the variations shows that ordinarily the copyists copied what they found in dull good faith to the best of their ability, often writing the same name differently in contiguous lines [3]. Moreover these dynasties of śūdras and foreigners offered little inducement to readers to alter the texts. Hence the variations that crept in were mostly due to clerical blunders or to misreadings of the MSS copied; and the mistake might be detected and corrected, or might not. If not detected, the erroneous letter remained; if detected, the correct letter was written or inserted, and the incorrect letter was sometimes cancelled but was not seldom left uncancelled. In that state

shape. They have no doubt been freely added to since, see § 28, note.

[1] P. 58, ll. 9, 12, and p. 61, l. 23.

[2] See Encycl. Brit., 'Hindu Chronology'.

[3] Cf. the corruptions in the well-known names, *Kauśāmbī* (p. 5, note [19]) and *Kāṇvāyana* (p. 34, note [11]). Yet sometimes errors were caused by a droll perversity or would-be cleverness, cf. p. 41, note [80]; p. 42, note [1]; and p. 47, note [71]: and sometimes where the text had become corrupt, it was boldly paraphrased afresh, cf. p. 26, note [42]; p. 33, note [62]; but the latter was probably the effort of a reader and not of a copyist.

the passage was repeated in subsequent copies, and misreadings are important chronologically if we can explain how they arose. If their divergent readings of the same name or passage be written in the ancient scripts, and resemble one another so closely in a particular script that an ordinary copyist might easily misread one for another, it may be inferred that the variation must have arisen out of a MS written in that script, and therefore that the text once existed in that script, that is, it had been written during the time when that script was in use. In this way it may be ascertained which are ancient and which are mediaeval or even modern corruptions. Most of the variations have arisen from misreadings of the Gupta and later scripts[1], but for the present purpose it is unnecessary to consider any that arose from misreading scripts that came into use after A.D. 330, the date when this account was finally compiled, and it is only essential to see whether any variations point to misreadings of Kharoṣṭhī or of Brāhmī.

27. It would overload this Introduction to examine such particulars here, and in Appendix II are noticed such cases as appear to throw light on this subject. It is shown there that errors are found in the Matsya, Vāyu, and Viṣṇu which point to misreadings of Kharoṣṭhī as their source. Hence it seems there is reasonable ground for inferring that this account of the dynasties was, in its earliest form, written in Sanskrit in Kharoṣṭhī, and, since Kharoṣṭhī was current only in Upper India, that the account was probably put together there: that is, since the earliest account was in the Bhaviṣya, that the Bhaviṣya account was written originally in Kharoṣṭhī and was put together in Upper India. If these conclusions are sound, it would follow that the account could not have been compiled later than about A.D. 330, because Kharoṣṭhī went out of use about that time. . Further, judging from the point of view displayed in the portion which was added to the Bhaviṣya to bring it up to date about the year 320[2], it would seem that the composers of this portion were probably in Madhyadeśa, and more particularly perhaps in the country between Magadha and Mathurā. The Viṣṇu account was probably based on the same original for three reasons: (1) its dynastic matter agrees closely with that in the Vāyu and Brahmāṇḍa, and also the ślokas where it has preserved them; (2) it closes its account where they close theirs; and (3) it is not probable that its account was a new and independent compilation from early chronicles when the compilations in the Bhaviṣya, Matsya, and Vāyu were available. At the same time it was composed early enough for its account to be drawn from Kharoṣṭhī MSS. It seems probable then that the main part of the Viṣṇu which is in prose was composed from those Purāṇas directly in Sanskrit not very long after the Gupta era, (say) perhaps before the end of the 4th century. The Bhāgavata was, as shown in Appendix II, composed afresh in Sanskrit, except in so far as it has incorporated old ślokas; and must have been based on the same materials for the same three reasons mentioned above, yet most probably on the Viṣṇu chiefly, to which it has

[1] Many such may be detected in the notes, such as mistakes of *p* and *y*, *n* and *r*, *l* and *n*. *r* and *v*, *c* and *v*, &c.

[2] See §§ 19–21.

the closest resemblances [1]; and it was probably not composed till the 8th century or even later. These conclusions strictly refer only to these dynastic accounts.

Sanskritization of the Account.

28. It has been shown that the account was first compiled for the Bhaviṣya Purāṇa about the middle of the 3rd century A.D., and there are reasons why that was appropriate. Since royal genealogies constituted one of the subjects which every Purāṇa should treat of, the Bhaviṣya, as a work professing to deal with the future, could hardly ignore the dynasties that reigned after his time; and the dynasties of the Kali age would hold the same position in it that the ancient genealogies held in the Purāṇas which dealt with ancient stories [2]. The account of

[1] See p. 18, note [7]; p. 25, notes [6, 16, 22]; p. 28, note [30]; and in its description of the evils of the Kali age, where the Viṣṇu and it have matter peculiar to themselves. It has resemblances to the Brahmāṇḍa in p. 22, note [46]; p. 35, note [42]; p. 41, note [80].

[2] The title Purāṇa indicates that such works narrated ancient stories, but the Bhaviṣya professed by its name to treat of the future, and the title Bhaviṣya Purāṇa is a contradiction in terms. Such a name could hardly have been possible, until the title Purāṇa had become so thoroughly specialized as to have lost its old meaning and become the designation of the kind of works now known by this title. The name Bhaviṣya Purāṇa therefore proves that the kind of composition that passed under the title Purāṇa had become stereotyped before the title could have been assumed by the Bhaviṣya; that is, that genuine Purāṇas must have preceded it so long before as to have specialized the title Purāṇa. It has been shown above that the Bhaviṣya existed in the middle of the 3rd century, hence some at least, if not many, of the true Purāṇas must be considerably older. This inference does not, of course, mean that the Purāṇas contained at their beginning all that they contain now, because there can be no doubt that they have been freely added to since. It is highly probable that they consisted at first mainly of ancient stories, genealogies, ballads, &c., which formed the popular side of ancient literature, and were quite probably in Prakrit originally. In fact, it seems to me that they were largely in an old literary Prakrit used by the higher classes, but that, as the spoken languages diverged in time more and more from Sanskrit through political vicissitudes, that literary Prakrit became unintelligible, while Sanskrit remained the only polished language of brahmanic Hinduism. Hence it was natural that this literature should be Sanskritized, if it was to be preserved, a process that was not difficult because the old literary Prakrit was not far removed from Sanskrit, yet it was not always effected completely, especially in poetry where the necessity of preserving the metre sometimes qualified that process, and hence Prakrit forms might survive embedded in good Sanskrit as *pravartayitvā* in p. 88, l. 14. It was the brahmans probably who saved and improved the status of those old compositions by converting them into Sanskrit, and afterwards, perceiving what an excellent means they provided for reaching popular thought, made use of them to propagate their own views and doctrines by freely augmenting them with brahmanical fables, philosophical discussions, and ceremonial expositions which were enforced with the authority of Vyāsa. I should say therefore, speaking generally, that what may be called the kṣatriya, or better perhaps the popular, matter of the Purāṇas constituted the really old and genuine *purāṇa*, and that the brahmanical and ritual matters now found in them were later additions and interpolations made from time to time. This inference is based on the fact that it is in the former portion of the Purāṇas that peculiarities occur such as are

these dynasties would then naturally have been required for the Bhaviṣya, and all that was necessary was to collect the Prakrit metrical chronicles and convert them into Sanskrit prophecies uttered by Vyāsa [1]. That was done as shown in Appendix I, and then the Matsya first, and the Vāyu and Brahmāṇḍa afterwards, borrowed the account from the Bhaviṣya. The original Bhaviṣya account has been lost, but these three Purāṇas have preserved and reveal what its contents were; otherwise it would have been impossible to know what it contained at that time. A comparison of their accounts with the present condition of the Bhaviṣya shows to what bold lengths pious fraud has gone.

29. Since the chronicles existed in the form of ślokas in literary Prakrit, all that was necessary was (1) to convert the Prakrit words into Sanskrit, and (2) substitute futures for past tenses, while maintaining the śloka metre. The first process appears to have been made word by word as nearly as possible [2], and the Sanskritization was crude as the many Prakritisms noticed in Appendix I indicate, for they must have existed in the Bhaviṣya account, otherwise it is difficult to see how they could appear in the Matsya, Vāyu, and Brahmāṇḍa. Indeed it would almost seem that the Bhaviṣya account may have been composed in a literary Prakrit rather than in true Sanskrit. Both processes of conversion would have upset the metre, since Prakrit words are sometimes a syllable longer or shorter than their Sanskrit equivalents, and future tenses are generally longer than past tenses; hence three correctives were adopted; (1) words were dropped which might be omitted without impairing the sense, such as 'reigned', 'years', &c.; (2) compensatory expletives were inserted; and (3) the sentence was occasionally recast [3]. Still the Sanskritization was imperfect and sometimes grammar or metre was sacrificed, and these blemishes have persisted, as pointed out in Appendix I, in spite of attempts to rectify them afterwards.

noticed in Appendix I. It seems highly probable too that it was largely through the Purāṇic literature, that brahmanism re-established itself over the people and secured the revival of Hinduism and the downfall of Buddhism. That was what actually happened in Bengal and has been called by Babu Dinesh Chandra Sen the 'Pauranik Renaissance', which he has described very clearly in his excellent work 'The History of Bengali Language and Literature' (ch, iv).

[1] This was, as has been pointed out above, the beginning of a pious fraud, whereby the prophetic matter has been continually revised and brought up to date in the Bhaviṣya. To be able to point to such prophetic accounts in the literature would have been a valuable weapon, moreover, in the hands of the brahmans against adversaries of other creeds; and it may be noted in this connexion, that the Veṅkaṭeśvara edition of the Bhaviṣya has incorporated a summary of the Biblical account from Adam to Abraham in the early chapters of Genesis (Bhav. iii, *4*, 17–19, 29–60; *5*, 1–20). There can hardly be any doubt that this interpolation has been made very recently in view of Christianity.

[2] See the phrase *aṣṭāviṁśati tathā varṣā* in Appendix I, § i.

[3] Cf. for instance the lines in the *Andhras* where the two versions are given, and the notes thereto.

soon after the middle of the 3rd century [1] in the shape found in the Matsya, and that they were extended to the rise of the Gupta kingdom before the year 335, which augmented compilation is what the Vāyu and Brahmāṇḍa contain and the Viṣṇu and Bhāgavata have condensed. It has been shown that the Matsya, Vāyu, and Brahmāṇḍa all obtained their accounts from the Bhaviṣya. Hence it would appear that the earlier compilation must have been incorporated in the Bhaviṣya about or soon after the middle of the 3rd century, and that its prophetic account was extended in the later compilation before the year 335. There is nothing improbable in this augmentation, because the Bhaviṣya account has been continually supplemented even up to the present time in order to keep its prophecies up to date, as shown above (§ 6). It follows then that the Bhaviṣya must have been in existence in the middle of the 3rd century [2]; and it would appear that the Matsya borrowed what the Bhaviṣya contained before the Gupta era, and that the Vāyu and Brahmāṇḍa borrowed the Bhaviṣya's augmented account about or soon after the year 330 or 335. Further remarks on these dates are offered in §§ 43 ff.

22. Further light is thrown on these points by the MS *e*Vāyu, which contains the full account but holds a position intermediate between the general Vāyu version and the Matsya version. The facts to be explained are these. The Matsya has one version which contains only the shorter compilation, the Vāyu generally has a somewhat different version containing the full account, the Brahmāṇḍa has the full compilation in a version resembling the Vāyu closely, *e*Vāyu has a version containing the full compilation in a text intermediate between the Matsya and all other copies of the Vāyu [3], and yet all these Purāṇas declare they borrowed their accounts from the Bhaviṣya.

23. The only theory which appears to me to explain all these facts is this. The Matsya borrowed from the Bhaviṣya the shorter account about (say) the last quarter of the 3rd century. The Bhaviṣya account was then extended down to the time when the Gupta kingdom had acquired the territories assigned to it, and its language was revised [4]; that would be (say) about 320–325. The Vāyu copied that extended and revised account from the Bhaviṣya almost immediately, and that is the version found in *e*Vāyu. Afterwards, the language of the Bhaviṣya version was revised again, and this must have been done very soon, (say) about 330–335, before the Gupta kingdom had developed into the Gupta empire by Samudragupta's conquests, because it could hardly have failed to notice that immense change if the revision had been later. This second revision was soon adopted by the Vāyu and is the version found now in Vāyu MSS generally. The fact that

[1] There is an apparent indication that a compilation was begun in the latter part of the 2nd century in the Andhra king Yajñaśrī's reign, for 5 MSS of the Matsya (of which three appear to be independent, namely, *b*, *c*, and *l*) speak of him as reigning in his ninth or tenth year; see p. 42, note [6]. If so, the Bhaviṣya may perhaps have existed in that century.

[2] But not of course in its present condition.

[3] The position of *e*Vā is best shown in the account of the Mauryas, pp. 27–9.

[4] This, as already pointed out, is what has been habitually done to it.

*e*Vāyu stands unique among all the Vāyu MSS suggests that no long interval could have separated the second revision from the first, and that the first revised version was quickly superseded by the second in the Vāyu. I cannot speak about the Brahmāṇḍa in any detail, because I have not been able to collate any MSS of it: yet two points may be noticed, *first*, it agrees closely with the general Vāyu version[1] and yet condenses the account sometimes[2]; and *secondly*, the probability is that it borrowed the second revised version from the Bhaviṣya not long after the Vāyu adopted that[3]. The Bhaviṣya existed in writing when the first revision appeared in it, because *e*Vāyu, as well as all other Vāyu MSS, uses the word *paṭhita* when acknowledging its indebtedness to the Bhaviṣya (see § 7). The Matsya uses the word *kathita* in the corresponding passage, which might imply that it borrowed the account orally at the earlier stage, but that is not probable because of the inferences brought out in Appendix II.

24. If this explanation be tenable, the Matsya version of these dynasties of the Kali age is older than those of the Vāyu and Brahmāṇḍa[4], and *e*Vāyu gives us the earliest text of the Vāyu. The styles of the versions appear to support this explanation, for the Matsya version is somewhat crude at times, and the Vāyu text has been revised more than the Matsya as shown by the story of king Janamejaya's dispute with the brahmans[5]. Though later than the Matsya, the Vāyu account may yet be more accurate at times by reason of the revision which it underwent[6]. The Vāyu has Prakritisms sometimes where the Matsya has correct Sanskrit[7], but this fact is not incompatible with that conclusion, and for either or both of two reasons; (1) the Matsya may have emended such defects at the time of taking the account from the Bhaviṣya, while the Vāyu may have copied them as they stood; and (2) a process of silent emendation has been in continual operation in the MSS[8]. Further it would seem that the three accounts may have been compared at times, for this would explain certain small variations which appear occasionally between the Vāyu and Brahmāṇḍa in the direction of the Matsya[9].

[1] The agreement is not only here, but large portions also of the Brahmāṇḍa are almost identical with the Vāyu.

[2] As in p. 22, note[46]; p. 35, note[42]. In those passages the Bhāgavata partially resembles it, and may have copied from it.

[3] Unless (what is possible) the Brahmāṇḍa copied its account from the Vāyu (see note[1]); and its paraphrase of *Aśoka-vardhanaḥ* as *aśokānāṁ ca tṛpti-daḥ*, if not a late attempted emendation of a text that was unintelligible, suggests that it could not have been composed until Aśoka was wholly forgotten.

[4] I differ therefore from Sir R. G. Bhandarkar, who estimated (without giving reasons) the Vāyu account to be older than the Matsya; but agree with him that the Viṣṇu is later and the Bhāgavata the latest: *Early History of the Dekhan*, 1895, p. 162. In all this discussion I am dealing only with the time when these accounts of the dynasties of the Kali age were incorporated in these Purāṇas, and not with the age of these Purāṇas themselves such as they were in that early period; see § 28, note.

[5] See Appendix III.

[6] As in the arrangement of verses (see pp. 27, 44), and in many of the readings in the concluding portion (pp. 55 ff).

[7] See Appendix I, § iii, first instance.

[8] *E.g.* p. 18, note[7]; see Appendix I, § ii.

[9] These conclusions do not imply that these Purāṇas existed then in their present

they no doubt, and many of the Purāṇas certainly, existed before the Bhaviṣya (§ 28, note). Metrical accounts of the dynasties, that reigned in North India after the great battle between the Pāṇḍavas and Kauravas, grew up gradually, composed in ślokas in a literary Prakrit and recited by bards and minstrels (§§ 15–17); and, after writing was introduced into India about seven centuries B.C., there could have been no lack of materials from which those accounts could have been composed and even written down (§ 17). Such accounts were composed in or near Magadha more particularly, which was one of the chief centres of political life and thought during those times (§ 13) and was famous for its bards and minstrels (§ 17); and the Prakrit in which they were expressed was no doubt a literary Māgadhī or Pali (§ 17).

49. The Bhaviṣya professed to treat of future events, subsequent to that battle which practically ushered in the Kali age (§ 14), and should therefore supply an account of the dynasties of that age, because royal vaṁśas were one of the prescribed topics of the Purāṇas (§ 28); and, as the Purāṇas professed to have been composed by Vyāsa, it took the same standpoint. Hence it appropriated the Prakrit metrical accounts, converted the Prakrit ślokas into Sanskrit ślokas, and altered them to the form of a prophecy uttered by Vyāsa (§§ 28, 29, Appx I); and this re-shaping was carried through generally yet not completely (§ 12). Some compilation seems to have been made, of the Andhras at least, in the reign of the Andhra king Yajñaśrī about the end of the second century A.D. (§ 21, note)[1]; but the first definite compilation is that which brought the 'history' down from the time of the battle to a little later than the end of the Andhras[2], together with the final portion[3], and was incorporated in the Bhaviṣya about or soon after the middle of the third century (§§ 19, 21, 24); and there are reasons for fixing its date as not later than A.D. 260–1 (§ 44). That account was apparently written in Kharoṣṭhī and composed in Northern India (§ 27). The Matsya borrowed it from the Bhaviṣya, probably during the last quarter of the third century (§ 23), and so has preserved what the Bhaviṣya contained then.

50. The Bhaviṣya account was revised about the years 315–320 and brought up to date by the insertion of the later dynastic matter[4] and much addition to the 'Evils of the Kali Age'[5]: it was still in Kharoṣṭhī, and was certainly written down then (§§ 23, 27). That version was borrowed by the Vāyu then, but exists now only in one MS, *e*Vāyu (§ 23). The language of the account in the Bhaviṣya was revised again about the years 325–330, and that version was adopted by the Vāyu, and soon afterwards by the Brahmāṇḍa[6], and now constitutes their general versions (§ 23). They have thus preserved what the Bhaviṣya contained at that time.

[1] It is possible that the use of the present tense for the three ancient Paurava, Aikṣvāku and Bārhadratha kings (§ 11) may have something genuine in it.

[2] P. 1 to l. 15 on p. 48.

[3] Pp. 55-63: see § 25.

[4] P. 48, l. 16 to p. 55.

[5] Pp. 55, 56.

[6] But the Brahmāṇḍa may have copied from the Vāyu (§ 23, note).

51. The Viṣṇu next utilized the account, perhaps before the end of the fourth century, and condensed it all in Sanskrit prose except the concluding portion (§ 27). The Bhāgavata also drew its materials from the same sources, from the Brahmāṇḍa and more particularly the Viṣṇu; it retained some of the old ślokas, but in the main condensed the matter into new Sanskrit ślokas; and it probably belongs to the 8th or even 9th century (§ 27). The Garuḍa utilized the same materials for the three great early dynasties only, and has merely a bald list of the kings in new Sanskrit ślokas; but its date is uncertain (Appx I, II).

52. Since those times a quiet process of small emendations in details has been at work in these Purāṇas; but the Bhaviṣya, the source of them all, has been unscrupulously tampered with in order to keep its prophecies up to date, and the text now presented in the Veṅkaṭeśvara edition shows all the ancient matter utterly corrupted, but the prophecies brought boldly down to the nineteenth century.

53. The sixty-three MSS of these Purāṇas that have been collated have yielded a great quantity of different readings, and no pains have been spared to state and arrange them correctly, so that I trust the notes will be found free from errors. The Index comprises all names and forms of names mentioned in the text, notes, translation, appendixes, and introduction, except such peculiar forms as are obviously erroneous or occur in single MSS of no particular trustworthiness.

54. In conclusion I have to tender my thanks to Dr. J. F. Fleet. He had long thought that a critical edition of the Purāṇa texts of these dynasties was greatly needed, and it was at his desire that I undertook this work, which has proved full of interest. He has done me the kindness to read most of this Introduction, and to offer me some criticisms and suggestions, which have been of great help and have also opened up some new questions that I have now endeavoured to elucidate; and he has supplied the valuable references to various inscriptions which mention certain kings named in these dynastic lists.

F. E. PARGITER.

OXFORD, *May* 15, 1913.

to diverge[1]; but this is a measure more of convenience than of accuracy, because it happens sometimes that the correct form is what would appear to be an aberrant form[2]; and in such cases what is, or would seem to be, the correct form is suggested sometimes in the notes[3].

39. The numbers present much difficulty. Those that occur oftenest are *viṁśati* and *triṁśati*, and their abbreviated forms *viṁśat* and *triṁśat*, *viṁśa* and *triṁśa*[4]; and the difficulty arises because *tr* and *v*, if written carelessly or if partially frayed, are hardly distinguishable in the later script[5], and *t* and *v* in the Prakrit forms of these words might have been confused from the first in Kharoṣṭhī. Hence in many cases either may be read as other data may indicate, irrespective of the weight of the MSS.

40. Various groups of misreadings will appear on an examination of the notes, and the most important may be mentioned here. First, *abda*, if the loop of the *b* be carelessly written so as to touch the top bar (as I have found it sometimes), may easily be misread as *aṣṭa*, and there can be no doubt that *abda* and *aṣṭa* have often been confused. Thus, where most MSS read *aṣṭapañcāśataṁ cābdan*[6], one has °*cābdā*, two °*cāṣṭān*, and one °*cāṣṭā*; and here *aṣṭa* is plainly a corruption of *abda* because it is impossible after *aṣṭapañcāśataṁ*. Again, one set of readings is *so smā daśa*, *so 'smād daśa* and *tasmād daśa*, and another set is *aṣṭāṁ daśa*, *aṣṭādaśa* and *so 'ṣṭādaśa*[7]: the latter suggest the reading *abdān daśa*, which (with the frequent use of anusvāra for nasals) would be often written *abdāṁ daśa* and might be misread as *aṣṭāṁdaśa* and so pass to *aṣṭādaśa*: thus *abdān daśa* would reconcile all the readings as regards the number and would seem to have been the original reading. The same confusion occurs in other places[8]. This liability of *abda* and *aṣṭa* to be confused may harmonize other passages where the numbers 10 and 18 are in conflict. Moreover, *abda*, if the initial *a* is elided by Sanskrit or Prakrit sandhi, becomes *bda*; and *bda* may be mistaken for *dva* (= *dvau*)[9]; hence *dvā* and *dvau* become a third alternative, and this possibility may harmonize other passages[10]. Secondly, *samā* and *sapta* have been confused sometimes, for it is not always easy to distinguish *m* and *pt* where written carelessly in the more modern scripts, as I have found. Thus two readings occur *saptāśītiṁ* and *samāśītiṁ*[11], and either might be derived from the other[12].

[1] See p. 39, note [45] for an instance.

[2] *E.g.* Vindusāra, whose name is given correctly only by the Viṣṇu (p. 28, notes [23, 24]).

[3] As in p. 6, note [29]; p. 42, note [98].

[4] In *n*Mt *ṣaḍviṁśati* looks like *ṣaḍgiṁśati* generally, and *ṣaṭtriṁśati* like *ṣaḍiṁśati*.

[5] For a clear instance see p. 57, note [4].

[6] P. 15, l. 17, and notes.

[7] P. 39, l. 5, and notes.

[8] See p. 19, note [46]; p. 30, note [45]; p. 43, note [33]; p. 47, note [77]; p. 60, notes [70, 86]; p. 61, note [1]; p. 62, note [35]. For the reverse cf. perhaps p. 29, note [31].

[9] I have not seldom found *bd*, *db*, and *dbh* inverted in the MSS, and *b* is generally written as *v*. See p. 22, note [43].

[10] Cf. probably p. 40, l. 13.

[11] That is, *samāḥ aśītiṁ* by double, or Prakrit, sandhi: p. 47, note [54].

[12] See also p. 29, note [44]; p. 31, note [13]; p. 40, notes [84, 85].

41. Misreadings could easily affect other numerals. Thus, *catvāriṁśa-t* occurs at times where it may be erroneous [1], and in such cases it might easily be a mistaken Sanskritization of Prakrit *cattāri sa* (or perhaps *ca*), for *cattāri* is both nomin. and accus., and is of all three genders [2]. Again *daśa* and *śata* are sometimes confused [3], and, since *daśa* appears in Prakrit as *daśa* and *dasa*, and *śata* as *śada* and *sada* [4], either word might easily be altered to the other, since metathesis occurs in the MSS [5]. Again the final *ti* of numerals, especially *saptati*, may be a misreading of *vi* which may in Prakrit represent *'pi* [6] or *vai* [7] (Pali *ve*), for *v* and *t* might easily be confused in Kharoṣṭhī, so that *saptati* should probably be *sapta vai* in some cases [8]. In short in dealing with all numerals, it must be remembered that they were Prakrit originally, and their Prakrit forms are of primary importance.

42. The combination of numerals is important. They are used in two ways, *first*, in correct Sanskrit compounds, such as *caturviṁśati*, 24; *aṣṭatriṁśac-chatam*, 138; *saptatriṁśac-chatam*, 137 [9]; and *secondly*, strung together in separate words. The latter construction alone requires notice, because it often follows what seems to me to have been a Prakrit arrangement and, if so, should be interpreted according to Prakrit usage. Thus, in Prakrit 'hundred' preceded by 'three' means 'three hundred', but followed by 'three' means apparently 'hundred (and) three'. The Prakrit numerals were Sanskritized as they stood, and were then declined regularly, so that 'three' appears as *trīṇi*, and 'hundred' seems to appear similarly in the plural as *śatāni*. If this view be right, *trīṇi śatāni* mean 'three hundred', but *śatāni trīṇi* 'hundred and three'. This conclusion may be tested by some cases, for it is very important if it is right.

43. The most important passage for this purpose is the statement that 18 Śakas would reign *śatāni trīṇy aśītiṁ ca* years [10]. This expression is ordinarily read as correct Sanskrit to mean 380, but there are cogent grounds to show that these words cannot have that meaning. These Śakas are, in Dr. Fleet's opinion, Nahapāna and his successors, whose kingdom began with (or about) the Śaka era, A.D. 78; and if these words mean 380, the conclusion could be and has been drawn that this Purāṇic notice was written after they had reigned 380 years, that is, about the year A.D. 458 [11]. Now this conclusion involves this consequence, that the account brings the notice of the Śakas down to A.D. 458 and yet wholly ignores the great Gupta

[1] See p. 14, l. 10; p. 21, ll. 3, 6; p. 22, l. 13; &c.

[2] Pischel's Prakrit Grammar, § 439.

[3] See p. 30, note [46]; p. 33, note [80].

[4] Pischel, *op. cit.*, §§ 442, 448.

[5] See p. 7, note [63]; p. 32, note [82]; p. 39, note [46]; p. 45, note [11]; p. 49, note [36]: also *nṛpaḥ* and *punaḥ* are confused through their Pkt forms *napa* and *pana*, see p. 11, note [51], and p. 45, note [4].

[6] Pischel, *op. cit.*, § 143.

[7] *Sapta vi* actually occurs for *sapta vai*, p. 53, note [4]. Similarly in names a final *vi* has been treated as a particle and the name curtailed, cf. p. 40, note [69], p. 42, note [88], and p. 43, note [24].

[8] *E.g.* p. 28, l. 7.

[9] P. 19, l. 10; p. 28, l. 9; p. 30, l. 15.

[10] *Various Local Dynasties*, p. 46, l. 9. The number of Śaka kings is given also as 10, or 16 (see p. 45, l. 3), which seem more probable.

[11] JRAS, 1912, p. 1047.

empire which was paramount in North India after A.D. 340 and was still flourishing in 458 [1]. This is incredible, because the Gupta kings were orthodox Hindus, guided by brahman advisers, and skilled in Sanskrit [2]; and this Purāṇic account, which was brahmanical, would unquestionably, if not closed till 458, have extolled their fame. The argument *ex silentio* is incontestable here. The fact then that the account knows nothing of events most congenial to brahmanism later than 330 shows that the rendering '380' leads to impossible results: indeed no date later than about A.D. 330 is possible. These words *śatāni triṇy aśītiṁ ca* occur in the Matsya as well as in the Vāyu and Brahmāṇḍa, and the Matsya account is that which was compiled in the Bhaviṣya about or soon after the middle of the 3rd century A.D. If we read these words as '380' with reference to that time, they take us back to about 130 or 120 B.C. as the beginning of these Śakas—a result that no one will accept. From both these alternative interpretations therefore it appears that the rendering of these words as '380' stultifies them.

44. We may now try reading these words as 'hundred, three, and eighty', 183. Applying them to Nahapāna and his successors and reckoning from A.D. 78 as before, we obtain the year A.D. 260–1 as the date of this notice of the Śakas, and this agrees entirely with the conclusion, reached above on other grounds (§ 21) that the account was first compiled about or soon after the middle of the 3rd century. This rendering '183' therefore brings all the particulars into an agreement which is strong evidence that it is the true meaning; and it further gives something like a precise date for the first compilation of the account in the Bhaviṣya as preserved in the Matsya, namely, A.D. 260–1. This statement, that the Śakas had reigned 183 years in A.D. 260, does not imply that they had come to an end then, but simply that the account being compiled then could say nothing about the future. So far as the account is concerned, they might have reigned, and in fact did reign, long afterwards, for there are coin-dates for them down to the year '311'. Such coin dates refer to a time after the account was compiled, and are in no conflict with the rendering '183'. This date A.D. 260–1 is a lower limit, for, if the Sakas formed a kingdom before their era was established, the reckoning would start from before A.D. 78, and the 183 years would have expired some little time before A.D. 260.

45. This conclusion is corroborated by the notice of the Hūṇas or Maunas along with the Śakas. They are said to have reigned, eleven for *śatāni triṇi* years [3]. It is not known when their rule began, so that exact calculations cannot be made for them; but, if these words be read as '300', difficulties occur precisely similar to those discussed with regard to the Śakas and show that that meaning cannot be right. Read as meaning '103' however the statement may be true; Hūṇas or Maunas may have formed some small kingdom for 103 years on the frontiers of

[1] V. Smith, *Early History of India*, 2nd ed., pp. 289–90.

[2] *Id.*, pp. 282, 287.

[3] P. 47, l. 14. Their number is also given less probably as 18 or 19 (cf. p. 46, l. 5).

India in A.D. 260. The corresponding line relating to the Tuṣāras is certainly corrupt, and their period should probably be 105 or 107 years[1], which would be possible in A.D. 260.

46. All the statements regarding the 'Various Local Dynasties' in pp. 45–47 must be read with reference to the date of the first compilation which is preserved in the Matsya. When the account was revised and brought up to date in the Bhaviṣya at the Gupta era in the version found now in the Vāyu and Brahmāṇḍa, the periods assigned to the Śaka and other mleccha dynasties should have been revised for the further period of 60 or 70 years, but that was not done, for the periods are the same in the two versions. The brahmans, who revised the account at that time, merely revised the language and not the statements. That was natural, for revision of the statements required fresh and precise calculations, for which they may have had few data and certainly had little inclination, as the dynasties were mleccha or śūdra. All they did was to extend the account by adding the fresh matter contained in p. 48, l. 16 to p. 55, l. 17; yet in that they do appear to have included further particulars about the Śakas on p. 49, for there can be little doubt that Nahapāna's successors are alluded to in l. 4[2], though the context is vague.

47. This examination of the circumstances thus leads to the conclusion that the numerals discussed here cannot be read as correct Sanskrit, and that read in the way now suggested they accord with the circumstances and also apparently with Prakrit usage. Hence I would submit that they must be interpreted in that way. This construction simplifies numerical statements remarkably and reduces to reasonable and probable totals figures that seem at first wild and extravagant. At the same time one must hesitate to assert that numerical statements must always be so read, for it certainly seems that the period assigned to the Andhras by the Matsya is 460 rather than 164 years[3].

Conclusion.

48. The foregoing results and inferences may be summarized thus. The Bhaviṣya was the first Purāṇa to give an account of the dynasties of the Kali age, and the Matsya, Vāyu, and Brahmāṇḍa got their accounts from it (§§ 7, 8), though

[1] P. 47, l. 11 with p. 45, l. 4. *Sahasrāṇi* is sometimes a corruption of *sa* (or *tu*) *varṣāṇi*, see p. 25, note[18]; p. 46, note[34].

[2] This would be natural, if they fostered brahmanism and Sanskrit learning during the 3rd century (V. Smith, *History*, p. 287); though they are treated so curtly in the earlier part, before they favoured Hinduism.

[3] It says there were 19 Andhra kings, and I may offer a tentative suggestion. The Andhra who overthrew the Kāṇvāyanas was not Simuka as these Purāṇic accounts say, but probably one of the kings, nos. 12–14 (V. Smith, *History*, p. 194). Possibly then the Matsya account may refer only to him and his successors, and they may have been 19: but the period if read as 164 years would be too short for them. Otherwise its reading *ekonaviṁśatir* should probably be *ekonatriṁśatir*, which is quite possible, see § 39.

shifting of names in a verse, and the disarrangement of lines would produce manifest disarrangement of groups of kings. Besides the Calcutta edition of the Viṣṇu and the Gaṇpat edition of the Bhāgavata, I have collated 10 MSS of the former and 18 of the latter, and also the French edition of the Bhāgavata so far as its Sanskrit text goes.

34. The Garuḍa is of use only for the names of the kings in the three earliest dynasties, and I have been able to collate only the Calcutta edition and two MSS. The Veṅkaṭeśvara edition of the Bhaviṣya is of no value as already explained.

35. As regards variations in words, these when small, such as errors in sandhi[1], or optional ways of writing[2], or obvious clerical mistakes[3], or mere trivial differences[4], are generally disregarded or corrected unless there is something noteworthy in them[5], for many of the MSS are carelessly written and abound in such blemishes; yet the notes will show that I have erred probably rather on the side of inclusion than of exclusion. Various letters are often written so much alike in the MSS as to be easily confused, such as *b* and *v*, *p* and *y*, *c* and *v*, *n* and *l*, *n* and *r*, subscript *r* and *u*, and the MSS often contain superfluous letters written by mistake and not cancelled. These flaws, when obviously purely clerical, have been disregarded in some cases, but otherwise, and especially where these particulars may prove significant in the matter of Prakritisms and scripts, have been cited in the notes as they stand, the superfluous letters being enclosed in square brackets. *B* and *v* when not distinguished in the MSS have been generally transcribed as they should be correctly, unless the actual letter seemed worthy of notice. Since the account is only a Sanskritized version of Prakrit ślokas, Prakrit forms have been admitted into the text if they are supported by the best authority, as more truly representing the original words especially in numerals. Variations of readings and corruptions of names have been arranged in the order of modification, so as to elucidate as far as possible the process of the changes, and when so placed, readings that are corrupt often prove to be highly instructive as regards both language and script[6].

36. Though I am not an advocate of the use of Roman characters in lieu of Devanāgarī, yet, as this work is intended for the use of all interested in Indian archaeology whether Sanskrit scholars or not, practical usefulness should be the chief consideration in this presentation of the Purāṇic accounts of the dynasties of the Kali age. Hence the Roman character has been used throughout, because it

[1] *E.g.*, in p. 60, note [63] *dflV*ā have *śatāt śatam* actually.

[2] As where conjunct nasals are written for convenience as anusvāra, or where consonants conjoined with *r* are optionally doubled.

[3] Thus the Calc. edition of the Vāyu has *Sneccha* sometimes instead of *Mleccha* by an obvious printer's error: see p. 47, note [76].

[4] As the insertion or omission of final anusvāra or visarga through mere carelessness.

[5] To have noticed such minutiae would have swollen the notes beyond all reason and usefulness.

[6] *E.g.* p. 39, note [45]; p. 40, note [69]; p. 47, note [72]; p. 49, note [14].

offers several advantages over Devanāgarī, namely, (1) words can be separated which would be all run together when written properly in Devanāgarī; (2) compound words and words that have fused together by sandhi can be divided by hyphens and so displayed distinctly; and (3) by so treating words capitals can be introduced for names, and names can be exhibited unmistakably, even when initial vowels have been modified by sandhi. The system of transliteration is that adopted by the Royal Asiatic Society and most other Oriental Societies. Where vowels are blended by sandhi, the resultant vowel has been marked with a circumflex, except *ai* and *au* where a circumflex is inconvenient and hardly necessary. Changes in sandhi, which are required by the variant readings, are treated as necessarily consequential and are not mentioned. It has been necessary to introduce the double hyphen (used in transliterating inscriptions and MSS) in order to distinguish separate words that have become fused by sandhi [1], and I trust this sign may be pardoned here, especially as this Purāṇic account is not literature but only patchwork Sanskritization.

Interpretation of the Account.

37. In interpreting the account the fact must be borne in mind that it was written in Prakrit originally, and this will throw light on many points, especially the variations in names and the meaning of numbers. It will explain how corruptions in names have sometimes occurred [2], it will help to elucidate doubtful passages [3], and will be the best guide in solving difficulties in readings which appear corrupt [4]. The best course in such cases is to convert the different readings into literary Prakrit, write the Prakrit forms in the various old scripts, compare them, and see whether one can divine what was probably the original Prakrit statement. These remarks apply especially to the Matsya, Vāyu, and Brahmāṇḍa versions.

38. There is often great variation in names. In some cases the correct form can be selected by reference to other books or to inscriptions, but where there is no such agreement I have not ventured to emend the Purāṇic forms from other sources, because it is my duty simply to edit the text and not to attempt to make it square with our present scanty knowledge of ancient Indian history—which is a separate matter. In such cases I have confined myself to estimating what form of the name is best attested by the MSS, and often the only feasible course is to adopt the most central form from which the other forms may be considered

[1] Chiefly where names have fused with other words by single or double sandhi, as *bhaviṣyôdayanas* (p. 7, l. 23; p. 82) and *bhavitâśoka* (p. 27, l. 2; p. 28, l. 4 in *e*Vā); these are printed as *bhaviṣy=Ôdayanas* and *bhavit=Âśoka* in order to bring out the name clearly. It could hardly be dispensed with in such cases of double sandhi as *Yavanâṣṭau* and *bhāvyânyāḥ* (see p. 82); and as no line could well be drawn regarding its use, the simplest course was to adopt it throughout, except in the Appendixes and Introduction.

[2] *E.g.* p. 40, note [69]; p. 41, note [74].

[3] *E.g.* p. 52, notes [37, 38, 42].

[4] P. 59, line 11 is an excellent crux for such solution.

LIST OF AUTHORITIES

Editions and Manuscripts collated.

BHĀGAVATA PURĀṆA.

*B*Bh. The edition published in part by Burnouf and continued afterwards. Skandha ix is in Skt, but sk xii only in translation. It differs very little from *G*Bh.

*G*Bh. The edition published by the Gaṇpat Kṛishṇājī Press, Bombay, 1889. Has a commentary, and some variant readings rarely.

MSS in the Bodleian Library.

*a*Bh. Wilson 22; Auf. Cat. no. 86. Dated 1711. In Bengali characters; fairly well written; contains sk x–xii only.

*b*Bh. Wilson 121–3; Auf. Cat. nos. 79–81. Dated 1813–6. Sk xii contains only the last portion, the Evils of the Kali Age, &c.

cBh. Mill 133–6; Auf. Cat. nos. 82–5. Dated 1823. Writing moderately good; many clerical errors.

*d*Bh. Fraser 2; Auf. Cat. nos. 809–10. Does not contain sk ix; sk xii is dated 1407. Genly accurate. A very valuable MS; it contains alterations by another and apptly later hand, which are not always sound.

*e*Bh. Walker 215–6; Auf. Cat. nos. 811–2. Dated 1794. Is close to *G*Bh and fairly correct; writing poor.

*f*Bh. Skt MS c. 54; W and K. Cat. no. 1180. Dated 1642. A very valuable MS in Śāradā script. Writing good and almost free from mistakes.

MSS in the India Office Library.

*g*Bh. No. 3206, E 3461. Date about 1650. Fairly good.

*h*Bh. Nos. 2759–60, E 3463–4. Dated 1762–3. Contains sk v–xii; writing poor but fairly correct, except for many small clerical errors.

*j*Bh. No. 976, E 3466. Modern. Contains sk viii–xii; well written and fairly correct.

*k*Bh. Nos. 654 and 656, E 3470 and 3472. Modern. Carelessly written.

*l*Bh. Nos. 1838–9, E 3474–5. Modern. Well written, with few clerical errors; is close to *G*Bh.

*m*Bh. Nos. 2502 and 2506, E 3489 and 3493. Dated 1779–81. Fairly good.

*n*Bh. Nos. 2756–7, E 3495–6. Dated 1780–1. Fairly well written, with few clerical errors.

*p*Bh. Nos. 2437 and 2439, E 3503 and 3505. Date, 18th cent. Fairly good.

*q*Bh. Jones MS; W 3*a*, T 32. Date, beginning of 17th cent. Fairly good.

*r*Bh. Jones MS; W 3*b*, T 33. Date, end of 18th cent. In Bengali characters; fairly good.

*s*Bh. Jones MS; W 3*c*, T 34. Date, 18th cent. Written on palm leaves; fairly good: does not contain sk ix.

*t*Bh. Tagore MS; no. 106; Auf. list no. 14. Date, about 1780. In Bengali characters on palm leaves.

There are two other MSS in the Bodleian—one, Wilson 117; Auf. Cat. no. 87, which contains sk x and not xii as stated in the Cat., and so has nothing about these dynasties: the other, Mill 145; Auf. Cat. no. 88, written on an extremely long narrow roll. There are also two similar MSS in the British Museum, Add. 16624 and 26419. These three are mere bijou MSS, written in minute characters and decorated with coloured pictures and designs.

BHAVIṢYA PURĀṆA.

Edition published by the Śrī-Veṅkaṭeśvara Press, Bombay. The Pratisarga-parvan deals with the dynasties of the Kali age, but the account is not genuine, see Introdn. §§ 6, 9, 28, and ZDMG, lvii, 276.

I have examined the following MSS, but none of them contain anything about these dynasties:—

in the India Office Library, two, no. 1314, E 3447, and no. 1429, E 3448;

in the Bodleian Library, three, Auf. Cat. nos. 75 (Wilson 103), 76 (Wilson 126), and 77 (Wilson 124);

in the Royal Asiatic Society, MS Tod 2;

in the Nepal State Library, one MS sent to Oxford with other selected MSS.

I have also made inquiries about MSS elsewhere, but have not found any in which this dynastic matter can be deemed genuine. The Sanskrit College, Calcutta, has a MS, ग no. 106, from which two extracts were sent me; it describes the founding of Calcutta. Queen's College, Benares, has a MS but it does not contain this dynastic matter, as Prof. Venis informs me. He sent me an extract from a MS belonging to the College Librarian, Paṇḍit Vindhyeśvarīprasād Dvivedī, but it deals with later events and especially with the Mohammedans.

BRAHMĀṆḌA PURĀṆA.

Bḍ. The edition published by the Śrī-Veṅkaṭeśvara Press, Bombay. It professes to be based on several MSS, yet gives variant readings only rarely, and leaves on my mind the impression that it has been silently emended at times; cf. p. 25, note [24]; p. 26, note [42]; p. 34, note [5]; p. 51, note [10].

I have also examined the following MSS, but they contain nothing about these dynasties:—

in the India Office Library, two, Burnell MS no. 458, and Tagore MS no. 10 (Auf. list, no. 11);

in the Bodleian Library, three, Auf. Cat. nos. 72 (Mill 51), 73 (Wilson 105), and 74 (Walker 130).

GARUḌA PURĀṆA.

*C*Gr. The edition published by Jīvānanda Vidyāsāgar, Calcutta, 1890. It contains no notes of variant readings.

MSS in the India Office Library.

*a*Gr. No. 1199 *c*, E 3353. Dated 1727? Far from correct. Account begins, fol. 114^{a}, l. 1.

*b*Gr. No. 2560, E 3355. Modern. Very incorrect. Account begins, fol. 103^{a}.

*c*Gr. No. 1199 *a*, E 3354. Dated 1800. Badly written. Account begins, fol. 127^{a}, l. 2.

The Bodleian Library has one, Skt MS c. 50; but it contains nothing about these dynasties.

MATSYA PURĀṆA.

*A*Mt. The Ānandāśrama (Poona) edition, 1907. It is based on 6 copies, the Veṅkaṭeśvara (Bombay) edition (marked क and cited here as *V*Mt), the Gondhaḷekar (Poona) edition (marked ख and cited here as *G*Mt), and 4 MSS marked ग, घ, ङ and च, and cited here as a^1, a^2, a^3, and a^4 respectively.

*C*Mt. The Calcutta edition by Jīvānanda Vidyāsāgar, 1876.

*G*Mt. The Gondhaḷekar edition; see *A*Mt.

*V*Mt. The Veṅkaṭeśvara edition; see *A*Mt.

*a*Mt. See *A*Mt.

MSS in the Bodleian Library.

*b*Mt. Wilson 21; Auf. Cat. no. 95. Dated 1729. Well written, fairly free from clerical mistakes, but errs widely in names and has corrupt readings, especially near the end. Has marginal notes of different readings by one or two other hands; these form no part of the text and are not noticed here. Where it varies from the general Mt text, it often agrees with the Vā and Bḍ.

*c*Mt. Fraser 1; Auf. Cat. nos. 813–4. Date, 17th cent. apptly. Fairly well written and genly correct. Where it varies from *A*Mt it agrees often with *A*Vā. Paurava kings, vol. i, fol. 113^{a}, verse 55; the rest, vol. ii, fol. 575^{b}, l. 1.

MSS in the India Office Library.

*d*Mt. No. 1918, E 3548. Dated 1525. Good, but with not a few inaccuracies. Where it differs from *A*Mt, it agrees often with *A*Vā. Paurava kings, fol. 63^{a}, l. 8; other dynasties, fol. 307^{a}, l. 2.

*e*Mt. No. 2032, E 3549. Dated 1767. Writing poor and full of clerical mistakes: agrees genly with *c*Mt and sometimes corruptly. Paurava kings, fol. 67^b, l. 13; other dynasties, fol. 321^b, l. 8.

*f*Mt. No. 1080, E 3550. Dated 1795. Fairly well written; many small clerical mistakes (as *s* for *ś* often) and a very few corrections. Paurava kings, fol. 62^a, l. 13; other dynasties, fol. 327^b, last line.

*g*Mt. Nos. 406–7, E 3551–2. Modern. Much like *f*Mt. Paurava kings, vol. i, fol. 79^a; other dynasties, vol. ii, fol. 437^b.

*h*Mt. No. 2831, E 3553. Modern. Contains only the first part of the Mt. Fairly well written; some special readings. Only Paurava kings, fol. 166^b, l. 9.

*j*Mt. No. 3347, Jackson Collection. Modern. Fairly well written; apptly copied carefully from a damaged MS and so has small blanks: many small errors. Valuable as it has several special readings, which are apptly ancient. Paurava kings, fol. 62^b, l. 6; other dynasties, fol. 330^a, l. 9.

MSS in the Dekhan College, Poona (collated for me by a paṇḍit through the kindness of the Professor of Sanskrit at the College).

*k*Mt. Skt MS no. 28 of 1871–2. Much like *ce*Mt.

*l*Mt. Skt MS no. 164 of 1887–91.

*m*Mt. Skt MS no. 340 of Viśrama (first collection).

MSS in the British Museum.

*n*Mt. Add. 14348. Date, 18th cent. Fairly well written; fairly accurate, though with some carelessness: resembles *c*Mt. Paurava kings, fol. 98^b; other dynasties, fol. 508^a.

*p*Mt. Add. 26414. Date, 18th cent. Fairly well written and genly correct; closely like *A*Mt. Contains only the Preface and Pauravas; begins fol. 42^b.

VĀYU PURĀṆA.

*A*Vā. The Ānandāśrama (Poona) edition, 1905. It is based on five copies, the Calcutta edition (marked क; see *C*Vā below), and 4 MSS marked ख, ग, घ, and ङ and cited here as a^1, a^2, a^3, and a^4 respectively.

*C*Vā. The Bibliotheca Indica edition, Calcutta. It is based on 6 MSS, but only rarely notes variant readings.

*a*Vā. See *A*Vā.

MSS in the Bodleian Library.

*b*Vā. Wilson 120; Auf. Cat. no. 104. Date, early 19th cent. Fairly well written, but with a good many mistakes and not a few repetitions. Account begins, fol. 237^a, l. 4.

*c*Vā. Wilson 355; Auf. Cat. no. 103. Date 15th cent. Unfortunately contains nothing about these dynasties.

MSS in the India Office Library.

*d*Vā. Jones MS; W 6*a*, T 37. Date, end of 18th cent. Valuable, because apptly copied from one MS and corrected by another: yet not accurate. Account begins, vol. ii, fol. 386^a, l. 9.

*e*Vā. Jones MS; W 6*b*, T 38. Not dated. Writing fairly good, but diction rather illiterate. Very valuable, because it has readings different from the printed editions, and some verses not contained therein; and where it differs therefrom, it often agrees with the Mt (see Introdn. § 22). Unfortunately it has a lacuna at the beginning. Account begins, fol. 198ᵃ, l. 11.

*f*Vā. No. 1869, E 3587. Date, about 1600. Fairly well written, but many small errors. It has a large lacuna at the beginning, and commences in fol. 358ᵇ, l. 5 with l. 23 of the Aikṣvākus.

*g*Vā. No. 2103, E 3589. Dated 1483. Fairly well written. Account begins, fol. 311ᵇ, l. 10.

*h*Vā. No. 1310, E 3590. Modern. Full of mistakes, especially at the beginning; agrees closely with *b*Vā even in the errors.

*j*Vā. No. 264, E 3591. Date, about 1800. Badly written, full of mistakes and gaps; has a lacuna at the beginning and commences only with l. 23 of the Aikṣvākus in fol. 347ᵃ, l. 7.

MSS in the Dekhan College, Poona (collated for me by a paṇḍit through the kindness of the Professor of Sanskrit at the College).

*k*Vā. Skt MS no. 8 of 1874–5. Has lost all the account after l. 17 on p. 48.

*l*Vā. Skt MS no. 110 of 1881–2.

MS in the Royal Asiatic Society.

*m*Vā. Tod 14. Writing poor, with many small mistakes; much like *f*Vā.

VIṢṆU PURĀṆA.

*C*Vṣ. The edition by Jīvānanda Vidyāsāgar, Calcutta, 1882. Has a commentary, but no notes of variant readings.

MSS in the Bodleian Library.

*a*Vṣ. Wilson 26; Auf. Cat. no. 112. Date, 18th cent. Beautifully written in Bengali characters. Account begins, fol. 102ᵃ.

*b*Vṣ. Wilson 108; Auf. Cat. no. 109. Dated 1703. Fairly well written and fairly correct. Much like *a*Vṣ.

*c*Vṣ. Wilson 107; Auf. Cat. no. 110. Dated 1740. Writing good but careless; close to *C*Vṣ.

*d*Vṣ. Wilson 130; Auf. Cat. no. 111. Date, late 18th cent. Well written and fairly correct: close to *C*Vṣ.

MSS in the India Office Library.

*e*Vṣ. No. 420, E 3606. Dated 1770. Writing poor, with not a few mistakes.

*f*Vṣ. No. 1380, E 3607. Modern. Fairly good.

*g*Vṣ. No. 1695, E 3608. Modern. Well written and accurate.

*h*Vṣ. Burnell MS no. 374. Fairly well written, with some variant readings.

MSS in the Indian Institute, Oxford.

*j*Vş. Malan MS; cat. no. 122. Date, 18th cent. Writing poor, with many small blunders and omissions, some of which have been corrected by a later hand in Bengali writing.

*k*Vş. Cat. no. 121. Dated 1736 (?). Fairly well written and genly correct, but has strange mistakes at times, probably through defects of the MS copied: contains several interesting readings.

MS in the Royal Asiatic Society.

*l*Vş. Whish MS no. 33. From South India; written on palm leaves in modern Grantha. Well and carefully written, but often shortens the connecting phrases in the first half, and omits the Bārhadrathas: agrees often with *h*Vş. A valuable MS, which checks the readings of North Indian MSS. Account begins, fol. 166ᵃ, l. 7.

ABBREVIATIONS.

* (prefixed) denotes a hypothetical word.
† (prefixed) denotes a corrupt reading.
apptly = apparently.
crp = corrupt, corruptly.
genly = generally.
MBh = Mahābhārata.
Pkt = Prakrit.
prob = probable, probably.
Skt = Sanskrit.
syll = syllable.

CORRIGENDA

p. xvii, line 8, *for* his *read* Vyāsa's

p. 48, line 14, *for* Kielhorn's Inscriptions of Northern India (Epig. Ind. v, Appendix) *read* Lüders' List of the Brāhmī Inscriptions (Epig. Ind. x, Appendix),

p. 50, line 17, *for* pp. *read* Lüders' List of the Brāhmī Inscriptions, nos.

THE PURĀṆA TEXT

OF THE

DYNASTIES OF THE KALI AGE

PREFACE

The Matsya and Vāyu Purāṇas introduce a preface into the middle of the account of the Paurava dynasty. Both bring the Paurava (or Aila) genealogy from the Pāṇḍavas to Abhimanyu, Parīkṣit, and Janamejaya [1], and then describe Janamejaya's dispute with Vaiśampāyana and the brahmans about his Vājasaneyaka doctrine [2]. They then continue the genealogy to Adhisīmakṛṣṇa, in whose reign was performed the twelve-year sacrifice during which these Purāṇas profess to have been recited [3]. At this point the rishis ask the Sūta for a full account of the Kali age [4], and he proposes to give it in verses which are here treated as the Preface [5]. Then starting from Adhisīmakṛṣṇa as the existing king, he carries on the dynasty to its close [6]. In order to simplify the arrangement, the prefatory portion is placed here first, and the separated parts of the Paurava genealogy are joined together in a continuous account and given next as the Paurava line. The story of Janamejaya's dispute [7], the rishis' questions, and the Sūta's resumption of his account are omitted as superfluous [8]. The Preface therefore consists of—

Text—*A*Mt *50*, 72–76; *A*Vā *99*, 264–269.

All copies contain this preface, except that *k*Mt omits lines 6–10; *h*Mt misplaces l. 11 after l. 5; *e*Vā has lost the first 5½ lines and it alone contains ll. 12–14; *g*Vā omits l. 11; and *fjm*Vā have nothing. All agree in the text except where noted, and where the Matsya and Vāyu are different, both versions are given, the Matsya on the left and the Vāyu on the right. The Brahmāṇḍa has lost the preface in a large lacuna. The Viṣṇu, Bhāgavata, and Garuḍa have no preface.

[1] *A*Mt *50*, 57; *A*Vā *99*, 249*b*–250*a*.
[2] *A*Mt *50*, 58–64; *A*Vā *99*, 250*b*–255.
[3] *A*Mt *50*, 65–67; *A*Vā *99*, 256–259.
[4] *A*Mt *50*, 68–71; *A*Vā *99*, 260–263.
[5] *A*Mt *50*, 72–76; *A*Vā *99*, 264–269.
[6] *A*Mt *50*, 77–89; *A*Vā *99*, 270–280*a*.
[7] This is given in Appendix III as it shows some brahmanical tampering with the Vāyu.
[8] See Introdn. § 14.

Sūta uvāca—
Yathā me[1] kīrtitam pūrvaṁ[2] Vyāsen⸗âkliṣṭa[3]-karmaṇā
bhāvyaṁ[4] Kali-yugaṁ[5] c⸗aiva tathā manvantarāṇi ca[6]
anāgatāni[7] sarvāṇi bruvato me nibodhata
ata ūrdhvam[8] pravakṣyāmi bhaviṣyā ye[9] nṛpās tathā[10]
Aiḍ-Êkṣvākv-anvaye[11] c⸗aiva | Ailāṁś[12] c⸗aiva tath⸗Êkṣvākūn[13]
Paurave c⸗ânvaye[14] tathā | Saudyumnāṁś[15] c⸗aiva pārthivān
yeṣu[16] saṁsthāpyate[17] kṣatram[18] Aiḍ-Êkṣvāku[19]-kulaṁ[20] śubham[21]
tān sarvān kīrtayiṣyāmi[22] Bhaviṣye[23] kathitān[24] nṛpān[25]
tebhyo 'pare 'pi ye[26] c⸗ânye[27] utpatsyante nṛpāḥ punaḥ[28]
kṣatrāḥ[29] pāraśavāḥ[30] śūdrās tath⸗ânye ye[31] vahiś-carāḥ[32]
Andhrāḥ[33] Śakāḥ Pulindāś ca Cūlikā[34] Yavanās tathā[35]

[1] *Yath⸗aiva* in *j*Mt.
[2] So Mt. Vā *sarvaṁ*.
[3] So Mt. Vā *°âdbhuta*.
[4] *Bhāvaṁ* in *e*Mt; *k*Mt *bhavet*.
[5] *Yuge* in *cejn*Mt.
[6] So Mt. Vā *tu*.
[7] *Atr⸗âgatāni* in *l*Mt.
[8] *Param* in *j*Mt.
[9] So Mt genly: *bd*Mt *bhaviṣy-ârthe*; *cejkn*Mt *bhāvino ye*. Vā *bhaviṣyanti*. For this half line *l*Mt reads *bhaviṣyān kathitān* (*nṛpān* omitted) as in l. 7.
[10] *Smṛtāḥ* in *fgj*Mt. Vā *tu ye*.
[11] So $a^{2}a^{4}$*befm*Mt; *CGVgp*Mt *°k-ânvaye*: *c*Mt *Ail-Êk°*; *j*Mt †*Ain-Êk°*; *h*Mt †*Aiṇâk°*; *d*Mt †*Eḍ-Êk°*; *n*Mt crp: a^{3}*k*Mt *Aiḍ-Êkṣvāku-nṛpe*: a^{1}Mt *Ikṣvākor anvaye*: *l*Mt †*Ekṣakasya*. *Aiḍa* = *Aila*.
[12] *Elāṁś* in *ghk*Vā.
[13] In *g*Vā *tath⸗Aik°*.
[14] But *n*Mt *v⸗ânvaye*; *e*Mt *c⸗ânya[ta]ye*. This is pleonastic because the Pauravas were Ailas, see JRAS, 1910, pp. 16, 20.
[15] This reading is better. The Saudyumnas were distinct from the Ailas and Aikṣvākus, being the descendants of Sudyumna, who was Manu's daughter Ilā when she gained man's form according to the fable; and they comprised the early kings of Gayā and the eastern region, Utkala and perhaps a country named Haritāśva or Vinatāśva in the west: see one version in Mt *12*, 17–18; and another in Vā *85*, 19, Bḍ iii, *60*, 18–19, and Hariv. *10*, 632.
[16] In *h*Mt *yehi* (Pkt for *yebhiḥ*?).
[17] So Vā, *ce*Mt: Mt genly *saṁsthāsyate*.
[18] So a^{2-4}Vā; *C*a^{1}*dghkl*Vā *kṣetram*, a frequent mistake for *kṣatram*. Mt genly *tac ca*; *cefghjn*Mt *tatra*.
[19] So Mt genly; *j*Mt *Ain-Êk°*: *h*Mt *Ail-Êkṣvākaṁ*, *e*Vā *°kuṁ*: *d*Mt *Eḍ-Êk°*. Vā genly *Aikṣvākavaṁ*: *l*Mt †*Ekṣâkasya*.
[20] So Mt. Vā *idaṁ*.
[21] *Śrutān* in *l*Mt; *smṛtam* in *d*Mt.
[22] *Kathayiṣyāmi* in *j*Mt.
[23] But *cl*Mt *bhaviṣyān*; *en*Mt *°ṣyā*; *j*Mt *°ṣyat*: see Introdn. § 7.
[24] So Mt. Vā *paṭhitān*; *b*Vā *paṭhito*.
[25] *Nṛpa* in *b*Vā.
[26] So Mt: *n*Mt omits *ye*. Vā *pare ca ye*.
[27] So Vā; *e*Vā *'py anye*. Mt genly *tv anye hy*; *bcdghjnp*Mt omit *hy*.
[28] So Mt; *e*Vā *nṛpās tathā*: Vā genly *mahīkṣitaḥ*.
[29] So Mt, Vā genly: *cjn*Mt, *e*Vā *kṣatra-*; a^{1}*k*Vā †*kṣetrāḥ*; *e*Mt †*kṣatriyāḥ*.
[30] So Mt, Vā genly: *fgp*Mt *pārasavāḥ*, so *m*Mt with *pāravaśāḥ* also; *b*Mt †*pāraśarāḥ*; *e*Vā †*pārāśarāḥ*; *e*Mt †*pāravā*; *n*Mt †*yâḥ-ravāḥ*; *l*Mt †*pāśavī*.
[31] So Mt genly; *j*Mt *ca* for *ye*: *h*Mt *tathā ye 'nye*. Vā *tathā ye ca*; *e*Vā *tathā c⸗aiva*.
[32] So Mt genly: *C*$a^{1}a^{4}$*bdmp*Mt *mahīśvarāḥ*. Vā *dvijātayaḥ*.
[33] So Vā genly, *chjlnp*Mt; *fg*Mt *Āndhrāḥ*: *dh*Vā, Mt often, *Andhāḥ*: *k*Vā *Adhryâḥ*.
[34] *AC*Mt *Cūlikā*; *e*Vā *Cul°*; *b*Vā *Vūl°*; *h*Vā *Vūn°* (or *Vūt°*); *d*Vā *Vrūl°*: Vā genly *Tūl°*; *h*Mt *Dhūl°*; *j*Mt *Mūl°*; *bmp*Mt *Cal°*; *e*Mt *Pulihāś*; *fg*Mt *Valiṁkā*; *d*Mt *Bālhikā*:

Kaivart-Âbhīra-Śabarā [36] ye c=ânye [37] Mleccha-sambhavāḥ [38]
Pauravā Vītihotrā vai Vaidiśāḥ [39] pañca [40] Kosalāḥ
Mekalāḥ Kośalāḥ Pauṇḍrā Gaunardāḥ Svasphrakāś ca ha [41]
Sunidharmāḥ Śakā Nīpā yāś c=ânyā Mleccha-jātayaḥ [42]
varṣ-âgrataḥ [43] pravakṣyāmi [44] nāmataś c=aiva tān nṛpān [45].

Pauravas.

Text—*A*Mt *50*, 57, 65[a], 66, 78–89 ; *A*Vā *99*, 249[b], 250[a], 256[a]–258[a], 271–280[a] ; Bḍ nil.

Corresp. passages—*C*Vṣ iv, *20*, 12—*21*, 4 ; *G*Bh ix, *22*, 34–45[a] ; *C*Gr i, *140*, 40—*141*, 4.

The arrangement of this dynasty has been explained above (p. 1). In the first portion the Matsya and Vāyu differ, and their versions are both given, the former on the left and the latter on the right ; otherwise they agree except where noted. The Brahmāṇḍa has lost the whole in a lacuna.

The Bhāgavata is somewhat full about the first seven kings, but combines the rest in a succinct list. The Viṣṇu agrees closely with it. The Garuḍa gives merely a list of names.

All copies of Mt give the whole except lines 5, 27 ; and besides *e*Mt omits l. 28 (second half) to l. 30 (first half) ; *f*Mt ll. 10 and 17 (second half) to 20 (first half); and *gj*Mt l. 10. The Vā MSS are complete, except that *e*Vā has lost ll. 1–6, 11 (first half) and 16 (second half) to 18 (first half): all copies, except *e*Vā, omit

*g*Vā omits this half line. *Cūlikā* appears to be the best form, see JRAS, 1912, p. 711.

[35] So Mt. Vā *Yavanaiḥ saha.*

[36] So Mt, Vā genly (*Śabarā* or *Śav°*); *e*Vā *Kaivartt-Âraibhīra-varāḥ*; *n*Mt *Kauvart-Ôbhīra-Śabaro.*

[37] So Mt, Vā genly: *n*Mt *ye v=ânye*: *e*Vā *yāś c=ânyā*, correcting the faulty grammar.

[38] So Mt. Vā *jātayaḥ*.

[39] This line only in *e*Vā, which reads *Rītihotrā vai Vaidikāḥ*; this should obviously be *Vītihotrā vai Vaidiśāḥ*, and has been emended so. For the Vītihotras see *Pradyotas*, line 1, *infra*; for Vaidiśas see *Dynasties of Vidiśā, &c., infra.*

[40] *Pañca* suggests that *Pañcālas* are meant, and that this name has been in some way curtailed. For them see *Early Contemporary Dynasties*, line 2, *infra.*

[41] This line only in *e*Vā. For Mekalas see *Dynasties of the 3rd Century*, line 5, *infra.*

[42] This line is only in *e*Vā.

[43] So Vā genly, *chjkn*Mt. Mt genly *paryāyataḥ*. Other copies intermediate, *e*Mt *vaṣāgratah*; *d*Vā *vaṣāyataḥ*; *b*Vā *varṣāyata*; *h*Vā *varyāyata.* *Varṣ-âgrataḥ* occurs in this context, *A*Vā *99*, 261—

varṣ-âgrato 'pi prabrūhi nāmataś c=aiva tān nṛpān.

Varṣ-âgra occurs in *A*Vā *21*, 16, 21 ; *22*, 3 ; where it means the 'total number of years' ; hence *varṣ-âgrataḥ* here, being applied to the kings, would mean 'according to the totals of their years'. *Paryāyataḥ* is also good.

[44] In *k*Mt *praviṣyāmi.*

[45] So Mt genly, Vā : *ceki/n*Mt read this half line, *bhaviṣyān* (*n*, *°ṣyāt*) *kathitān* (*l*, *kāśikān*) *nṛpān*, which should no doubt be *Bhaviṣye kathitān nṛpān*; see l. 7.

ll. 10 and 20 (second half) to 25 (first half); *h*Vā omits ll. 15 (second half) to 18 (first half); *l*Vā ll. 17 (second half) to l. 20; and *fjm*Vā have nothing. Also *ade*Bh have nothing; and *ab*Gr omit all kings after the second Śatānīka.

For notices of the earliest of these kings elsewhere see Introdn. § 2. The kings named are 29 altogether, 25 from and including Adhisīmakṛṣṇa; but the list of *Early Contemporary Dynasties*, l. 6, *infra*, mentions '36 Kauravas'.

Abhimanyoḥ Parīkṣit tu [1]	Uttarāyāṁ tu Vairāṭyām
putraḥ para-puraṁ-jayaḥ	Parikṣid [1] Abhimanyu-jaḥ [2]
Janamejayaḥ [3] Parīkṣitaḥ	Parikṣitas tu dāyādo [4]
putraḥ parama-dhārmikaḥ	rāj=âsīj [5] Janamejayaḥ
Janamejayāc Chatānīkas [6]	tasya putraḥ Śatānīko [6]
tasmāj jajñe sa vīryavān [7]	balavān satya-vikramaḥ

putro 'śvamedhadatto 'bhūc [8] Chatānīkasya vīryavān
putro 'śvamedhadattād vai jātaḥ para-puraṁ-jayaḥ [9]
Adhisīmakṛṣṇo dharm-âtmā [10] sāmprataṁ yo [11] mahā-yaśāḥ [12]

[1] *Parikṣita-su-* in *m*Mt. All agree in this name. Parīkṣit's name is often written in the MSS in other ways, as *Parīkṣita*, *Parīkṣi*, *Parīkṣa*, &c.; these variations are left unnoticed here. Bh begins with a verse about his birth as told in the MBh, and Vṣ amplifies it in high literary style.

[2] *Abhimanyunā* in *b*Vā.

[3] All agree in this name. There is a redundant syllable in this and the next line, and it occurs elsewhere with the name Janamejaya. The name was sometimes treated as *Janmejaya* (as in *cefj*Mt here), thus obviating the superfluous syllable.

[4] *Parīkṣitasya* (omitting *tu*) in *b*Vā. Bh says Parīkṣit had three other sons—

Tav=ême tanayās tāta Janamejaya-pūrvakāḥ
Śrutaseno Bhīmasena Ugrasenaś ca vīryavān.

Vīrasena for *Bhīmasena* in *rt*Bh. Vṣ concurs in this; so also MBh i, *3*, 661–2.

[5] *Rājā sa* in *k*Vā.

[6] All agree in this name. Vṣ styles him *aparaḥ Śatānīkaḥ*, with reference to an earlier Śatānīka, who was son of Nakula and Draupadī and was killed in the great battle. Bh is fuller and contains these two lines—

tasya putraḥ Śatānīko Yājñavalkyāt trayīm paṭhan
astra-jñānaṁ kriyā-jñānaṁ Śaunakāt param eṣyati.

Vṣ agrees, and expands this statement, improving it by reading *Kṛpāj jñānaṁ* instead of *kriyā-jñānaṁ*. MBh says Janamejaya had a second son, Śaṅkukarṇa (i, *95*, 3837–8).

[7] *Su-vīryavān* in *j*Mt.

[8] So Vā; *h*Mt agrees but has *vai* for *'bhūc*. Mt crp *ath=Âśvamedhena tataḥ* (*fg*Mt *sutaḥ*); *k*Mt omits this line. Vṣ and Gr give the name as *Aśvamedhadatta*; *k*Vṣ °*dātṛ*; Bh as °*medhaja*. Between him and the preceding Śatānīka Bh inserts a king *Sahasrānīka* thus—

Sahasrānīkas tat-putras tataś c=aiv=Âśvamedhajaḥ:

but no other authority supports it.

[9] So Vā: *k*Vā *pura-puraṁ*°. Mt omits this line, condensing it with the next.

[10] So Vā except that the name varies; all have a superfluous syllable: *h*Vā *Adhisīma-[tta]kṛṣṇo*; *Ca*^{2}*a*^{4}Vā °*sāmak*°; *g*Vā °*sāmaḥ Kṛṣṇo*; *a*^{1}Vā °*māsąk*°; *a*^{3}Vā °*masak*°; *k*Vā *Adhimak*°. Mt genly *jajñe 'dhisomakṛṣṇâkhyaḥ*; *fg*Mt °*sīmak*°; *j*Mt both; *e*Mt °*sīmaḥ Kṛṣṇ*°; *n*Mt †*Adhinsamak*°; *p*Mt *Adhisomakṛṣṇāsyaḥ*; *b*Mt °*kṛṣṇasya*; *d*Mt °*sīmaḥ Kṛṣṇāsyaḥ*; *g*Mt °*sīmakṛṣṇaś ca*; *h*Mt *āsīt Kṛṣṇa sutas tasya*: *j*Mat misplaces this line after l. 3. Mt readings seem to

Adhisīmakṛṣṇa-putro [13] Nicakṣur [14] bhavitā nṛpaḥ [15]
Gaṅgay≈âpahṛte [16] tasmin nagare Nāgasāhvaye [17]
tyaktvā Nicakṣur nagaraṁ [18] Kauśāmbyāṁ sa [19] nivatsyati [20]
bhaviṣy≈âṣṭau [21] sutās tasya [22] mahā-bala-parākramāḥ [23]

Bhūrir [24] jyeṣṭhaḥ [25] sutas tasya
tasya [27] Citrarathaḥ [28] smṛtaḥ

| bhaviṣyad Uṣṇas tat-putra [26]
Uṣṇāc Citrarathaḥ [28] smṛtaḥ

be corruptions of *Adhisīmakṛṣṇo'sya* in Pkt form °*kṛṣṇa asya*. Vṣ *Adhisīmakṛṣṇa*; *k*Vṣ °*sīmaḥ Kṛṣ*°: Gr °*sīmakaḥ Kṛṣ*°. Bh *Asīmakṛṣṇas tasy≈âpi*; *h*Bh *Aśiśāk*°; *f*Bh *avātsīt Kṛṣ*°; *g*Bh crp. In two later lines (omitted here) $a^1a^2a^4$Mt (verse 77) and a^3a^4Vā (verse 270) have *Adhisīmak*°. The correct name appears to be *Adhisīmakṛṣṇa*, with a shorter form *Asīmak*°. The longer form is best supported here, though the shorter would improve the metre.

[11] So Mt: *j*Mt *sa*. Vā *sāmprato 'yam*. See corresponding lines about Divākara of the Aikṣvākus and Senājit of the Bārhadrathas, *infra*.

[12] So Vā, Mt genly: a^3*ceknMt* *mahārathaḥ*. After this line Mt and Vā insert three lines stating that the twelve-year sacrifice was performed during his reign; see Introdn. § 10.

[13] So Mt, Vā, except that there are variations in the name; *c*Mt adds *'bhūt* and *CGV*a^3a^4*j*Mt *tu* superfluously: a^1a^2*de*Mt, *gh*Vā *Adhisīmaḥ Kṛṣṇa-putro*; *k*Mt °*māsaḥ K*°; *d*Vā *Asīmak*°; *n*Mt merely *Kṛṣṇa-putro*; *e*Vā *Dadhīcikṛṣṇa-suto*. Bh says *tat-sutaḥ*, 'son of the preceding'.

[14] There is great variation in this name here and in l. 9. Mt often *Vivakṣu*; *bg*Mt *Vicakṣus*; *d*Mt both; *h*Mt *Nṛcakru*; a^2*cen*Mt *Nṛcaka*: afterwards *f*Mt *Nicakṣus*, *l*Mt *Nṛvakṣu*, *k*Mt *Nṛcaka*. Vā genly *Nirvaktra*; *e*Vā *Nṛvadha* here. Vṣ genly *Nicakṣus*; *bcdefgj*Vṣ, *j*Mt, *t*Bh *Nicakru*; *l*Vṣ *Niścakru*; *k*Vṣ crp: *a*Gr †*Nivadra*?; *b*Gr †*Nivaha*?; *CGr Aniruddha*. Bh genly *Nemicakra*; *e*Bh *Nemiṁśc*°; *n*Bh *Naimic*°; *r*Bh, *a*Vṣ *Nic*°. I have adopted *Nicakṣus* as the most central form; but the true name may be *Nṛcakṣas*, a word occurring in Rigv. x, 14, 11.

[15] So Mt. Vā *kila*.

[16] So Vā, *cen*Mt. Mt genly *Gaṅgayā tu hṛte*; *b*Mt °*dhṛte*; *m*Mt both; *d*Mt *bṛte*.

[17] Similarly Vṣ—yo Gaṅgay≈âpahṛte Hastināpure Kauśāmbyāṁ nivatsyati. Bh also—

Gajāhvaye hṛte nadyā Kauśāmbyāṁ sādhu vatsyati:

where *g*Bh °*sa tu vat*°; *r*Bh °*sa nivat*°; *p*Bh ends *neṣyati*.

[18] So Mt genly with variations in the name, see note [14]: a^2a^3*ceknMt* *Nṛcako nagaraṁ tyaktvā*; *h*Mt °*svaṁ vaṁśaṁ tyaktvā*: *e*Vā *tyaktvā Nṛbandhu vāsam* (with a syll. lost). Vā genly *tyaktvā* (*g*Vā *kṛtvā*) *ca taṁ sa vāsaṁ ca*; *C*Vā °*su-vāsaṁ*°; *d*Vā °*taṁ tu vāsaṁ svam*; *h*Vā °*naṁ sarvāsa va*; *b*Vā †*nya*[*ttakaṁ*]*tkāṁ ca naṁ sa vāsa va*. These variations suggest the reading *tyaktvā ca taṁ sva-vāsaṁ* (or *vaṁśaṁ*) *ca*.

[19] So Vā genly (*g*Vā omits *sa*) and *r*Bh; *l*Vā †*Kauśāṁdyāṁ*°; *f*Mt *sa Kauśāmbyāṁ*; *g*Mt *sa Kauśāvyā*. Mt genly *Kauśāmbyāṁ tu*; *j*Mt °*su*; *d*Mt †*Kauśānāṁ*; *h*Mt †*Kauśālyāntu*. Vṣ, Bh corroborate; *e*Bh †*Kauśikyāṁ*; *k*Vṣ *Kauśak*°.

[20] So Mt, Vā genly, Vṣ: *b*Vā *niveśyati*; *h*Vā *niveṣ*°; *d*Vā *niveśmani*; *g*Vā *sannivetsyati*.

[21] This line is only in Mt, but not in *dfgj*Mt: a^3Mt *bhaviṣyāś ca*; *h*Mt °*ṣye yaḥ*; *mp*Mt °*ṣyākṣau*; *k*Mt omits *aṣṭau*: *e*Vā has only the first half line, *bhaviṣyas tu sutas tasmāt*.

[22] *C≈aiva* in a^3Mt.

[23] In *h*Mt *Uṣṇa Citraratha smṛtaḥ*.

[24] *Bhūri* in *bdfgjkp*Mt; *h*Mt *Bhūvi*; *l*Mt *Bhūmi*.

[25] In *h*Mt *śreṣṭhaḥ*.

[26] So Vā. Vṣ *tasy≈âpy Uṣṇaḥ putro*. *CGr Uṣṇa*; *ab*Gr *Uśca*?; Bh *Ukta*; *t*Bh *Upta*.

[27] *Tataś* in *bcefghnp*Mt; *m*Mt both; *j*Mt *tatra*.

[28] All agree in this name, except *e*Vā *Tvaṣṭā Dhitrarathaḥ*.

Śucidrathaś [29] Citrarathād [30] Vṛṣṇimāṁś [31] ca Śucidrathāt
Vṛṣṇimataḥ Suṣeṇaś ca [32] bhaviṣyati śucir nṛpaḥ [33]
tasmāt Suṣeṇād bhavitā Sunītho [34] nāma pārthivaḥ [35]
Rucaḥ [36] Sunīthād [37] bhavitā [38] Nṛcakṣur [39] bhavitā tataḥ [40]
Nṛcakṣuṣas [41] tu dāyādo bhavitā vai [42] Sukhībalaḥ [43]
Sukhībala-sutaś c≠âpi [44] bhāvī [45] rājā Pariplavaḥ [46]
Pariplava-sutaś c≠âpi [47] bhavitā Sunayo [48] nṛpaḥ

[29] So Vā, *fj*Mt; *C*Gr agrees: *ceghn*Mt *Sucidratha*; a^2a^3kMt *Suvid°*; *h*Vṣ either; *b*Mt, *k*Vā *Śucidravya*, so *dp*Mt with *°dravāt* at the end: other Mt *Śucidrava*. Vṣ genly *Śuciratha*; *c*Vṣ *Suvir°*. Bh *Kaviratha* and *Kuvir°* about equally; *j*Bh *Tuvir°*; *f*Bh *Kathir°*; *rs*Bh *Sucir°*. The proper form should probably be *Śucadratha*. Omitted in *dl*Vṣ, *ab*Gr.

[30] *Caitraratho* in a^2a^3kMt; *en*Mt *Cit°*. Bh says *sutaḥ*.

[31] So Mt genly; Vṣ, *fgjklq*Bh, *C*Gr agree in the name: *mp*Mt *Viṣṇumāṁś*; *cejn*Mt *Vṛṣṭim°*: in next line *p*Mt *Vṛṣṇimataḥ*; *l*Mt *Vṛṣṭi°*; *n*Mt *Vṛṣi°*. Vā genly *Dhṛtimāṁś*; *d*Vā *Dhṛtam°*; *g*Vā *Vṛttim°*; *b*Vā *Vṛtyam°*; *h*Vā *Vṛnam°*; *k*Vā *Vṛttirmāś*. Bh genly, *ab*Vṣ *Vṛṣṭimat*; *t*Bh *Vṛti°*; *r*Bh *Dhṛti°*; *e*Bh *Dhṛṣṭi°*; *c*Bh *Kṛṣṭi°*. Omitted in *ab*Gr.

[32] So Mt genly: *e*Vā *Suṣeṇa Dhṛtimato* (with one syll. short). Vā genly *Suṣeṇo vai mahāvīryo*. Bh, Vṣ, *C*Gr agree in the name; *k*Vṣ *Susena*. With the dialectical modification of *ṣ*, *cen*Mt read *Sukheṇas tu*, so *g*Vā and *h*Vṣ; *b*Vṣ, *knp*Bh *Sukhena*: *l*Mt *Sukhanas tu*. Omitted in *ab*Gr.

[33] So Mt genly: *cfghjkln*Mt *punar nṛpaḥ*; *e*Mt *panu°*. Vā genly *mahāyaśāḥ*; *e*Vā *punaḥ punaḥ*.

[34] So Mt genly, *e*Vā. Vṣ, Bh agree; *C*Gr *Sunīthaka*; *k*Bh *Sunitha*: *j*Mt *Sunīyo*; *mp*Mt *Sunīpo*, *p*Mt *Sunīthād* in next line. Vā genly *Sutīrtho*. Omitted in *ab*Gr.

[35] *Dhārmikaḥ* in *e*Vā.

[36] So Vā genly; *g*Vā *Rucih*. Vṣ genly *Ṛcaḥ*; *k*Vṣ *Ṛta*; *j*Vṣ *Aṁca*; *e*Vā *sa vai*. Mt *nṛpāt*. Bh, *hl*Vṣ, Gr omit him.

[37] *Sunīto* in *e*Vā. Vā *Sutīrthād*.

[38] *Saṁjanye* in *k*Mt.

[39] So Mt genly; Vṣ, Bh, Gr agree genly: *ckn*Mt *Nṛcakra*, *e*Mt *Nuc°*. Vā genly *Tricakṣo*; *bd*Vā *°vakṣyo*; *g*Vā *Citrākṣo*; a^3klVā *Vivakṣo*; *e*Vā *Nṛvandhur*. Others, *p*Bh *Nṛcakru*; *c*Bh *Nṛpakṣu*; *f*Bh *Sucakṣus*; *a*Vṣ *Nuc°*, *k*Vṣ *Ntac°*, *b*Vṣ *Tric°*: see note [41].

[40] So Vā. Mt *su-mahāyaśāḥ*; *d*Mt *sa°*; *fgh*Mt *tu°*.

[41] Readings here genly follow those in note [39]: but *bp*Mt *Nṛcakṣuṣasya* (omitting *tu*), *l*Mt *Vivakṣasas*: *l*Vā *Trivakṣasya*, *k*Vā *°kṣyāsya*, *b*Vā *°vikṣyasya*; *g*Vā *Citrākhyasya*; *e*Vā *Nṛvandhuyas*.

[42] In *fg*Mt *°ca*: *cehkn*Mt *bhaviṣyati*.

[43] So Mt, Vā genly, here and in next line: *bd*Vā *Suṣib°*; *n*Mt *Sukhīlava*, *j*Mt *Sukhel°*, *c*Mt *Mukhīl°*; *ek*Mt *na saṁśayaḥ*: but in next line *c*Mt *Sukhīlava*, *ek*Mt *°ītala*, *b*Vā *Suradhīla*. Vṣ genly *Sukhābala*, *l*Vṣ *Sukhab°*, *abhk*Vṣ *Sukhīb°*. Bh genly *Sukhīnala*, *p*Bh *°nara*; *f*Bh *Suṣīnara*; *r*Bh *Sakhānana*. *C*Gr *Mukhābāṇa*; *a*Gr *Surabala*, *b*Gr *°baja*. This name omitted in *e*Vā. After him Gr adds, *medhāvī ca nṛpañjayaḥ*, implying apptly two other kings, but no authority supports it.

[44] In *d*Vā *sutaḥ sūta*; *b*Vā †*suta[mṛ]tasi*; *ek*Mt †*vaśaś c≠âpi*. Bh *sutas tasmāt*.

[45] So Mt genly. Vā, *cn*Mt *bhāvyo*, *e*Mt *bha°*; *h*Mt *bhaviṣyati* (omitting *rājā*).

[46] So many Mt, a^3a^4Vā, here and in next line. Vṣ, Bh agree genly; and *ab*Gr: *bgrt*Bh, *C*Gr *Pāriplava*; Ca^1a^2Vā *Paripluta*. *CG*Va^3lMt, *gh*Vṣ, *c*Bh *Pariṣṇava*; *k*Mt *°ṣṇuva*. The letters *pl* and *ṣṇ* are often written very much alike; so *e*Mt *°ṣṇura* here, *°pluva* in next line: *g*Vā *°pluta*, *°ḷava*; *k*Vā *°pluva*, *°plava*: *b*Vā *°śraya*, *°plava*; *k*Vṣ *°puna*; *d*Vā *°ślagha*; *cf*Vṣ *Paritmava*: *l*Vā substitutes here *Daṇḍapāṇir bhaviṣyati* from l. 25.

[47] This line omitted in some, see p. 3.

[48] So Vā genly, *h*Mt; Vṣ genly, *C*Gr agree: also Bh impliedly, *Medhāvī Sunay-âtmajaḥ*. Mt genly *Sutapā*; *j*Mt *°tamā*: *t*Bh *°tapa*; *p*Bh *°daya*; *k*Vṣ *°vaya*; *k*Mt *°nṛpo*; *e*Vā

Medhāvī [49] tasya dāyādo [50] bhaviṣyati narādhipaḥ [51]
Medhāvinaḥ sutaś c-âpi [52] bhaviṣyati Nṛpañjayaḥ [53]
Durvo [54] bhāvyaḥ sutas tasya [55] Tigmātmā [56] tasya c=âtmajaḥ [57]
Tigmād [58] Bṛhadratho [59] bhāvyo Vasudāno [60] Bṛhadrathāt
Vasudānāc [61] Chatānīko [62] bhaviṣy=Ôdayanas [63] tataḥ [64]
bhaviṣyate c=Ôdayanād [65] vīro rājā [66] Vahīnaraḥ [67]
Vahīnar-âtmajaś [68] c=aiva [69] Daṇḍapāṇir [70] bhaviṣyati
Daṇḍapāṇer Nirāmitro Nirāmitrāt [71] tu [72] Kṣemakaḥ [73]

°*ratho*: *bg*Vā, *acdegh*Vṣ, *ab*Gr *Munaya*; *h*Vā *Mumapa*; *l*Mt *Muṣṇavo*; *ce*Mt *Putrayo*; *n*Mt *Putrāpo*; *r*Bh *Vijana*.

[49] So all: but *h*Bh *Modhāvin*; *k*Bh *Meghāvin*.

[50] So Mt, *e*Vā. Vā genly *Sunayasy=âtha*; *bg*Vā *Munay°*; *h*Vā *Munany=âtha*. Bh *Sunay-âtmajaḥ*.

[51] So Vā: *e*Vā *nṛpaḥ sa tu*; *h*Mt *nayasya tu*. Mt genly *na saṁśayaḥ*.

[52] So Mt and Vā.

[53] So *e*Vā. Bh, Vṣ, Gr agree. Mt *Purañj°*; *b*Vṣ *Ripuñj°*; *l*Vṣ *Nṛpanaya*. See p. 3.

[54] There is great variation in this name. Mt mostly *Urvo*; *ce*Mt *Ūru*; *h*Mt *Uror*; *j*Mt *Ūrvyā*; *g*Mt *Urvyau*, *f*Mt *Ūr°*; *n*Mt *Ūru* (or *Kuru*); *p*Mt *Kurvo*; *d*Mt *Jayo*. But *e*Vā *Durvi*. Bh genly *Dūrva*; *n*Bh *Dur°*; *ct*Bh *Dar°*; *r*Bh *Dār°*; *p*Bh *Purva*. Vṣ genly *Mṛdu*; *f*Vṣ *°da*; *h*Vṣ *Durva*, *l*Vṣ *Dūr°*; *ab*Vṣ *Durbala*; *k*Vṣ *Durddharṣa*. Gr *Hari*. *Durva* is the most central form.

[55] *C=âpi* in *e*Vā.

[56] So Mt genly; *e*Vā shortly *Tigmāṁs*. Vṣ, Gr *Tigma*, which Mt and *e*Vā use in next line. Bh *Timi*; *h*Mt *Tīmātmā*, *cekn*Mt *Nirm°*; *fg*Mt *Nirm-âkhyas*; *j*Mt †*Nindātmā*.

[57] In *e*Vā *tasmād bhaviṣyati*; Bh *°janiṣyati*.

[58] So Mt genly, *e*Vā: *b*Mt *°mātmād*, *d*Mt *°mātmano*, with excess syll: *p*Mt *Tigmā*; *h*Mt *Timād*; *cefgkn*Mt *Nirmād*; *j*Mt †*Nindā*.

[59] All agree in this name.

[60] So *h*Mt, *e*Vā; Vṣ agrees: *d*Mt *Vasudānā*. Mt genly *°dāmā*; *k*Mt *°dhānā*; *e*Mt *°dhāmā*; *cn*Mt *°dhāma*; *j*Mt *°devo*: *l*Vṣ *°da*; *b*Vṣ *°manas*. *C*Gr *Sudānaka*; *ab*Gr †*Tudānava* misplacing him after the next king Śatānīka. Bh *Sudāsa* indirectly, *Śatānīkaḥ Sudāsajaḥ*; *b*Bh *Sudāru-jaḥ*.

[61] So *h*Mt, *e*Vā. Mt genly *°dāmnaḥ*; *b*Mt *°dāmnā*; *en*Mt *°dhāmā*; *c*Mt *°dhāmāc*; *j*Mt *°dāsuḥ*.

[62] All agree; *e*Mt *Sat°*: *ab*Gr *Sadānīka*, Pkt. Vṣ calls him *aparaḥ Śatānīkaḥ*; for the former see note [6]. Bh says 'son of the preceding', see note [60].

[63] So Mt genly; Vṣ: *e*Vā *bhavit=Ôdanaya[ṁ]s* here, *Udayanād* in next line: *j*Mt *bhaviṣy=Ôdayinaḥ*; *e*Mt *°ṣyadayanaḥ*; *dmp*Mt *°ṣy=Ôdathanaḥ*; *k*Mt *°ṣyadanayaḥ*. *C*Gr *Udāna*. Bh genly *Durdamana*; *en*Bh *Durd°* or *Urd°*; *c*Bh *Umanasu* (or *Dum°*).

[64] *Tathā* in *bchjnp*Mt, *e*Vā.

[65] See note [63]. Other variations here are, *cjn*Mt *°ṣyataś c°* (so *k*Mt crp); *C*Mt *°ṣyate ca Dayanād*; *dp*Mt *°c=Ôdathanād*; *e*Mt *bhavitaś c=Ôvayanād*; *e*Vā *bhaviṣyaś c=âpy Udayanād*.

[66] *Jāto* in *d*Mt.

[67] So Mt genly; Bh, *abl*Vṣ agree: *p*Bh *Vrahī°*: Vṣ genly *Ahī°*; *h*Vṣ *Ahā°*; *C*Gr *Ahni°*: *g*Bh *Vahīnana*: *cehln*Mt *Mahīnaraḥ*, *fg*Mt *°rataḥ*, here and in next line.

[68] So Mt; *e*Vā *°ra-sutaś*: *l*Mt *Mahīṣar-âtm°*.

[69] *C=âpi* in *e*Vā; *mp*Mt *c=Aindro*.

[70] So Mt; and Vā which resumes the list here. Bh, *bkl*Vṣ, *C*Gr agree. Vṣ genly *Khaṇḍa°*; *f*Vṣ that or *Khaḍga°*.

[71] So Vā, *Cbcdefgjn*Mt; *j*Vṣ. *Ap*Mt, *bgh*Vṣ *Nira°*; *h*Mt *Nirva°*. Vṣ genly *Nara°*; *a*Vṣ *Ni°*. *C*Gr *Nimittaka*. Bh genly, *kl*Vṣ *Nimi*; *c*Bh *Nima*; *n*Bh *Nini*; *t*Bh *Nidhi*; *j*Bh *Niti*; *r*Bh *Muni*. This half line in *e*Vā is *bhavitā Kṣemakas tathā*.

[72] So Mt. Vā *ca*.

[73] All agree in this name; but *l*Vṣ *Kṣema*; a^3a^4*gk*Vā *Kṣepakaḥ*; *j*Vṣ, *l*Bh *Kṣamaka*; *k*Vṣ *Cākṣuka*. All agree in *Kṣemaka* in l. 30.

pañca-viṁśā [74] nṛpā hy ete [75] bhaviṣyāḥ Pūru[76]-vaṁśa-jāḥ
atr=ânuvaṁśa[77]-śloko 'yaṁ gīto vipraiḥ purātanaiḥ [78]
brahma-kṣatrasya [79] yo yonir vaṁśo [80] deva-ṛṣi[81]-satkṛtaḥ [82]
Kṣemakam prāpya rājānaṁ saṁsthām prāpsyati vai Kalau [83]
ity eṣa Pauravo vaṁśo [84] yathāvad anukīrtitaḥ [85]
dhīmataḥ Pāṇḍu-putrasya Arjunasya [86] mahātmanaḥ [87].

Aikṣvākus.

Text—*A*Mt *271*, 4–17ᵃ; *A*Vā *99*, 280ᵇ–293; Bḍ iii, *74*, 104–107ᵃ.

Corresp. passages—*C*Vṣ iv, *22*; *G*Bh ix, *12*, 9–16; *C*Gr i, *141*, 5–8.

The Matsya and Vāyu give the whole. The Brahmāṇḍa has a lacuna and its account begins only at l. 23. The Bhāgavata gives a list of names with a few particulars. The Viṣṇu and Garuḍa have only a list of names.

Line 1 is only in Vā. Otherwise all copies of Mt and Vā have the dynasty complete, except that *j*Mt omits ll. 4–7; *e*Vā ll. 19–21; *g*Vā ll. 5, 7–14, 24, 25; *l*Vā l. 24; *hp*Mt have lost the whole; and *fjm*Vā begin only at l. 23. In *j*Bh kings Śākya to Kṣudraka (inclusive) are omitted; in *n*Bh Śākya to Suratha; in *p*Bh Raṇañjaya to Śuddhodana: in *c*Vṣ Śākya to Kulaka; in *k*Vṣ all after Śākya except the genealogical verse; and *ads*Bh have nothing.

There is confusion regarding the first two kings, for Vā, Vṣ, and Bh name two, but Mt and Gr make them one only. This piece of the dynasty, with so much of the various readings as concerns these two kings, stands thus:—

[74] This line is only in Vā; *d*Vā °*śan*; *g*Vā °*śa*: *e*Vā °*triṁśan*. These 25 kings are Adhisīmakṛṣṇa and his successors, see l. 6; but see *Early Contemporary Dynasties*, l. 6, *infra*.

[75] *Nṛp-âdyā te* in *b*Vā.

[76] Vā genly *pūrva*; *e*Vā *Puru*. The correct reading is clearly *Pūru*, from whom the Pauravas were descended.

[77] In *h*Mt °*vaṁśaḥ*; *n*Mt °*vaṁśya*: *bdp*Mt *ato 'nuvaṁśa-ḥ*; *e*Vā *tatr=ân*°: *d*Vā *Puru-vaṁśasya*; *k*Vā *anuv*°, *h*Vā °*śayā*: *g*Vā omits *atra*.

[78] So Mt genly; *n*Mt †*surāt*°; *fg*Mt *sanāt*°. Vā genly *purā-vidaiḥ*; *e*Vā *paurāṇikair dvijaiḥ*.

[79] This verse is in Mt, Vā, Vṣ, Bh.

[80] In *h*Mt *yā yonir*°; *Brt*Bh *vai yonir*°. Bh genly *vai prokto*°; *bfhjknpq*Bh *vaṁśo 'yam prokto*.

[81] Vṣ *rājarṣi*; *al*Vṣ *devarṣi*.

[82] In *n*Mt *saṁk*°; *c*Mt *saṁsk*°; *e*Mt †*sajñitaḥ*; *k*Mt †*saṁjñinaḥ*.

[83] So Vā, Bh, *l*Vṣ. Mt MSS have two endings (1) *saṁsthāsyati Kalau yuge*, (2) *saṁsthāsyati sa* (or *ca*) *vai Kalau*; *j*Mt °*sthāpyanti ca ye*°. Vṣ *sa saṁsthām* (*k*, *saṁsthānam*) *prāpsyate Kalau*. Cf. p. 12, note [78].

[84] But *e*Vā *ity evam Pauravaṁ vaṁśam*.

[85] So Vā, *cekn*Mt; *e*Vā °*tam*. Mt genly *iha kīrtitaḥ*.

[86] So Vā, Mt genly; *Abklm*Mt *c=Ârjunasya*; *d*Vā *dharma-jñasya*; *e*Vā reads this half line *Pārthasya prathit-âtmanaḥ*.

[87] Gr after naming Kṣemaka says, *tataḥ śūdraḥ pitā pūrvas tataḥ sutaḥ*, suggesting that two śūdra kings, father and son, reigned after him.

Mt. Bṛhadbalasya dāyādo vīro rājā hy [1] Urukṣayaḥ [2]
Urukṣaya[3]-sutaś c-āpi [4] Vatsadroho mahāyaśāḥ [5].
Vā. Bṛhadrathasya [6] dāyādo vīro rājā Bṛhatkṣayaḥ [7]
tataḥ Kṣayaḥ sutas [8] tasya Vatsavyūhas tataḥ Kṣayāt.
Vṣ. Vṛhadbalasya putro Vṛhatkṣaṇaḥ [9]
tasmād Gurukṣepaḥ [10] tato Vatsaḥ [11] Vatsād Vatsavyūhaḥ.
Bh. Bṛhadbalasya bhavitā putro nāma Bṛhadraṇaḥ [12]
Urukriyas [13] tatas tasya Vatsavṛddho bhaviṣyati.
Gr. Vṛhadbalād [14] Urukṣayo Vatsavyūhas tataḥ paraḥ.

A comparison of these readings with possible mistakes in letters in the various old scripts suggests that Vā, Bh, and Vṣ are right in naming two kings, that their names appear to be Bṛhatkṣaya and Urukṣaya, and that Mt and Gr have confused them as one. Hence it seems the text of Mt and Vā should be emended thus:—

Bṛhadbalasya dāyādo vīro rājā Bṛhatkṣayaḥ
Urukṣayaḥ sutas tasya Vatsavyūha Urukṣayāt.

The number of kings in this dynasty is not stated, but 29 are named, excluding Siddhārtha: see however *Early Contemporary Dynasties*, *infra*.

Ata ūrdhvam pravakṣyāmi Ikṣvākūṇām mahātmanām [1]
Bṛhadbalasya [2] dāyādo vīro rājā Bṛhatkṣayaḥ [3]
Urukṣayaḥ [3] sutas tasya Vatsavyūha [4] Urukṣayāt
Vatsavyūhāt [5] Prativyomas [6] tasya putro [7] Divākaraḥ [8]

[1] *Hy* omitted in *bcdefgjkn*Mt.
[2] In *j*Mt *Urūk°*; *dk*Mt *Ruruk°*; *ce*Mt *Nurak°*; *l*Mt *Nuk°*.
[3] See note [2]; *e*Mt *Surak°*: *n*Mt *Urukṣayas*.
[4] In *n*Mt *tu tasy-āpi*.
[5] In *g*Mt *mamā°*; *n*Mt *mahātapāḥ*.
[6] *Bṛhadbalasya* in *e*Vā.
[7] In *h*Vā *°tkṣavaḥ*; *d*Vā *°tvayaḥ*; *b*Vā *°drathaḥ*.
[8] *Kṣaya sutas* in *b*Vā: *e*Vā omits this line.
[9] In *k*Vṣ *°kṣvenaḥ*; *g*Vṣ *°kṣetraḥ*; *b*Vṣ *°kṣantaḥ*; *f*Vṣ *Bṛhatakṣaṇaḥ*.
[10] So *d*Vṣ or *Ūruk°*: *j*Vṣ *Urukṣapraḥ*: *abh*Vṣ *Urukṣayaḥ*; *k*Vṣ *Varūk°*; *l*Vṣ †*Puruṣak°*.
[11] But *l*Vṣ omits him.
[12] In *hn*Bh *°vraṇaḥ*; cBh *Dharudraṇaḥ*.
[13] In cBh *°kriśas*?; *h*Bh *Kurukriyas*; *r*Bh *Upāvṛttas*.
[14] *Vṛhanraṇād* in *ab*Gr.

[1] This line is only in Vā. Vṣ, Gr have similar statements.

[2] Vā genly, *fg*Mt *°rathasya*, but *Bṛhadbala* correctly in l. 24. Bṛhadbala, king of Kosala, is mentioned in the MBh.
[3] For this line, see above.
[4] So Vā genly, *a*[1]*a*[3]*a*[4]*bkl*Mt. Vṣ, Gr agree. In *kl*Vā *°vyūhās*; *fg*Mt *°vyāho*, *d*Mt *°dāho*, in next line *dg*Mt *°dvyăhāt*; *j*Mt crp; *e*Mt *Vaśavyūho*; *n*Mt *Vṛtsamūho* and *Vatsavyūhāt*. Mt genly *Vatsadroho*: Bh *°vṛddha*, *t*Bh *°vrīha*: *h*Vṣ *Vyūha*. Vṣ (except *l*Vṣ) inserts a king Vatsa before him (see above), but no other authority supports it.
[5] *Vyūdhāt* merely in *e*Vā.
[6] So Mt genly. Vṣ, Bh, *ab*Gr agree. In *e*Vā *Prativyomnas tu*. Vā genly, *l*Vṣ *°vyūhas*; *g*Mt *°vyogo*; *r*Bh *°vyota*; *j*Vṣ *°cyoma*; *k*Vṣ *Praticyāma*. *C*Gr, *h*Vṣ omit him.
[7] *Vyoma-putro* in *fg*Mt.
[8] So Mt, Vā, Vṣ. Bh *Bhānur Divāko vāhinī-patiḥ*, where *Bep*Bh read correctly *Divārko*. *Sūrya* in *ab*Gr. *C*Gr, *h*Vṣ omit him.

tasy≠aiva [9] Madhyadeśe tu | yaś ca sāmpratam adhyāste
Ayodhyā nagarī śubhā | Ayodhyāṁ [10] nagarīṁ nṛpaḥ
Divākarasya bhavitā [11] Sahadevo [12] mahā-yaśāḥ
Sahadevasya [13] dāyādo [14] Bṛhadaśvo [15] mahā-manāḥ [16]
tasya Bhānuratho bhāvyaḥ [17] Pratītāśvaś [18] ca tat-sutaḥ
Pratītāśva-sutaś c≠âpi Supratīko [19] bhaviṣyati
Marudevaḥ [20] sutas tasya [21] Sunakṣatraś [22] ca tat-sutaḥ [23]
Kinnarāśvaḥ [24] Sunakṣatrād bhaviṣyati paraṁ-tapaḥ
Kinnarād Antarikṣas tu [25] | bhavitā c≠Ântarikṣas tu [26]
bhaviṣyati mahā-manāḥ [27] | Kinnarasya suto mahān
Suṣeṇaś [28] c≠Ântarikṣāc ca [29] | Antarikṣāt Suparṇas [30] tu [31]
Sumitraś c≠âpy [32] Amitrajit [33] | Suparṇāc c≠âpy [34] Amitrajit [33]

[9] So Mt genly: °*aiṣā* in *cdefgmn*Mt. Cf corresponding lines about Adhisīmakṛṣṇa (p. 4, l. 6) and Senājit (p. 15, l. 13).

[10] So Vā: *g*Vā omits this line.

[11] *Sahitā* in *e*Mt.

[12] So all, except that *g*Vā reads—
Divākara-sutaś c•âpi cakravartī bhaviṣyati.
*C*Gr, *h*Vṣ omit him.

[13] In *Cm*Mt °*devāc ca*.

[14] So Vā. Mt *bhavitā*.

[15] So Vā. Vṣ, Bh, Gr agree: *k*Vṣ °*drutha*. Mt genly *Dhruvāśvo vai*; *cen*Mt °*v-âkhyo*°: *h*Vṣ omits him.

[16] So Mt: *cn*Mt °*yaśāḥ*. Vā *bhaviṣyati*.

[17] So Vā genly; Vṣ, Gr agree: *bh*Vā *Bhātu*°. Bh *Bhānumant*; *h*Bh *Vān*°: *bh*Vṣ omit him. Mt corrupts this half line, *gj*Mt *bhāvya-ratho bhāvyaḥ*, *f*Mt *bhăvya*°, *b*Mt *bhāvyo*°, *dm*Mt *bhāvyo rathā*°; *l*Mt °*rathodbhāv*°: genly *bhāvyo mahābhāgaḥ*. Vṣ says, 'son of the preceding', *tat-sūnur*.

[18] So Vā, *bdfgn*Mt; *abhkl*Vṣ agree. Mt genly *Pratīpāśvaś*; *k*Mt *Praṇītā*°. In *b*Bh *Pratikāśva*: Bh genly *Pratīkāśva*; *cfhknpr*Bh °*kāśa*: *C*Gr °*vya*; *ab*Gr °*cyu*: *j*Mt *Pracetās tasya* (omitting *ca*), but *Pratatāśva* in next line: *l*Mt *marutaś c≠âpi*. Vṣ genly omits him.

[19] So *k*Mt; Vṣ, Bh agree. Vā genly *Supratīto*; *e*Vā °*ṇīto*: Mt genly °*tīpo*; *fg*Mt °*tāpo*: *m*Mt *Suprītāyo*; *l*Mt *Suvratopo*. *C*Gr *Pratītaka*; *r*Bh *Pratīka*; *ab*Gr °*tikṣaka*. Bh says, 'son of the preceding', *tat-sutaḥ*.

[20] So Mt; Vṣ, Bh agree: *j*Bh *Marad*°; *l*Vṣ *Maru[da]d*°; *m*Mt, Gr, *bp*Bh *Manud*°; Vā *Sahad*°; *c*Bh *Suhud*°.

[21] *C•âpi* in *e*Vā.

[22] So all; except *r*Bh *Svan*°; *e*Bh *Sutaḥk*°; *h*Bh *Sunakṣetra*: *c*Mt *Sukṣatras tat*; *e*Mt †*Svakṣatrasvat*; *m*Mt *Sutakṣas tu*, but *Sutakṣatāt* in next line; *j*Mt *Sutaḥkṣatas*, but *Sutakṣattād* in next line.

[23] So Vā: *ce*Mt *suto 'bhavat*. Mt genly *tato 'bhavat*; *dkn*Mt °*bhavet*.

[24] So Mt genly, *e*Vā; *k*Mt °*raśva*: *n*Mt °*raś ca*; *l*Mt °*rāḥ*; *d*Mt °*rākṣaḥ*; *fgm*Mt °*r-âkhyaḥ*; *j*Mt †°*rakṣāt*. Vā genly *Kinnaras tu*; Vṣ, Gr agree: *b*Vā †*Kanarasya*: *r*Bh *Kandara*; Bh genly *Puṣkara*; *k*Bh °*kalu*; *c*Bh *Puṣpara*; *t*Bh *Rūṣkara*. But *c*Mt *Kinnaraś cākṣaras tadvad*; so *e*Mt crp.

[25] So *cdefgjklmn*Mt (with some corruptions); so *b*Mt, but altered to *Kinnarāśvād Antarikṣas* which *AC*Mt have. Vṣ, Bh *Antarikṣa*; *bfgjk*Vṣ °*rīkṣa*; *C*Gr °*rīkṣaka*: *ab*Gr *Anurakṣaka*.

[26] So Vā; *k*Vā °*rikṣasya*: *e*Vā *c•Âkṣavīkṣas tu*, but *Antarīkṣāt* in next line.

[27] *Mahāyaśāḥ* in *dfm*Mt.

[28] So Mt genly: *m*Mt °*ṣarṇaś*; *cek*Mt °*varṇaś*; *dfg*Mt °*parṇaś*; *b*Mt °*parvaś*; *l*Mt °*pparvaḥ*; *n*Mt °*kṣatraś*; *j*Mt °*varṇāc*.

[29] So Mt genly; *cen*Mt °*rikṣasya*.

[30] So Vā: *bhl*Vṣ, Gr agree. Vṣ *Suvarṇa*; *j*Vṣ *Sarvaṇa*. Bh *Sutapas*.

[31] *Tu* wanting in *k*Vā.

[32] So Mt genly; *j*Mt *tu*: *n*Mt *Sumitrasy-âpy*; *b*Mt *Sumantr*°; *ce*Mt *Suvarṇ*°. Sumitra Amitrajit would be one king.

[33] All agree in this name, except *b*Mt

putras tasya [35] Bṛhadbhrājo [36] Dharmī [37] tasya sutaḥ smṛtaḥ
putraḥ [38] Kṛtañjayo [39] nāma Dharmiṇaḥ sa [40] bhaviṣyati
Kṛtañjaya[41]-suto vidvān [42] bhaviṣyati [43] Raṇañjayaḥ [44]
bhavitā Sañjayaś [45] c*â*pi [46] vīro rājā Raṇañjayāt
Sañjayasya [47] sutaḥ Śākyaḥ [48] Śākyac [49] Chuddhodano [50] 'bhavat [51]
Śuddhodanasya [52] bhavitā Siddhārtho [53] Rāhulaḥ [54] sutaḥ [55]
Prasenajit [56] tato bhāvyaḥ [57] Kṣudrako [58] bhavitā [59] tataḥ [60]
Kṣudrakāt Kulako [61] bhāvyaḥ Kulakāt [62] Surathaḥ [63] smṛtaḥ [64]

Amantrajit; *C*Gr *Kṛtajit*; *ab*Gr *Śatajit*: *j*Mt *tato bhavet*.

[34] So Vā; *d*Mt also: *d*Vā *Parṇāc*.

[35] So Vā. Mt genly *Sumitra-jo*; *b*Mt °*triyo*; *j*Mt °*trāt tu*.

[36] Mt genly *Bṛhadrājo*; Vṣ, Bh genly agree. But *hl*Vṣ, *bqt*Bh, *C*Gr °*dbhrāja*; *hjklp*Bh °*dbhāja*; *n*Mt, *ab*Gr °*dvāja*; *f*Bh °*dgātra*; *c*Bh °*dbhānu*; *g*Bh °*jjāta*; *e*Bh *Brahmadrāja*; *c*Mt *Mahārājo*. Vā *Bharadvājo*. *Bṛhadbhrāja* appears to be the probable name.

[37] So Vā; Vṣ agrees: *e*Vā *Dharma*; Gr *Dhārmika*. Mt reads this half line *Bṛhadrājasya* (*d*, °*rājyasya*; *n*, °*vājasya*) *vīryavān* (*b*, *vīrya-bhāk*; *j*, *kīrtanāt*), where *vīryavān* is probably a mistake for *Dharmavān* or *Dhārmikaḥ*; see note [40]. Bh *Barhis*.

[38] So Vā, *CbcdejkmnMt*. Other Mt *punaḥ*.

[39] So Mt genly, Vā, Vṣ, Bh, Gr agree. But *fg*Mt read thus—

Kṛtiñjaya iti khyātaḥ su-putro yo bhaviṣyati:

but *f*Mt *Kṛtañj*° in next line. In *b*Vṣ *Kṛtiñj*°: *j*Mt *Vṛhaṁj*°, but *Kṛtañj*° in next line.

[40] So Vā: for *sa d*Vā has *sam-*, *e*Vā *tu*. Mt genly *Dhārmikaś ca*; *c*Mt °*keś ca*; *m*Mt †*tathākaś ca*. Mt reading should probably be *Dhārmikasya* (see note [37]). But *g*Vā reads this half line, *rājā parama-dhārmikaḥ*.

[41] In *deg*Vā °*jayāt*; *k*Vā °*jayā*; *l*Mt *Raṇañjaya-*.

[42] So Mt. Vā genly *Vrāto*: *g*Vā *suta vrāto*, *d*Vā °*vrāta*, *k*Vā *vrato*; *e*Vā *suvrato vai*. These suggest a king Vrāta or Suvrata, of whom the other authorities know nothing.

[43] So Mt. Vā *tasya putro* to accord with the insertion of Vrāta.

[44] So Vā, *cefgkn*Mt; Vṣ, Bh agree. Mt genly *Raṇej*°; *ab*Gr *Raṇaj*°; *q*Bh *Ṛṇañj*°; *e*Vā *Rathāj*°: *C*Gr †*Dhanastraya*.

[45] So all; but *g*Bh *Suñjaya*: *l*Mt reads this half line †*Raṇaṁjayaś capisuno*.

[46] *C*·*âto* in *b*Mt.

[47] *Raṇañjaya-* in *cen*Mt.

[48] So all genly: but *cde*Mt, *ab*Vṣ, *cf*Bh *Śak*°; *b*Mt *Śāṭh*°; *g*Mt *Śāj*°; *f*Mt *Sāj*°; *ab*Gr *Kāśyapaṇya*: *k*Vā omits this name in a blank.

[49] So all; except *ce*Mt *Śak*°; *dg*Mt *Śāj*°; *f*Mt *Sāj*°; *b*Mt *Śāṭh*°: *g*Vā *rājā*.

[50] So Vā, *bcdj*Mt; *bghl*Vṣ, Gr agree: *efg*Mt *Sud*°. Mt genly *Chuddhaud*°; *n*Mt crp. Bh *Śuddhoda*. Vṣ genly *Kruddhodana*; *d*Vṣ *Krod*°; *a*Vṣ crp.

[51] So Vā; *b*Vā *bhavet*: *e*Vā *smṛtaḥ*. Mt genly *nṛpaḥ*; *cejn*Mt *punaḥ*.

[52] So Vā, *cden*Mt. Mt genly *Śuddhaud*°; *bfg*Mt *Suddhod*°.

[53] So Mt genly; *c*Mt *Śuddhārddha*, *e*Mt *Śru*°. Vā *Śākyārthe*; *a*[1]*a*[3]*bdh*Vā *Śak*°. Vṣ, Bh, Gr omit him.

[54] So *Ca*[3]*a*[4]Vā; *l*Vṣ *Rāhuḷa*. Vṣ genly *Rātula*; *a*[1]*a*[3]*dgkl*Vā *Nāhula*; *abh*Vṣ, *C*Gr *Bāh*°; *ab*Gr *Vāph*°; *bh*Vā *Nah*°; *j*Vṣ *Gār*°. Bh *Lāṅgala*. In *j*Mt *Prāhula*; *fg*Mt *Prahuta*; Mt genly *Puṣkala*; *e*Mt *Hasata*; *k*Mt *Hasanaḥ* (*c*Mt *sanaḥ*); *l*Mt *Sukṛtaḥ*.

[55] So Mt. Vā *smṛtaḥ*; *j*Mt *dhruvaḥ*. Bh *tat-sutaḥ smṛtaḥ*.

[56] So Mt genly, Vā. Vṣ, Bh agree. *Ce*Mt *Prasenaji*; *l*Mt °*sannaji*; Gr *Senajit*: *l*Vṣ omits him.

[57] *Kṛto*° in *e*Mt; *j*Mt *tato bhavyāt*.

[58] So all; but *l*Vṣ *Kṣudrajit*: *a*Vṣ omits him.

[59] *Mavarā* in *e*Mt.

[60] In *ce*Mt *nṛpaḥ*; *n*Mt *na saḥ*.

[61] So Mt genly: *a*[3]*d*Vā *Kuliko*, *Ca*[1]*a*[2]*a*[4]Vā *Kṣul*°; *c*Mt *Kṣullako*, *e*Mt *Kṣall*°; *j*Mt *Tūlako*. Vṣ *Kuṇḍaka*; *f*Mt *Ku*[*va*]*nako*;

Sumitraḥ [65] Surathasy=âpi [66] antyaś ca [67] bhavitā nṛpaḥ
eta Aikṣvākavaḥ [68] proktā [69] bhaviṣyā ye [70] Kalau yuge [71]
Bṛhadbal-ânvaye jātā [72] bhaviṣyāḥ kula-vardhanāḥ [73]
śūrāś ca kṛta-vidyāś ca satya-sandhā jit-êndriyāḥ [74]
niḥśeṣāḥ kathitāś c-aiva nṛpā ye vai purātanāḥ [75]
atr=ânuvaṁśa[76]-śloko 'yaṁ viprair gītaḥ purātanaiḥ [77]
Ikṣvākūṇām ayaṁ vaṁśaḥ Sumitr-ânto bhaviṣyati [78]
Sumitram prāpya rājānaṁ saṁsthām prāpsyati vai Kalau[79].

ity evam Mānavo vaṁśaḥ [80]
prāg eva [82] samudāhṛtaḥ [83]

ity evam Mānavaṁ kṣatram [81]
Ailaṁ ca samudāhṛtam [84]

*l*Vṣ *Kuraṇḍaka*: *p*Bh *Kaṇaṁka*; *f*Bh *Gaṇaka*; *g*Bh *Sun*°; Bh genly *Raṇ*°; *c*Bh *Rūn*°: *er*Bh omit him. *C*Gr *Kuḍava*; *ab*Gr *Kuḍara*. Gr inserts a king *Sumitra* before him, misplacing apptly the next king Suratha.

[62] In *j*Mt *Kūl*°; *f*Mt *Krul*°; *ce*Mt *Kṣull*°.

[63] So Mt, Vā. Vṣ, Bh agree: *k*Bh *Suretha*; *f*Mt *Surasaḥ*: *h*Vṣ *Adhiratha*; *l*Vṣ *Viḍūr*° or *Vimyūr*°: *c*Bh *Sunaya*; *er*Bh omit him. Gr apptly *Sumitra*, see note [61].

[64] *Sutaḥ* in *cen*Mt. Bh *tanayas tataḥ*.

[65] So all: *e*Vā omits this name.

[66] So Vā, *bcdfgjkn*Mt; *e*Mt °*thaś c=âpi*: other Mt °*thāj jāto*; *A*Mt adds *hy*: *e*Vā °*thāt tasmād*: *l*Vṣ says *tat-putraś*.

[67] So Vā, *n*Mt; *e*Vā °*sa*; Mat genly °*tu*; *b*Vā *antya ca*. *Antyaḥ* crp to *antaḥ* in *b*Mt, *ab*Gr; to *anyaḥ* in *Ccefgj*Mt, Vṣ genly; to *ataḥ* in *C*Gr; to *tataś* in *d*Vā: so *antyaś ca* to *antasya* in *gk*Vā. Bh *niṣṭhânta*.

[68] So *bdh*Vā, Bḍ. *AC*Mt *ete c=Aik*°; *cen*Mt, *e*Vā *ete Ik*°; *bdfg*Mt *ity et=Êk*°, *j*Mt °*ev=Êk*°. Vā genly *eta Aikṣvākavāḥ*; *m*Vā *ete Ai[la]kṣvākavaḥ*.

[69] *Bhūpā* in *j*Mt.

[70] So Mt genly, *e*Vā: *cejn*Mt °*ṣyanti*. Vā, Bḍ *bhavitāraḥ*.

[71] *Kilau purā* in *j*Vā.

[72] So Vā, Bḍ; *e*Vā °*tv ete*; *bcn*Mt °*ânvayā ye tu*. Mt genly °*ânvavāye tu*: *j*Mt *Vṛhadba..nṛpā ye tu*; *cjq*Bh °*balā nṛpāḥ*. Vṣ °*bal-ânvayāḥ*. Bh genly *ete Bārhadbal-ânvayāḥ*: *rt*Bh *ete c=ânāgatā nṛpāḥ*.

[73] So Mt genly: *d*Mt *kṣudra-vaṁdh*°, *bfg*Mt °*bāndhavāḥ*, *e*Vā *putra-bāndh*°; *k*Mt *kṣatra-bandhavaḥ*: *j*Mt *kruddha-vaṁdhanaḥ*; *cen*Mt *śuddha-vaṁśa-jāḥ*. Bḍ reads this half line, *mahā-vīrya-parākramāḥ*. Vā repeats *bhavitāraḥ Kalau yuge*.

[74] This line is only in Va and Bḍ.

[75] This line is only in *cen*Mt.

[76] *Atr-ânubandha* in *k*Mt.

[77] So Mt genly; *bcfgjn*Mt *gīto vipraiḥ*. Vā *bhaviṣya-jñair udāhṛtaḥ*; Bḍ *bhaviṣyajjñ*°; *d*Vā *bhaviṣyatair* (or °*nair*)°: see Introdn. § 8.

[78] So all; but *j*Mt *Sumitrā te bh*°: *e*Mt omits the second half line.

[79] So all: except that Vṣ, Bh begin *yatas tam*; *r*Bh *eṣyati* for *prāpsyati*; *l*Vṣ *tasmāt* for *saṁsthām*. Vṣ reads the second half line, *sa saṁsthām* (*h*, *saṁsthānam*) *prāpsyate Kalau*. This line in *j*Mt is—

Sumitraś c=âpi rājā vai saṁsthām prāpsyati kevalam.

[80] So this line is in Mt genly: *b*Mt *Mānavaṁ vaṁśam*.

[81] So this line is in Vā, Bḍ: *Cgk*Vā †*kṣetram*: *e*Vā blunders thus—

ity etat Soma-jaṁ kṣatram Aila-jaṁ samudāhṛtam;

for *Aila-ja* = *Soma-ja*, and neither term applies to the Aikṣvākus who were Mānavas.

[82] In *b*Mt *Pāṇḍavam*; *cn*Mt *Ailasya*; *e*Mt *Elaś ca*; *k*Mt †*malasa*; *j*Mt *etaiḥ ca*; *d*Mt crp.

[83] In *b*Mt °*tam*: *e*Mt *su-mah-âdṛtaḥ*; *c*Mt *su-mah-âdbhutaḥ*.

[84] *Su-suhṛd-gatam* in *b*Vā.

Bārhadrathas.

*Text—A*Mt *271,* 17b–30a; *A*Vā *99,* 294–309a; Bḍ iii, *74,* 107b–122a.

*Corresp. passages—C*Vṣ iv, *23*; *G*Bh ix, *22,* 45b–49; *C*Gr i, *141,* 9–11.

The Matsya, Vāyu and Brahmāṇḍa give the whole, and agree except where noted. The Viṣṇu, Bhāgavata and Garuḍa give merely a list of names. There is some confusion in the Matsya in lines 20, 22, and 24 compared with l. 26, and its version and that of the Vāyu and Brahmāṇḍa are both given, the Matsya on the left and the other on the right.

Scarcely any copies are complete. L. 15 is only in Vā and Bḍ, and ll. 30, 31 only in *j*Mt. All copies of Mt omit ll. 26–28, except that l. 26 is in *dfgk*Mt and ll. 27, 28 in *cdefgjkm*Mt. Other omissions are: *ce*Mt ll. 8, 9, 13, 20, 21, 23–25, and *e*Mt also ll. 29, 32, 33; *j*Mt ll. 8–12, 17–19, 32, 33; *k*Mt ll. 12, 13, 17–23; *l*Mt ll. 8–12, 21–29; *m*Mt ll. 10–12, 14, 24, 25 and misplaces 18–20 after 23; *n*Mt ll. 19 (second half)–22 (first half): *a*[1]*a*[2]Vā ll. 23–25; *b*Vā ll. 16 (second half)–18 (first half); *e*Vā ll. 7–9, 15; *f*Vā l. 25; *g*Vā ll. 21–29; *j*Vā ll. 1 (second half)–2 (first half), 10–12; *l*Vā ll. 8–12; *m*Vā ll. 23–25: *hp*Mt and *l*Vṣ have lost the whole. Vṣ and Bh omit Nirvṛti; *r*Bh also Kṣema, Suvrata, Dharmanetra and Suśrama; and *ab*Gr Senājit and all after Dṛḍhasena.

Lines 30, 31 in *j*Mt are perhaps valuable. This dynasty was founded by Bṛhadratha, son of Vasu Caidyôparicara, and he and his 9 successors reigned down to the great battle; see JRAS, 1910, pp. 11, 22, 29. From the battle to Senājit 6 kings are named, excluding Senājit who is spoken of as the then reigning king; and from and including him to the end 16 kings are mentioned. There were thus 32 kings altogether, 10 before the battle and 22 after; or from the standpoint of Senājit's reign 16 past and 16 future. Lines 30–31 in *j*Mt take the standpoint of his reign and speak of him and his successors as the 16 future kings, and say *prima facie* their total duration was 723 years; see note [98]. Lines 32–33, which are not in *j*Mt, reckon (in a way) from the beginning and speak of all the 32 kings as future since most of them were posterior to the battle; and thus they say the whole dynasty lasted 1000 years. These two statements are not contradictory but are hardly compatible, because taken together they assign 723 years to the last 16 kings and only 277 to the first 16. The total of 1000 years for 32 kings is excessive, and that of 723 years for 16 kings is absurd. But if we can read lines 30–31 as two independent sentences, and treat *teṣām* as applying, not merely to those 16 future kings, but to the Bṛhadrathas generally, their purport stands thus—"These 16 kings are to be known as the future Bṛhadrathas: and[1] their kingdom (that is, the kingdom of the Bṛhadrathas) lasts 723 years." The total duration then, 723 years, would be within possibility, for the average reign would be about 22½ years. This rendering would of course discredit lines 32–33. If we read *vayo* in *j*Mt with that construction (see note [98]), the total period would be 700 years and would give an average reign of just under 22 years, which would be *viṁś-âdhikam.*

[1] The position of *ca* does not necessarily discredit this rendering, for *cas* are often inserted anywhere in these accounts.

Ata ūrdhvam pravakṣyāmi Māgadhā ye Bṛhadrathāḥ [1]
Jarāsandhasya ye vaṁśe [2] Sahadev-ânvaye [3] nṛpāḥ
atītā vartamānāś ca [4] bhaviṣyāś ca tathā punaḥ [5]
prādhānyataḥ pravakṣyāmi gadato me nibodhata [6]
saṅgrāme Bhārate vṛtte [7] Sahadeve nipātite [8]
Somādhis [9] tasya dāyādo [10] rāj=âbhūt [11] sa Girivraje [12]
pañcāśataṁ [13] tath=âṣṭau ca [14] samā rājyam akārayat
Śrutaśravāś [15] catuḥ-ṣaṣṭiṁ [16] samās tasy=ânvaye [17] 'bhavat [18]
Ayutāyus [19] tu [20] ṣaḍ-viṁśad [21] rājyaṁ varṣāṇy [22] akārayat

catvāriṁśat [23] samās tasya	samāḥ śataṁ [24] Nirāmitro
Niramitro [25] divaṁ gataḥ	mahīm bhuktvā divaṁ gataḥ

[1] So Mt, $a^{2}a^{3}a^{4}$*bdfgh*Vā; also *l*Vā (reading *yo*): *fkm*Vā *Māgadha* (*m*, °*dhe*) *ye Bṛhadrathaḥ*, Bḍ *Māgadho yo B°*, *j*Mt *Māgadhêśo B°*: other Vā *Māgadheyān Bṛhadrathān*: *e*Vā *vaṁśe ye vai Vṛhadrathāt*. Bh says—
Atha Māgadha-rājāno bhavitāro vadāmi te;
which is not Skt but Pali; see Appendix I, § ii. Vṣ says—
Māgadhānāṁ Vārhadrathānām bhaviṣyāṇām (*k*Vṣ *bhāvinām*) anukramaṁ kathayāmi.

[2] So Vā, Bḍ. Mt *pūrveṇa ye Jarāsandhāt*, which should prob. be *pūrve tu ye J°*, cf. *j*Mt *sarve ye tu J°*. Vṣ says—
atra hi vaṁśe mahābalā Jarāsandha-pradhānā babhūvuḥ.
See JRAS, 1908, p. 316; and 1910, p. 29.

[3] In *j*Mt °*devās tu ye*; *d*Mt crp.

[4] Both accus. pl. in *cefgn*Mt; both nom. sing. in *j*Mt.

[5] So Vā, Bḍ. Mt °*ṣyāṁś* (*bdj*, °*ṣyāś*) *ca nibodhata* (*j*, *nibodha tān*).

[6] This line only in Vā, Bḍ: *e*Vā *prādhānyās tān*.

[7] So Mt; *j*Mt *matte*. Vā, Bḍ *tasmin*.

[8] So Mt, *e*Vā. Vā, Bḍ °*devo nipātitaḥ*: *ce*Mt *yaiś ca bhuktā mahī drayam* (*c*, *duyam*).

[9] So Mt, Vā genly. Bḍ, *cdefgj*Vṣ, *C*Gr *Somāpi*; *e*Vā, *bh*Vṣ °*āvi*; *bn*Mt °*ādi*; Vṣ genly °*āmi*; *k*Vṣ °*āri*: *a*Vṣ *Semāvi*; *j*Mt, *b*Vā *Samādhi*, *h*Vā *Sām°*. Bh *Mārjāri*. For *Somādhis tasya* *c*Mt has *Sahadevasya*, *e*Mt °*devo 'sya*.

[10] So Mt. Vā, Bḍ *tanayo*.

[11] So Mt: *e*Vā *rāj=āsīt*. Vā, Bḍ *rājarṣiḥ*.

[12] In *l*Mt *Giri*[*saṁ*]*vrajan*; *ce*Mt *samiti-dhvajaḥ*.

[13] *Pañcāśac ca* in *fg*Mt; *j*Mt reads this half line, *pañcāśat sapta ca tathā*.

[14] *Tathā c=aiva* in *b*Mt; *e*Vā omits *th=âṣṭau ca*.

[15] So Mt, a^{1-4}*m*Vā, Bḍ. Bh, *bk*Vṣ, *C*Gr agree. *C*Vā °*śruvāś*; *f*Bh °*śruva*; *ab*Gr °*ścavās*: *g*Bh *Śataśravas*, *t*Bh *Vyutaś°*. Vṣ genly *Śrutavān*; *a*Vṣ †*Tukṣata*.

[16] So Mt, *C*a^{1}Vā: a^{2-4}*bdfghjklm*Vā, Bḍ *sapta-ṣaṣṭi*; but *d*Vā repeats the line thus—
Śrutaśravā ṣaṣṭi samās tatas tasya suto 'bhavat:
so *b*Vā also, crp.

[17] So Mt genly; *b*Mt °*ânvayo*; *d*Mt °*ântayo*; *n*Mt *tasya nayo*. Vā, Bḍ *tasya suto*.

[18] *Bhavet* in *bk*Mt.

[19] So Vā, Bḍ. Vṣ, Bh, *C*Gr agree; *g*Vṣ °*tāyuta*, *ab*Gr °*tāmus*, *r*Bh °*dhāyus*; *f*Bh '*dhutaś ca*; *j*Vṣ *Uyus*. Mt genly *Apratīpī*; $a^{1}a^{2}$*dfgm*Mt *Apratāpī* (which would be an easy misreading of *Ayutāyī*); *n*Mt *Anayāpaṁ*; *k*Mt *Asutā*.

[20] *Ca* in Mt.

[21] So *bk*Mt, Bḍ; Vā genly *ṣaḍ-viṁśaṁ*: *m*Vā that or *ṣaṭ-triṁśaṁ*. Mt genly, $a^{1}a^{2}$*fgjn*Vā *ṣaṭ-triṁśat* or °*śaṁ*: but *dfg*Mt, *bdh*Vā *ṣaḍ-triṁśat* or °*śa*, where the *ḍ* suggests the correct reading is *ṣaḍ-viṁśat*, for *v* and *tr* are often confused.

[22] So Vā, Bḍ. Mt *samā* (*k*Mt *abdaṁ*) *rājyam*.

[23] So Mt: *k*Mt °*śati*.

[24] So Vā, Bḍ: *e*Vā omits these words.

[25] So Mt genly; *bn*Mt *tasmān Nir°*; *n*Mt *Nirāmitro*: but *ce*Mt *samā Mitro bhuktvā c=aiva*; *k*Mt *Śarmamitro bhogān bhuktvā*; *dfg*Mt *Nirāmitro* (*g*, °*titro*) *bhuktvā c=êmāṁ*.

pañcāśataṁ samāḥ ṣaṭ ca [26] Sukṣatraḥ [27] prāptavān mahīm
trayo-viṁśad Bṛhatkarmā [28] rājyaṁ varṣāṇy [29] akārayat

Senājit [30] samprayātaś ca [31]	Senājit [30] sāmpratam [32] c=âpi
bhuktvā [33] pañcāśatam [34] mahīm	etā vai [35] bhokṣyate [36] samāḥ [37]

Śrutañjayas [38] tu [39] varṣāṇi [40] catvāriṁśad [41] bhaviṣyati
mahā-balo [42] mahā-bāhur [43] mahā-buddhi[44]-parākramaḥ
aṣṭā-viṁśati [45] varṣāṇi mahīm [46] prāpsyati vai [47] Vibhuḥ [48]
aṣṭa-pañcāśataṁ [49] c=âbdān [50] rājye sthāsyati vai Śuciḥ [51]
aṣṭā-viṁśat [52] samā rājā [53] Kṣemo [54] bhokṣyati vai mahīm [55]

Vṣ, *e*Vā, Bh, Gr *Nirāmitro.* Bh adds *tat-sutaḥ.*

[26] But *fg*Mt *ṣaḍva*; *n*Mt *ṣaḍga*; *c*Mt *ṣaṣṭaḥ*; *e*Mt *hy aṣṭaḥ*; *e*Vā *tasya.*

[27] So *df*Mt, a^3*e*Vā, Bḍ; Vṣ agrees: *k*Vā *Sukṣatrā*; a^4*fgm*Vā °*kṣattā.* *C*a^1a^2Vā °*kṛttaḥ*, *h*Vā °*kṛttā*, *b*Vā °*kṛtā*, *d*Vā °*kṣakṛt*; *g*Mt *Kṣukṣatraḥ*; *b*Mt *Sukṣaraḥ.* Mt genly *Surakṣaḥ*; *ce*Mt *Sumitraḥ*; *k*Mt *Nakṣatraḥ*; *n*Mt crp. Bh, *b*Vṣ *Sunakṣatra*; *ab*Gr *Suhakṣ*°; *C*Gr *Svakṣetra.* Vṣ adds *tat-tanayaḥ.*

[28] So Vā, Bḍ, with °*śad*, °*śaṁ*, or °*śa.* Mt *Bṛhatkarmā trayo-viṁśad*; *ce*Mt °*tu dvā-triṁśat.* Vṣ *Vṛhatkarman.* Bh °*tsena*; *h*Bh *Vihaśena.* *C*Gr *Bahukarmaka*; *ab*Gr *Varukarmaṇa.*

[29] So Vā, Bḍ; *e*Vā *varṣāṇi 'kār*°. Mt genly *abdaṁ rājyam*, *fg*Mt *abdān*°: *cen*Mt read this half line, *prāptā* (*n*, °*taś*; c, °*tvā*) *c=êmāṁ vasundharām.*

[30] So Mt, Vā genly, Bḍ: a^2*bdj*Mt, a^2a^3Vā, Vṣ, *C*Gr *Sena*°; *n*Mt *Śena*°, *m*Mt *Śyena*°; *k*Vā *San-jit.* Bh genly *Karmajit*, *n*Bh *Kār*°, *hk*Bh *Kūr*°; *r*Bh *Dharmavid*: *e*Vā *Manīṣī.* *C*Gr inverts this king and the next. See the corresponding lines about Adhisīmakṛṣṇa (p. 4, l. 6) and Divākara (p. 10, l. 5).

[31] So Mt genly: *bfgn*Mt *sāmprataś c=âyam*, *j*Mt *samprajic c*°.

[32] So Vā, Bḍ: *e*Vā *sāmprataś.*

[33] *Bhoktā* in *bdfgjln*Mt.

[34] So a^1a^2*bdl*Mt; *fgj*Mt °*śatā.* Mt genly *pañca-śatam.*

[35] So Vā genly, Bḍ. *C*Vā *etāṁ vai*, 'this (earth)'. But *e*Vā *pañcāśad*, thus bringing this version into similarity to the corresponding verses, p. 4, l. 6 and p. 10, l. 5.

[36] *C*Vā *bhujyate*; *fm*Vā *bhokṣyase.*

[37] In *m*Vā *tava*; *f*Vā *tave.*

[38] So all; except *j*Mt *Śrutiñj*°; a^3*k*Vā *Śatañj*°; *g*Mt *Śrītañj*°; *b*Mt *Stutañj*°; *d*Vṣ *Kṣatañj*°; *b*Vṣ *Ripuñj*°: *e*Vā *Śataṁyajñas.* Bh names him *Sṛtañjaya* indirectly, *Sṛtañjayād Vipraḥ*; *c*Bh *Mutañj*°. *C*Gr inverts him and Senājit.

[39] *Ca* in *cen*Mt.

[40] In *en*Mt *varṣāṇāṁ*; *j*Mt *varṣān vai.*

[41] *Pañca-triṁśad* in *fg*Mt, *e*Vā.

[42] This line is only in Vā, Bḍ. *C*Vā °*bāhur.* Bḍ *ripuñjayo.*

[43] *C*Vā °*buddhir.*

[44] *C*Vā *bhīma*; *g*Vā *bala.*

[45] So Mt; *e*Vā *aṣṭa-viṁśat tu*: *gm*Vā *pañca-viṁśat tu.* Vā, Bḍ *pañca-triṁśat tu.*

[46] *Masvā* in *e*Vā.

[47] So Mt genly; *j*Mt *pāsyati*°; *cen*Mt *samprāpsyate.* Vā, Bḍ *pālayitā.*

[48] So Mt genly, *e*Vā; *b*Mt *vibho*; *cefg*Mt *Prabhuḥ*; *l*Mt *prabho*: *djk*Mt *vīryavān* for *vai Vibhuḥ.* Vṣ, Bh genly *Vipra*; *p*Bh *Dhipra*; *j*Vṣ *Pipra*; *k*Vṣ *Ripu*; *b*Vṣ *Ripuñjaya.* *C*Gr *Bhūri*; *ab*Gr *Saṁvi.* Vā, Bḍ *nṛpaḥ*, giving no name; *m*Vā [*vṛ*]*nṛpaḥ.*

[49] *Aṣṭau pañcāśatā* in *e*Vā.

[50] So *dfg*Mt, Vā, Bḍ: *c*Mt *c=âbdā*; *n*Mt, *h*Vā *cāṣṭān*; *e*Mt *cāṣṭā.* Mt genly *ṣaṭ ca*: *e*Vā *śūnho.*

[51] So all: except *n*Bh *Suci*; *b*Mt *Muciḥ*; *e*Mt *Śruciḥ*; *g*Bh *Śuśi.* Vṣ adds *tasya putraḥ.*

[52] In *cde*Mt *aṣṭā-triṁśat* (or °*śa*); *m*Mt *dvātriṁśaś ca.*

[53] So Mt. Vā, Bḍ *pūrṇāḥ.*

[54] So all: except *e*Vā *Kṣamo*; *l*Mt *Kṣaimo.* Vṣ genly, *C*Gr *Kṣemya*: *fg*Mt *Pakso* or *Yakṣo.*

[55] So Mt genly; *cefgn*Mt *bhokṣyati* (*f*, *bhojyati*) *medinīm.* Vā, Bḍ *rājā bhaviṣyati.*

Suvratas tu [56] catuḥ-ṣaṣṭiṁ [57] rājyam prāpsyati vīryavān [58]
pañca-triṁśati [59] varṣāṇi | pañca varṣāṇi pūrṇāni [60]
Sunetro [61] bhokṣyate mahīm [62] | Dharmanetro [63] bhaviṣyati
bhokṣyate [64] Nirvṛtiś [65] c=êmām [66] aṣṭa-pañcāśataṁ samāḥ [67]
aṣṭa-viṁśat [68] samā rājyaṁ | aṣṭa-triṁśat [69] samā rājyaṁ [70]
Trinetro [71] bhokṣyate tataḥ [72] | Suśramasya [73] bhaviṣyati
catvāriṁśat tath=âṣṭau ca [74] Dṛḍhaseno [75] bhaviṣyati
trayas-triṁśat tu [76] varṣāṇi | trayas-triṁśat tu varṣāṇi
Mahīnetraḥ [77] prakāśyate [78] | Sumatiḥ [79] prāpsyate tataḥ [80]
dvā-triṁśat tu [81] samā rājā [82] Sucalas [83] tu bhaviṣyati [84]

[56] So Bḍ. Vṣ, Bh, *C*Gr agree: also *e*Vā *Suvratas tha* (for *Suvrato 'tha*); *Cbfghm*Vā *Suvatas tu*. Vā genly *Bhuvatas tu*; *j*Vā, 2 MSS of *C*Vā *Yuvatas°*; *d*Vā †*savatsara*; *j*Bh *Suvṛta*; *ab*Gr *Sujāta*. Mt genly *Anuvrataś*, *g*Mt *°traś*; *f*Mt *Anuvṛta*: *ce*Mt *Kṣemakasya*.

[57] So Mt, Vā, Bḍ (*°ṭi*, *°ṭī*, *°ṭiṁ*, *°ṭīṁ*): *cde*Mt *sutaḥ ṣaṣṭi*; *d*Vā *tu ṣaṣṭiṁ vai*; *m*Mt *ṣaṣṭi samā*.

[58] In *ce*Mt *yatnataḥ* (for *Suvrataḥ*? see note [56]).

[59] So *Cb*Mt; *fgjkm*Mt *°triṁśat tu* (*m*, *ca*; *k* omits *tu*). *Al*Mt *°viṁśati*; *d*Mt *pañcāśac ca* (with a syll. short).

[60] So Vā, Bḍ: *e*Vā *varṣāṇi* repeated.

[61] In *j*Mt †*Snānātro*; *l*Mt *pañcāśan*.

[62] *Mahān* in *j*Mt.

[63] So Vā, Bḍ; also *h*Vṣ, *hjk*Bh, and v. r. in *G*Bh: *h*Vā *°nepro*. Bh genly *Dharmasūtra*; *n*Bh *°putra*; *bq*Bh *°kṣetra*. Vṣ, Gr briefly *Dharma*.

[64] *Bhojyate* in *m*Mt, *em*Vā.

[65] So Mt; *j*Mt *Ninṛtiś*; *e*Vā *Nṛbhṛtaḥ*. Vā, Bḍ *nṛpatiś*.

[66] So Mt. Bḍ *c=êmā*; $a^1a^2a^4$*fkm*Vā *caimā*; *h*Vā *caibhā*; *d*Vā *c=ôbhā*; other Vā *c=aiva*: *e*Vā *pṛthvīm*.

[67] In *f*Mt *aṣṭam p°*: *b*Mt *aṣṭā-pañcāśa vai samām*.

[68] So Mt: *cde*Mt *°viṁśa*.

[69] So Vā, Bḍ. *C*Vā *aṣṭā°*.

[70] So Vā. Bḍ *rāṣṭraṁ*.

[71] So Mt genly; *j*Mt *Train°*: *cdefg*Mt *Sun°*.

[72] In *cefgj*Mt *nṛpaḥ*; *d*Mt *mahīm*.

[73] So Bḍ; Vṣ genly *Suśrama*: *k*Vṣ *Suśruma*, *e*Vṣ and *ab*Gr *Śuś°*, *C*Gr †*Śmaś°*: *d*Vṣ *Śuśuma*; *t*Bh *Śrama*. Bh genly *Śama*; *hknp*Bh *Sama*; *b*Vṣ *Susava*; *h*Vṣ *Suvrama*. Vā genly *Suvratasya*, *e*Vā *Suśrut°*.

[74] So Mt; *e*Vā *°śatam aṣṭau ca*. Vā, Bḍ *°śad* †*daś=âṣṭau ca*.

[75] So a^2*dj*Mt, Vā genly, Bḍ. Vṣ genly, *Bcrt*Bh agree; *C*Gr *°senaka*; *j*Vṣ *°śnena*; *ab*Gr *Daṭhasenaka* (Pkt): *m*Mt *Dṛḍhanetā*; *fg*Mt and *e*Vā *Vṛhatseno*; *b*Mt *Mahats°*, *n*Mt *Mahās°*, *CVa*$^1a^3a^4$Mt *Dyumats°*, and so *Gp*Bh (altered in *p* to *Dṛḍhas°*).

[76] So Mt genly; *dj*Mt *°śac ca*; *fg*Mt *°śati*: *k*Mt *pañca-triṁśad* (omitting *tu*).

[77] So *CVa*$^3a^4$*kn*Mt: a^1a^2*bdfgj*Mt *mahīṁ N°*.

[78] So Mt genly: a^1*bf*Mt *praśāsyate*, *dg*Mt *°ti*; a^2*k*Mt *praśasyate*, *gjn*Mt *°ti*. The root *praśās* appears to be treated as belonging to the *ya* class, see *Various local dynasties*, note [54], *post*.

[79] So Vā, Bḍ, Vṣ, Bh, *C*Gr: *d*Vṣ *Sumanti*.

[80] In *e*Vā *°te mahīm*; *d*Vā *viṁśatiḥ samāḥ*.

[81] So Mt genly, *e*Vā; *dfgk*Mt *°śac ca*; *n*Mt *°śataṁ*. Vā *dvā-viṁśati*; *j*Mt *°śat tu*. Bḍ *catvāriṁśat*.

[82] So Mt; *fg*Mt *rājan*. Vā, *d*Mt *rājyam*. *Ak*Mt add *hy*.

[83] Mt genly *Acalas*; *b*Mt *Abalas*: a^1a^2*jl*Vā *Sucalo*; *C*Vā *Sucălo*; a^3a^4*bhk*Vā *Sucālo*. Vṣ, *n*Mt, Bh, *C*Gr *Subalas*; *h*Bh *Subāla*; *c*Bh *Surbola*: *e*Vā *Sudhanvā*; *r*Bh *Bhūvana* or *Bhūbala*; one *C*Vā MS *Yuvāno*. *Sucalo* seems the best form. Bḍ omits this line: *d*Vā reads it—

rājyaṁ Sucālo bhokṣyati atha śatru-jayī tataḥ;

which suggests a king *Śatrujayin*, but no other authority supports this. Bh adds *janitā tataḥ*, 'son of the preceding'.

catvāriṁśat samā rājā [85] Sunetro [86] bhokṣyate [87] tataḥ [88]
Satyajit [89] pṛthivīṁ rājā [90] try-aśītim [91] bhokṣyate [92] samāḥ [93]
prāpy⸗êmāṁ Viśvajic [94] c⸗âpi pañca-viṁśad [95] bhaviṣyati
Ripuñjayas [96] tu varṣāṇi [97] pañcāśat prāpsyate mahīm
ṣoḍaś⸗aite [98] nṛpā jñeyā bhavitāro Bṛhadrathāḥ
trayo[99]-viṁś-âdhikaṁ teṣāṁ rājyaṁ ca śata-saptakam
dvā-triṁśac [1] ca [2] nṛpā hy ete [3] bhavitāro Bṛhadrathāḥ [4]
pūrṇaṁ varṣa-sahasraṁ [5] vai [6] teṣāṁ rājyam bhaviṣyati [7].

Pradyotas.

Text—*A*Mt *272*, 1–5 ; *A*Vā *99*, 309b–314a ; Bḍ iii, *74*, 122b–127a.

Corresp. passages—*C*Vṣ iv, *24*, 1–2 ; *G*Bh xii, *1*, 2–4.

The Matsya, Vāyu, and Brahmāṇḍa give the whole dynasty. The Viṣṇu and Bhāgavata name all the kings.

All are complete, except thus: *Ck*Mt omit lines 9, 10; *g*Mt ll. 5, 6; *b*Mt

[84] So Mt. Vā *bhokṣyate tataḥ*; *e*Vā *bhojyate*°.

[85] As to this line, see p. 13: *dfyk*Mt *rājyaṁ*.

[86] So Mt, Vā, Bḍ. Vṣ genly, *frt*Bh *Sunīta*, *d*Vṣ °*nāta*; Bh genly, *a*Vṣ °*nītha*. *C*Gr *Nīta*.

[87] In *k*Mt *bhojyate*; *e*Vā *bhavitā*.

[88] In *dfgk*Mt *nṛpaḥ*.

[89] So all (see p. 13); except *jk*Mt *Saptajit*; *cdem*Mt *Sarvajit*.

[90] So *cdefkm*Mt, *e*Vā; *gj*Mt °*vī-rājā*. Vā genly °*vī-rājyaṁ*. Bḍ °*vī-rāṣṭraṁ*.

[91] So Vā, Bḍ: *cefgkm*Mt *aśītiṁ*; *d*Mt *aśītiḥ*: *e*Vā *triṁśatam*: *j*Mt reads this half line, '*śītim prāpsyati vai samāḥ*. *Tryaśītim* may be a mistake for *hy aśītim*, or (by metathesis of vowels) for *triṁśatam*.

[92] In *e*Vā *bhojyate*; *cdefgkm*Mt *prāpsyate*.

[93] In *dfykm*Mt *tataḥ*; *ce*Mt *nṛpaḥ*.

[94] So all (see p. 13): but *k*Vā *Vīṣyajic*; Vā genly *Vīrajic*: *cdefgjkm*Mt read this half line, *Viśvajic c⸗aiva* (*d*, *sarba*) *varṣāṇi*.

[95] So *ek*Mt, *dfm*Vā, Bḍ. Vā genly, *cdjm*Mt °*triṁśad*: *g*Mt *tri-pañcaśad*, *f*Mt °*cād*.

[96] So Mt, *e*Vā. Vṣ, Bh agree: see *Pradyotas*, note [1]. Vā, Bḍ synonym. *Ariñj*°; *d*Vā †*Acirañj*°; *C*Gr *Iṣuñj*°: *g*Mt omits this line and repeats l. 24 here. Vṣ adds *tasya putraḥ*.

[97] So Mt, Vā. Bḍ *varṣāṇām*.

[98] So *j*Mt (see p. 13) with *ṣoḍaśaiste*, which no doubt means *ṣoḍaś⸗aite*, because from Senājit to the end there were 16 kings, though its list is imperfect.

[99] So *j*Mt (see p. 13) reading *vayo*, which is no doubt a misreading of *trayo*, *tr* and *v* being often confused. If we keep *vayo*, the line may perhaps mean, 'Their periods exceeded 20 years, and their kingdom lasted 700 years'; yet the first of these two statements, if it can be sō rendered, seems inept: see p. 13.

[1] So Mt genly, Vā. *Cbl*Mt °*śati* (omitting *ca*). Bḍ *dvāviṁśac*, which is the total number of kings mentioned. This half line in *g*Vā is, *ete mahābalāḥ sarve*.

[2] Mat *tu*; *e*Vā omits.

[3] *C*Mt *nṛpārhyate* (misprint): *e*Vā *ete hi nṛpā*.

[4] So Mt, Bḍ. Vā genly °*thāt*. *C*Vā *Dṛhadrathāḥ*; *e*Vā *dṛḍha-vratāḥ*.

[5] In *d*Mt *pūrvaṁ v*°; *fy*Mt *pūrṇe varṣa-sahasre*. Vṣ *varṣa-sahasram ekam*. Bh *sāhasra-vatsaram*.

[6] Mt *tu*.

[7] After this line *Abc*Mt insert l. 3 from the next dynasty.

inserts l. 2 of the next dynasty after l. 8: *e*Vā omits ll. 9 (second half), 10; *m*Vā omits ll. 5, 6 and reads then ll. 8, 9, 7–10: *n*Bh has lost Viśākhayūpa to the end; and *hp*Mt and *bt*Bh the whole.

The total of the reigns agrees with the period assigned to the dynasty, which is 138 years according to Vā, Bḍ, Vṣ, and Bh. Mt generally says the duration was 52 years, or at most (if *dvi-pañcāśat* could mean *dviḥ pañcāśat*) 100 roundly; but several copies make it 152 years (see note [30]).

Bṛhadratheṣv [1] atīteṣu [2] Vītihotreṣv [3] Avantiṣu [4]

Pulikaḥ [5] svāminaṁ hatvā [6] | Sunikaḥ [7] svāminaṁ hatvā
sva[8]-putram abhiṣekṣyati | putraṁ samabhiṣekṣyati [9]
miṣatāṁ [10] kṣatriyāṇāṁ [11] ca [12] | miṣatāṁ kṣatriyāṇāṁ hi [13]
Bālakaḥ [14] Pulik-ôdbhavaḥ [15] | Pradyotaṁ [16] Suniko [17] balāt [18]

sa vai praṇata[19]-sāmanto [20] bhaviṣyo [21] naya-varjitaḥ [22]

[1] In a^1bMt °*rathe*: *n*Mt *Bārhadratheṣv*, *e*Mt °*ratheśa*.

[2] In *be*Mt *vyatīteṣu*; a^1Mt °*te tu*; *b*Vā omits '*tīteṣu*.

[3] So Mt genly: Vā genly and *cden*Mt *Vīta*°; *e*Vā *Rīti*°. Bḍ *Vīrahantṛṣv*. *Vītihotreṣv* is right; see *Early Contemporary Dynasties*, l. 7, where all three read it right; the name occurs often in the Purāṇas.

[4] So Mt genly. Bḍ, a^2a^3bfghVā *a-vartiṣu*. Other Vā °*hotreṣu vartiṣu*, *e*Vā °*varṇiṣu*, *fgjk*Mt °*bandhuṣu*; *l*Mt °*bhaviṣyati*.

[5] So $a^{1-3}bcdefgkmn$Mt. *CGVa*^4lMt *Pulakaḥ*; *j*Mt *Palikāḥ*.

[6] *Kṛtvā* in *e*Mt.

[7] So *fm*Vā; and Vṣ genly. Bḍ, Bh *Śunaka*; *d*Bh *Śanaka*. Vā genly, *hk*Vṣ *Munikaḥ*; *l*Vṣ *Munīka*. Vṣ says—

yo 'yaṁ Ripuñjayo nāma Bārhadratho 'ntyaḥ tasya Suniko nām=âmātyo* bhaviṣyati. Sa c=ainaṁ svāminaṁ hatvā sva-putram Pradyota†-nāmānam abhiṣekṣyati: where * *k*Vṣ *âpatyo*; † *e*Vṣ *Pradyotana*. Bh reads—

yo 'ntyo * Purañjayo † nāma bhaviṣyo Bārahadrathaḥ ‡

tasy=âmātyas tu Śunako hatvā svāminam ātmajam

Pradyota-sañjñaṁ rājānaṁ kartā:—

where * *l*Vṣ '*nyaḥ*; † *d*Bh *Ripuñjayo* correctly, see p. 17, note [36]: ‡ *Bārahadrathaḥ* for the metre; *e*Bh *Bārhayad*°; *cp*Bh *Vāvṛhad*°; *d*Bh '*tha Bārhad*°, *afnrs*Bh *Bārhad*°, in disregard of metre: *q*Bh and v.r. in *G*Bh amend this half line, *bhāvyo Bārhadratho nṛpaḥ*.

[8] *Svam* in *bcd*Mt; *e*Mt †*sūṁ*.

[9] So Vā, Bḍ; *sam-* was probably *svam* originally: *d*Vā *rājye 'bhi*°.

[10] So Mt genly: *b*Mt *jiyatāṁ*; *l*Mt *niyatāṁ*; *n*Mt *niyantā*; *d*Mt †*maṣilām*: see p. 17, note [7].

[11] In *d*Mt °*yāyāṁ*.

[12] *Tu* in *cdefgjn*Mt.

[13] *Ca* in *e*Vā.

[14] So Mt genly: *b*Mt *bālakaiḥ*; *j*Mt *Mālikaḥ*; see note [27].

[15] So *cejn*Mt; see note [5]. *AC*Mt *Pulak*°; *k*Mt *Pulako* merely. But *bd*Mt *Puliko balāt*, *l*Mt *Pulako*°, *fgm*Mt *Pālako*°. The accus. seems to be required.

[16] So Vā genly. Vṣ, Bh corroborate, see note [7]. Bḍ °*tiṁ*; *e*Vā *Sudyotaṁ*. Ca^1a^3kVā *Pradyoto*.

[17] See note [7]; *f*Vā *Śunike*. Vā genly *Muniko*, *m*Vā °*ke*. Bḍ *nṛpatim*.

[18] To its statement in note [7] *h*Vṣ adds †*kyi saṁnati pārśva svayam evą rājā svayāmava bhăvino*.

[19] In *e*Mt *prajāta*; *k*Mt *prajāṁtāḥ*.

[20] In *l*Mt *śrīmanto*.

[21] So Mt genly, *e*Vā. Vā genly, a^1a^2bdMt °*ṣye*; *j*Mt *bhavitā*.

[22] So $Ca^3a^4cejkln$Mt, *cfghjklm*Vā; so *A*Vā which prints it '*naya*°. But *d*Mt *nava-v*°; *e*Vā *na ca v*°; *f*Mt *na ca dhārmikaḥ*, GVa^1a^2mMt °*dharmataḥ*, *b*Mt °*dharma-jit*:

trayo-viṁśat samā rājā [23] bhavitā [24] sa nar-ôttamaḥ [25]
catur-viṁśat samā rājā [26] Pālako [27] bhavitā tataḥ [28]
Viśākhayūpo [29] bhavitā nṛpaḥ pañcāśatīṁ [30] samāḥ
eka-viṁśat samā rājā [31]
Sūryakas [33] tu bhaviṣyati
eka-viṁśat [32] samā rājyam
Ajakasya [34] bhaviṣyati
bhaviṣyati [35] samā [36] viṁśat [37] tat-suto Nandivardhanaḥ [38]
dvi-pañcāśat tato [39] bhuktvā [40]
praṇaṣṭāḥ [44] pañca te nṛpāḥ.
aṣṭa-triṁśac [41]-chatam [42] bhāvyāḥ [43]
Prādyotāḥ [45] pañca te sutāḥ [46].

*d*Vā *mitra-varjitaḥ*; *b*Vā merely *varjitaḥ*. Bḍ reads this half line *bhaviṣyeṇa pravartitaḥ*.

[23] In a^2a^4Vā *rājya*.

[24] In *n*Mt *bhaviṣyat*.

[25] In *bln*Mt *manmath-âturaḥ*.

[26] So Vā, Bḍ. Mt genly *aṣṭā-viṁśati varṣāṇi*: *b*Mt °*viṁśati tathā varṣā* (with an extra syll.), see Appendix I, § i: *k*Mt °*viṁśat tato yo* (with a syll. short).

[27] So all, except *h*Bh *Pal*°; *d*Bh *Yāl*° (*p* and *y* confused); *k*Vṣ *Gopāl*°; *ce*Mt *Bāl*°; *bn*Mt *Til*°: *j*Mt *Pāśako*; *l*Vṣ *Baka*; *l*Mt *Nalakṣo*. Vṣ adds, *tasy=âpi Pālaka-nāmā putro*; Bh *yat Pālakaḥ sutaḥ*.

[28] So Vā, Bḍ: *e*Vā *punaḥ*. Mt *nṛpaḥ*.

[29] So genly, except *d*Vṣ °*yapa*, *b*Vṣ °*yūgha*, *c*Bh °*ṣūpa*, *b*Mt and *a*Vṣ °*bhūpo*, *fm*Vā °*dhūpo*, *j*Bh °*dūya*, *fg*Mt °*rūpo*, *r*Bh °*nṛpa*. With the dialectical variation of *ṣ* and *kh*, *n*Mt and *de*Vā *Viśaṣa-yūpo*, *bh*Vā °*sūyo*, *k*Bh °*mūpa*. Otherwise *d*Mt *Viśvākhayūpo*; *h*Bh *Visvay*°; *k*Vṣ *Viśāśvaṁy*°. Bh adds *tat-putro*; Vṣ implies it.

[30] So $Ca^1a^2a^4$Vā; *bghk*Vā °*tī*; a^3lVā °*tīḥ*: Bḍ °*taṁ*. Mt reads this half line, *tri-pañcāśat* (*j*Mt *pañcāśa drā*) *tathā samāḥ*; *e*Vā *kṣatriyāṇāṁ samā śatam*.

[31] So Mt: *k*Mt *rājye*.

[32] So *ef*Vā, Bḍ: *m*Vā first *trayo-viṁśat* (part of l. 5?) but in repeating has *eka*°. Vā genly *eka-triṁśat*.

[33] So Mt genly: *l*Mt *Sūryabas*; *d*Mt *Mūrjakas*; *m*Mt *Mṛjukas*.

[34] So Vā, Bḍ; *f*Vā *Ajyak*°, *d*Vā *Akark*°: *e*Vā reads this half line *Ajakaḥ sa kariṣyati*. Bh genly *Rājaka*; Vṣ *Janaka*: *d*Bh *Cājaka*; *ak*Vṣ *Ajaka*; *h*Vṣ *Aja*.

[35] In *b*Mt *Śiśunākaḥ*.

[36] So Vā, Bḍ, *b*Mt. Mt genly *nṛpas*; *f*Mt *bhṛśas*.

[37] Mt *triṁśat*; *j*Mt *tadvat*.

[38] So Mt, Bḍ. Vṣ, Bh agree: *d*Bh *Nanda*° altered to *Nandi*°; *c*Vṣ *Nakṣi*°. Vā genly *Varti*°; one MS of *C*Vā *Vardhi*°; a^1Vā *Kīrti*°. Bh adds *tat-putraḥ*; Vṣ implies it.

[39] So *ACbklm*Mt: *d*Mt *chate*; *fgjn*Mt *chatam*; *ce*Mt *satam*.

[40] In *cdefgj*Mt *bhūtvā*; *l*Mt *bhāvyaḥ*.

[41] So Vā genly, Bḍ; Ca^4Vā *aṣṭā*°; *j*Vā *aṭṭi-triṁśat*; *d*Vā †*aṣṭāttaśa*.

[42] In *jm*Vā *satam*; *dh*Vā *tatam*; *g*Vā *samā*.

[43] In *g*Vā *rājā*.

[44] In *g*Mt *prāṇaṣṭhāḥ*; *b*Mt *praṇanyāḥ*; *f*Mt *prāṇāṁdyāḥ*; *l*Mt *prothotāḥ*.

[45] So Vā genly, Bḍ: $a^1a^3a^4km$Vā, Vṣ *Prad*°. Bh *Pradyotanāḥ*; *d*Bh *Prād*°.

[46] So Vā. Bḍ *nṛpāḥ*. Similarly Vṣ—

ity ete aṣṭa*-triṁśad†-uttaram abda‡-śatam pañca Pradyotāḥ pṛthivīm bhokṣyanti:

where * *a*Vṣ *ṣaṭ*, *h*Vṣ *dvā*; † *bhk*Vṣ *viṁśad*; ‡ *j*Vṣ *ardda*, *h*Vṣ *aṣṭa*, and *k*Vṣ *arū*, all corruptions of *abda*. Bh says—

pañca Pradyotanā ime
aṣṭa*-triṁś†-ôttara-śatam bhokṣyanti
pṛthivīṁ nṛpāḥ:

where * *fm*Bh *aṣṭā*; † *m*Bh *viṁś*.

Śiśunāgas.

Text—*A*Mt *272*, 6–13ᵃ; *A*Vā *99*, 314ᵇ–322ᵃ; Bḍ iii, *74*, 127ᵇ–135ᵃ.

Corresp. passages—*C*Vṣ iv, *24*, 3; *G*Bh xii, *1*, 5–8ᵃ.

The Vāyu and Brahmāṇḍa give the whole, and the Matsya all except lines 11, 12. The Viṣṇu and Bhāgavata name all the kings and state the duration of the dynasty. All copies of the Matsya erroneously introduce the first two Kāṇvāyana kings (see note [24]) after l. 7; and the Vāyu and Brahmāṇḍa put l. 8 before ll. 6 and 7 contrary to all the other authorities.

The defects are these. *C*Mt omits l. 1; *ce*Mt ll. 13, 14; *j*Mt ll. 6 (second half), 7 (first half); *k*Mt ll. 2, 3, 10; *l*Mt ll. 5, 6: *a*⁴Vā omits ll. 6–end; *e*Vā ll. 8–10; *f*Vā ll. 15, 16, 17 (first half); *g*Vā ll. 7–14, 16, 17; *h*Vā has only ll. 1–3: *m*Bh omits Kṣemadharman to Udayin; *n*Bh has only the verses stating the duration of the dynasty; and *hp*Mt, *bt*Bh have nothing.

All the authorities say there were 10 kings, and do not differ much in their names. The duration of the dynasty appears to have been 163 years, for the Mt reading in l. 16 can well mean 'hundred, three, plus sixty' (see Introdn. §§ 42 ff.), though it would mean '360' if taken as literary Sanskrit; moreover '163' is a probable figure while '360' is an impossible one. The terms certainly admit of ambiguity, and an examination of the other versions shows how it developed.

The Bḍ and Bh reading *ṣaṣṭy-uttara-śata-trayam* (see note [46]) can also mean 163, if it represents a Pkt original of (something like) *saṭṭhy-uttara-satam tao*, but means 360 if taken as correct Skt. The former interpretation seems preferable, because this expression is used with *varṣāṇi* in Bḍ and with *samāḥ* in Bh, and these combinations do not constitute correct Skt but would be good in Pkt: still an ambiguity does appear there. It seems to have affected the two other versions. The Vā reading (see note [46]) taken as Pkt means 'hundred, three, plus sixty-two', but this is an impossible style of reckoning, and the only tenable construction is to read it as correct Skt meaning 362. As this is an impossible figure, I would suggest that the *dvi* is a corruption of *abda* [1], that the initial *a* blended with or was elided after the word that represented *varṣāṇi* in the Pkt original [2], and that the remaining *bda* was mistaken for *dvā* (or *dvi*). If this suggestion be tenable, the Vā reading agreed with Mt and meant 163. The Vṣ following upon the ambiguity and mistake says explicitly '362 years' in correct Skt.

[1] Compound consonants are sometimes inverted in the MSS, see note [43].

[2] Such elisions do take place in Pkt, and appear in Sanskrit, cf. p. 15, note [29]; p. 17, note [31]; *Various local dynasties*, note [48], *infra*; and to that cause are no doubt due the elisions in the middle of the following lines, *A*Vā *88*, 81, 115; *94*, 21:—

apadhvaṁs-eti bahuśo 'vadat krodha-samanvitaḥ.
devaiḥ sārdham mahātejā 'nugrahāt tasya dhīmataḥ.
rathī rājā 'py anucaro 'nyo 'gāc c-aiv-ânudṛśyate.

Instances might be easily multiplied from the Purāṇas.

Hatvā [1] teṣāṁ yaśaḥ kṛtsnaṁ Śiśunāgo [2] bhaviṣyati

Vārāṇasyāṁ sutaṁ sthāpya [3] śrayiṣyati [5] Girivrajam	Vārāṇasyāṁ sutas tasya [4] sa yāsyati [6] Girivrajam [7]

Śiśunāgaś ca [8] varṣāṇi catvāriṁśad bhaviṣyati
Kākavarṇaḥ [9] sutas tasya [10] ṣaṭ-triṁśat [11] prāpsyate mahīm [12]

ṣaṭ-triṁśac c=aiva [13] varṣāṇi Kṣemadharmā [15] bhaviṣyati	tatas tu viṁśatiṁ [14] rājā Kṣemadharmā [16] bhaviṣyati

catvāriṁśat [17] samā rājyaṁ [18] Kṣatraujāḥ [19] prāpsyate tataḥ [20]
aṣṭā-viṁśati [21] varṣāṇi [22] Vimbisāro [23] bhaviṣyati [24]
Ajātaśatrur [25] bhavitā pañca [26]-viṁśat samā nṛpaḥ
pañca [27]-viṁśat [28] samā rājā Darśakas [29] tu bhaviṣyati

[1] In a⁵Vā *hṛtvā*; kVā *hate*; cMt *kṛtvā*.

[2] So mMt, Bd. Vṣ, Bh agree: nMt *Śiṣunāgo* here. Mt, Vā genly *Śiśunāko*; bMt *Śigru°*; eMt *Suśruvāko* here; kVā *Śiśuko*; kVṣ *Śiśunāma*.

[3] So Mt: jMt *°sthāpyo*; dfMt *tu saṁsthāpya*.

[4] So Vā and Bd.

[5] So Mt genly; so bMt *ante*, see p. 18, but *śraṁyāsyati* here: cenMt *vrajiṣyati*; dfgmMt *adhyāsyati*, jMt *'dhiṣṭhās°*; lMt *†avyameti*.

[6] So a²a³a⁴dVā, 3 MSS of CVā; bfgjlmVā *so y°*: hVā *yo y°*; kVā [*so yosya*] *yo y°*. Bd *saṁy°*: a¹Vā, 3 MSS of CVā *samprāpsyati*.

[7] In klVā *°vratam*.

[8] So Bd. Vā *Śiśunākasya* for *°nākaś ca*, as in fMt. Mt genly *Śiśunākas tu*; egMt *Śiśru°* (g, *ca*); bMt *Śigru°*.

[9] So Mt, Bd. Vṣ, Bh agree; lMt *Kākev°*: kMt and fBh *Kākakarṇaḥ*; mMt *Kāṣṇivarṇaḥ*. Vā *Śakavarṇaḥ*; fVā *Śavarṇa*.

[10] Vṣ, Bh corroborate.

[11] So Vā, bcdfgjMt, Bd: eMt *ṣaḍ-triṁśat*, which suggests *ṣaḍ-viṁśat*, as in Mt genly: nMt *ṣaḍ-giṁśat* (= *ṣaḍ-viṁśat*).

[12] So Mt, eVā (which has only these two words). Vā, Bd *ca bhaviṣyati*.

[13] So Mt genly (jMt *°c=āpi*): bceMt *°śati ca* (b omits *ca*); nMt *ṣaḍiṁśati* (= *ṣaṭ-triṁśati*) *ca*.

[14] So Vā and Bd.

[15] So Mt genly. CMt *°dhomā*; nMt *°dhanvā*; dMt *Ṣyemadharmā*, where *ṣ* is dialectic variation in writing of *kh* which = *kṣ*: bMt *†Lemacarmā*.

[16] So eVā, Bd. Vṣ, Bh agree. Vā genly *°varmā*; bVā *°vama*; lVā *°vam*: dehlpsBh *°dharmā*, and yet say the next king was *Kṣetradharma-ja*; similarly fBh *Kṣemadhanvā* and *°dharma-ja*. Vṣ adds *tat-putraḥ*; Bh *tasya sutaḥ*.

[17] So Vā, ceknMt, Bd. Mt genly *caturviṁśat*, dMt *°śati*.

[18] So Vā, bMt. Bd *rāṣṭraṁ*; cMt *rājā*. Mt genly *so 'pi*.

[19] So Vā genly, Bd. Vṣ genly agrees; bdfglVā *°trojāḥ*: eVā *Kṣetrojā*, mVā *°jaḥ*, kVā *°yaḥ*. Bh *Kṣetrajña*; kBh *°trata*; qBh *Kṣetra*. Mt mostly *Kṣemajit*; gMt *°mavit*; fMt *°māṁvit*; dMt *°mābiḥ*; kMt *°mārvi*; ceMt *°mārciḥ*; nMt *Hemajit*. Bh adds *Kṣemadharma-ja*; Vṣ implies it.

[20] So Vā, Bd. Mt *mahīm*; nMt *mahī*.

[21] So Mt. Vā *°śat* (bVā *°śe*). Bd *aṣṭa-triṁśat*.

[22] So Mt. Vā, Bd *samā rājā*, eVā *°nṛpaḥ*.

[23] There is great variation in this name: aVṣ *Vinviśāra*; jVṣ *Vimis°*. Vṣ genly *Vidmis°*. Bd, Bh, hlVṣ *Vidhis°*. Vā, kVṣ *Vivis°*; bVṣ *Suvindus°*; mMt *Viduśāno*: jMt *Vindumāno*, bfglMt *°duseno*: dMt *Bindunāśo*. Mt genly *Vindhyaseno*, nMt *Vidh°*: kMt *Kṣemadharmā*. Vṣ adds *tat-putro*.

[24] After this line Mt inserts the two lines about Kāṇvāyana and Bhūmimitra of the Kāṇvāyana dynasty (see *infra*), and repeats them in their proper place there. It is a clear error of misplacement.

[25] So all: nMt *Ajātāś°*; kVā *Ajaś°*. Bh adds *sutas tasya*.

[26] So Vā, Bd. Mt genly *sapta*; cegnMt *saptā*; blMt *aṣṭā*.

[27] So Vā, Bd. Mt *catur*.

Udayī[30] bhavitā tasmāt[31] trayas-triṁśat samā nṛpaḥ
sa vai pura-varaṁ rājā pṛthivyāṁ Kusum-âhvayam[32]
Gaṅgāyā dakṣiṇe kūle[33] caturthe 'bde[34] kariṣyati
catvāriṁśat[35] samā[36] bhāvyo rājā[37] vai Nandivardhanaḥ[38]
catvāriṁśat trayaś[39] c=aiva Mahānandī[40] bhaviṣyati
ity ete bhavitāro[41] vai[42] Śaiśunāgā nṛpā daśa[43]
śatāni[44] trīṇi varṣāṇi[45] ṣaṣṭi-varṣ-âdhikāni tu[46]
Śiśunāgā[47] bhaviṣyanti[48] rājānaḥ kṣatra-bandhavaḥ[49].

28 Bḍ, a³Vā *triṁśat.*

29 Mt genly *Vaṁśakas*; eMt *Vaṁs°*; cMt *Vas°*; nMt *Viś°*; jMt *Vaśyagas*; kMt *Śakaś c=aiva* (omitting *tu*). Vā *Darśakas.* Bḍ, Vṣ, Bh *Darbhaka*; fBh *Dambh°*. *Darśaka* seems the most central form.

30 There is great variation in this name. Mt genly *Udāsī*; nMt *Udātir*; lMt *Udambhī*; dfMt *Udāmbhī*, gMt *°bhīr*; bMt *Udībhir*. Ca²Vā *Udāyī*; a¹a³lVā, Bḍ *Udayī*, bVā *°yaṁ*: kVā *Tradapī* (an easy misreading); jMt *Tedāṁnī*; mVā *Uda*. Vṣ genly *Udayāśva*, acfgjkVṣ *°yana*, lVṣ *°ya*: bVṣ *Anaya* (or *Dan°*); hVṣ *Ovaya*. Bh *Ajaya* or *Ājaya*, (but see note[38]). *Udayī* seems the best form.

31 In a¹⁻³Vā *yasmāt*; bMt *tasyās*; jMt *bhūpās*.

32 This line and the next only in Vā, Bḍ.

33 In a³blVā *koṇe*; kVā *ko[va]ṇe*.

34 So Vā. Bḍ *'hni*: eVā *caturutpraṁ* (for *catur-abdaṁ* ?).

35 So Mt, a³klVā, Bḍ. Vā genly *dvācatvāriṁśat*, with a syll. too much (*dvā* cancelled in dVā): eVā *dvi-c°*.

36 In eVā *satir*.

37 *Rājā* wanting in eVā.

38 So all: kVā *Rand°*; nMt *Nandivardanaḥ*. Bh gives him the patronymic *Ājeya*; qBh *Ājñeya*: see note[30].

39 CVā *trayaṁ* (which AVā adopts); jMt *bhayaṁ*; nMt *tataś*.

40 So Mt, Vā genly. Vṣ agrees: Bh *°diḥ*; bjMt, kVā *°dā*; nMt *Mahāṁnandi*; fVā *Mahīnandī*. Bḍ *Sahānandir*. Bh adds *sutas tataḥ*.

41 In eVā *saṅkhyayā bhavitārā*.

42 In a¹⁻⁴Mt *'tra*.

43 So Vā, except that it gives the name as *Śaiśunākā*; mVā *Śaiṣu°*; gVā *Śaiśukāś ca*: see note[47]. The correct number of kings is ten, as Vā, Bḍ, Vṣ, Bh say (see notes[46] and[48]). Mt is confused. Its original reading was probably *daśa vai Śiśunāka-jāḥ*, but, since the first two Kāṇvāyana kings were erroneously inserted (see note[24]), the number of names in it became 12, and attempts were made to reconcile the discrepancy: hence *CGVcdfgm*Mt boldly read *daśa dvau* (*fg*, *bdau*) *Śiśunāka-jāḥ*, eMt *daśādvā Śiśru°*, kMt [*daśa*] *dvādaśa Śiśu°*; jMt crp [*vai*] *daśa dve Śiśvanekatāḥ*: other copies evade inconsistency by an indefinite statement, thus a¹⁻⁴blnMt *vaṁśe vai* (*n*, *'smin*) *Śiśunākataḥ* (*j*, *°jāḥ*; *b*, *Śigrunākataḥ*); and eVā, which often agrees with Mt, *Śiśunāg-âdayo nṛpāḥ*. For Bḍ, Vṣ, Bh, see note[46].

44 In bVā *etāni*.

45 In eVā *varṣāṇāḥ* (for *°ṇāṁ*). Mt genly *pūrṇāni*; dMt *pūrbāṇi*: fMt omits this word.

46 So Mt; cenMt *ca* for *tu*: bMt *ṣaṣṭir vā adhikāni ca*; jMt *ṣaṣṭi varṣāṇi kāni ca*. Vā genly *dvi-ṣaṣṭy-abhyadhikāni tu*; a¹⁻³bdmVā *dvā°*; lVā *dvā-ṣaṣṭy=âbh°*; eVā *dvi-ṣaṣṭyaś c=âdhik°*. Bḍ condenses this and the preceding line into one—

bhaviṣyanti ca varṣāṇi ṣaṣṭy-uttara-śata-trayam.

Bh agrees, condensing the same two lines and the next into two lines—

Śiśunāgā* daś=aiv=aite ṣaṣṭy-uttara-śata-trayam†
samā bhokṣyanti pṛthivīṁ, Kuru-śreṣṭha, Kalau nṛpāḥ;

where * *adrs*Bh *Śaiś°*; † *h*Bh *trayaḥ*. Vṣ agrees with Vā—

ity ete Śaiśunāgā¹ daśa bhūmi-pālās trīṇi varṣa-śatāni dvi²-ṣaṣṭy-adhikāni bhaviṣyanti;

where ¹ *CV*ṣ *Śauś°*; ² *kV*ṣ crp *°trīṇi varṣa-sahasrāṇi śatāni dve.* See discussion, p. 20.

47 So Bḍ, eVā. Mt genly *Śiśunākā*; eMt

Early Contemporary Dynasties.

Text—*A*Mt *272*, 13b–17 ; *A*Vā *99*, 322b–325 ; Bḍ iii, *74*, 135b–138.

Corresp. passages—Vṣ and Bh, *nil*.

The Matsya, Vāyu, and Brahmāṇḍa give the whole of this passage, except that the latter two have not got l. 8 and remove l. 2 to l. 8 : *j*Mt omits ll. 1, 5, 6 ; *a*[2]Vā ll. 2, 6, 7 ; *m*Vā ll. 6–8 (first half) ; and *hp*Mt and *a*[4]*h*Vā have nothing. Here *e*Vā gives ll. 1, 3, 4, 6 only, but long afterwards, out of place, namely after the first line about Viśvasphāṇi, inserts ll. 6, 7, 5, and 2 in modified form.

Etaiḥ sārdham means contemporary with the Bārhadrathas and their successors, the Pradyotas and Śiśunāgas, for none of these are mentioned here, but the Aikṣvākus and the Kurus (who are probably the Pauravas) are included, whose dynasties have been fully set out *ante*. The next king Mahāpadma Nanda is called 'destroyer of all the kṣatriyas', and 'monarch of the whole earth which was under his sole sway'—which terms imply that he overthrew all the kingdoms mentioned in this list, so that all subsequent dynasties except the Kāṇvāyanas were śūdras (see *Nandas*, ll. 2–6). This list of contemporary dynasties means therefore all the old kṣatriya dynasties, which reigned from the time of the great battle till they and the Śiśunāgas in Magadha were swept away by the Nandas, whose dynasty follows this list.

Etaiḥ [1] sārdham bhaviṣyanti tāvat[2]-kālaṁ [3] nṛpāḥ pare [4]
tulya-kālam bhaviṣyanti sarve hy ete [5] mahīkṣitaḥ
Aikṣvākavaś catur-viṁśat [6] Pañcālāḥ [7] sapta[8]-viṁśatiḥ
Kāśeyās [9] tu catur-viṁśad [10] aṣṭā-viṁśatir [11] Haihayāḥ [12]

Śiśru°. Vā, *k*Mt *Śaiśu°*; *c*Mt *Śauśu°*: *b*Mt *Śiśunākād.*

[48] So Mt, Vā. Bḍ *daś=aiv=aite.*

[49] So Mt, Bḍ; *f*Vā *°vāḥ*. Vā, *dl*Mt *°bāndhavāḥ*; *f*Mt *vandhanāḥ*; *b*Mt *°vīcavaḥ* with marg. note *°bandhavaḥ*. *C*Vā confuses this with the first line of the following dynasties, reading—

Śaiśunākā bhaviṣyanti Tāvat-kālaṁ nṛpāḥ pare
rājānaḥ kṣatra-bāndhavāḥ etaiḥ sārdham bhaviṣyati :

and so *j*Mt which has the first line only, reading *yāvat-k°*. Hence perhaps the words *rājānaḥ kṣatra-bandhavaḥ* should be read with the following list.

[1] See above, note [49] : *k*Vā *ete*.

[2] So Vā, Bḍ. Mt *yāvat*; *b*Mt *yāna* (with marg. note *yāvat*).

[3] So Vā, Bḍ, *fg*Mt: *d*Mt *kāli*; Mt genly *Kali*; *e*Mt *kila*; *b*Mt *eka* (with marg. note *Kali*).

[4] *Ca te* in *g*Vā. For this half line *kl*Vā have *rājānaḥ kṣatra-bāndhavāḥ* (see above, note [49]), and *k*Vā then adds as in the text.

[5] So Mt. Vā, Bḍ *sarva eva.*

[6] So *bfgm*Vā, Bḍ. Vā genly *Aikṣākavāś* (*d*Vā *°vaś*); *e*Vā *Ikṣvākavaś*. Mt genly *catur-viṁśat* (*ce*Mt *°viṁśas*, *bj*Mt *°viṁśa*) *tath=Aikṣvākāḥ*; *bcdfgj*Mt *°Êkṣvākāḥ*; *j*Mt *°mah-Êkṣvākaḥ*; and so *n*Mt crp. This number does not agree with the Aikṣvāku list, see p. 9.

[7] So *bcdfgjn*Mt, *a*[1–3]*bdfgm*Vā, Bḍ: other Mt and Vā *Pāñc°*.

[8] So Mt. Vā, Bḍ *pañca* (perhaps by influence of *Pañcālāḥ*).

[9] So Mt genly: *cek*Mt *Kāṣeyās*; *l*Mt, *e*Vā *Kāśayās*; *b*Mt *Kāśasās*; *dj*Mt *Kāleyās*. Vā genly, Bḍ *Kālakās*. See Appendix II, § ii.

Kaliṅgāś [13] c≠aiva dvā-triṁśad [14] Aśmakāḥ pañca-viṁśatiḥ [15]
Kuravaś c≠âpi ṣaṭ-triṁśad [16] aṣṭā-viṁśati [17] Maithilāḥ
Śūrasenās [18] trayo-viṁśad [19] Vītihotrāś [20] ca viṁśatiḥ [21]
ete sarve bhaviṣyanti eka-kālam [22] mahīkṣitaḥ.

Nandas.

Text—*A*Mt *272*, 18–22 ; *A*Vā *99*, 326–330 ; Bḍ iii, *74*, 139–143.

Corresp. passages—*C*Vṣ iv, *24*, 4–7 ; *G*Bh xii, *1*, 8^b–12.

The Matsya, Vāyu, and Brahmāṇḍa give the whole and have a common version in the main. Here for the first time the Bhāgavata gives the tradition in ślokas, which agree in their purport with those three Purāṇas, and are not a mere list of names. Both versions are placed here, side by side, as they are independent and valuable. The Viṣṇu in prose agrees closely with the Bhāgavata.

All the versions are complete, except that *a*²*d*Mt omit ll. 6–10; *m*Mt l. 9 with a space; *b*Vā ll. 7–9 (first half); *k*Vā ll. 2 (second half), 3, 7, 8; *hp*Mt, *a*⁴*h*Vā, and *bt*Bh have lost the whole; and *l*Vṣ the matter of the last three Bh verses: *e*Vā omits the whole here, but long afterwards, out of place, inserts it after the first line about Viśvasphāṇi.

The time assigned to Mahāpadma may mean the entire length of his life, as Mt seems to imply; and if so, the whole dynasty may have lasted about a hundred years as stated.

[10] In *j*Mt °*śā*; *ce*Mt °*śa*: *f*Mt blends this and the next number into one, thus *catur-viṁśat tu*, and so *k*Mt *ṣaṭ-triṁśat tu*.

[11] So *GVa*¹*a*³*a*⁴*n*Mt, violating the metre. Others save it thus, *b*Mt °*śati*; *Cg*Mt, *e*Vā °*śat tu*; *a*²*m*Mt °*śās tu*; *j*Mt °*śā tu*; *cde*Mt °*śas tu*: *l*Mt †*aśāti*. Vā *catur-viṁśat tu*; *g*Vā, Bḍ °*śas tu*, where the number seems to be a mere repetition of the preceding number.

[12] In *j*Mt *Hehayaḥ*; *e*Vā *Tehayāḥ*.

[13] So Mt genly, Vā: *fg*Mt *Kāl*°; *l*Mt *Kalindaś*; *e*Mt *Kaliḥśāś*. Bḍ †*Ekaliṅgās*.

[14] So Mt genly. Vā reads this half line *dvā-triṁśad vai Kaliṅgās tu*; Bḍ *dvā-triṁśad Eka*°. But *cen*Mt °*dvā-viṁśa-d*; *l*Mt °*catvāriṁśat* (with a syll. extra); *b*Mt °*catvārid*: *e*Vā reads this line—

Aśmakāḥ pañca-viṁśac ca ṣaḍ-viṁśac ca Kaliṅgakāḥ.

[15] So Mt; *b*Mt *Asmākāḥ*. Vā, Bḍ *pañca-viṁśat tath≠Âśakāḥ*, prob. Pkt for *tath≠Âśmakāḥ*: *m*Vā crp: for *e*Vā see note [14].

[16] So Mt, Vā genly, Bḍ; *n*Mt *ṣaḍ-iṁśad* (= *ṣaṭ-triṁśad*); *k*Vā merely *triṁśad*. *Cb*Vā, *b*Mt *ṣaḍ-viṁśad*: *e*Vā *pañcāśad* here, but afterwards (see p. 23) indefinitely *ūnaviṁśat tathā c≠âbhūd*. These numbers do not agree with the Paurava list, see p. 4.

[17] So *fg*Mt, Vā, Bḍ. Mt genly °*śās tu*; *dn*Mt °*śat tu*; *b*Mt °*śa tu*: *e*Vā *varṣāṇy aṣṭādaś≠aiva tu* here, but afterwards (see p. 23) agrees with the text.

[18] In *bc*Mt, *d*Vā *Sūras*°; *n*Mt *Suras*°.

[19] In *ce*Mt, *e*Vā °*śa*; *j*Mt °*śā*.

[20] In *ce*Mt *Vīta*°; *e*Vā *Rītihotraś*.

[21] In *el*Vā °*tim*.

[22] In *j*Mt *Kali-kāle*. See p. 23.

Mt, Vā, and *Bḍ.*	*Bh* (with *Vṣ*).
Mahānandi[1]-sutaś c=âpi	Mahānandi[1]-suto rājan[2]
śūdrāyāṁ[3] Kalik-âṁśa-jaḥ[4]	śūdrā[5]-garbh-ôdbhavo[6] balī[7]
utpatsyate Mahāpadmaḥ	Mahāpadma-patiḥ[8] kaścin
sarva-kṣatr-ântako[9] nṛpaḥ	Nandaḥ kṣatra-vināśa-kṛt[10]
tataḥ prabhṛti rājāno	tato nṛpā bhaviṣyanti
bhaviṣyāḥ śūdra-yonayaḥ	śūdra-prāyās tv[11] adhārmikāḥ
eka[12]-rāṭ sa[13] Mahāpadma	sa eka-cchattrām[14] pṛthivīm
eka-cchattro[15] bhaviṣyati	an-ullaṅghita-śāsanaḥ[16]
aṣṭâśīti[17] tu varṣāṇi[18]	
pṛthivyāṁ ca bhaviṣyati[19]	śāsiṣyati Mahāpadmo
sarva-kṣatram[20] ath=ôddhṛtya[21]	dvitīya iva Bhārgavaḥ[22]
bhāvin=ârthena coditaḥ[23]	
Sukalp-âdi[24]-sutā[25] hy aṣṭau[26]	tasya c=âṣṭau[27] bhaviṣyanti

[1] In *fgn*Mt °*dī*; *k*Bh °*da*.

[2] This vocat. expletive has no doubt ousted some genuine word, which may have been *lubdhaḥ*, because Vṣ genly describes him as *ati-lubdha*; *h*Vṣ *lubdha*; *c*Vṣ *'bhilubdha*; *djl*Vṣ *ati-buddha*; *k*Vṣ crp.

[3] In Bḍ, *j*Mt °*yāḥ*; *b*Vā *śūdrā vā*.

[4] So Mt genly; *d*Mt °*âṁśu-jaḥ*; *cen*Mt °*âṁśataḥ*; *bk*Mt °*âṁśakaḥ*; *f*Mt °*āṁ-jayaḥ*; *j*Mt *kālikā..jaḥ*. Vā, Bḍ *kāla-saṁvṛtaḥ*; *e*Vā °*samṛtaḥ*; *b*Vā *kāla-[paṁ]saṁvṛtaḥ*.

[5] So *ahrs*Bh, Vṣ. Bh genly *śūdrī*.

[6] In *j*Vṣ [*bha..rno*] *garbh-ôd*°; *d*Vṣ *jar-mod*°.

[7] In *f*Bh *'rdhalī* apptly; cf. *Andhras*, note [2]. Vṣ has no corresponding word.

[8] Vṣ *Mahāpadmo Nandaḥ*: *l*Vṣ °*patma* always.

[9] So Mt. Vā °*ântare*, altered in *d*Vā to °*ântako*. Bḍ, *e*Vā °*ânta-kṛn*.

[10] Vṣ *akhila-kṣatr-ânta-kārī*.

[11] *Tv* omitted in *adr*Bh. Vṣ *śūdrā bhūmi-pālāḥ*.

[12] In *k*Vā *saka*.

[13] In *cek*Mt *rājā*; *m*Mt *padma*; *f*Mt *ehya*; *l*Vā *su* for *sa*.

[14] In *d*Bh °*cchattra-*; *jk*Bh °*kṣatrām*; *f*Bh *eka-cchattrāṁ sa*.

[15] In *l*Mt °*kṣatro*; *b*Mt °*mātro*: *j*Mt *ekaś chatro*; *k*Vā †*ekatro*.

[16] Vṣ has the same expressions; *k*Vṣ *c=aika-chātrā-samullaṅgh-ânamita-śāsano*.

[17] So all genly: *Ajklm*Mt °*tis*; *c*Mt, *d*Vā °*tiṁ*; *j*Vā *aṣṭāsīti*. *Cekl*Vā *aṣṭā-viṁśati* (omitting *tu*), which *A*Vā adopts.

[18] In *cdfgjn*Mt *sa v*°; *e*Mt *saṁv*°; *b*Mt *sahasrāṇi*.

[19] So Mt genly; *bcejn*Mt *tu bh*°; *d*Mt *sa bh*°: *fg*Mt *pṛthivī śobhayiṣyati*. Vā, Bḍ *pṛthivīm pālayiṣyati*.

[20] In *Ca*[2]*a*[3]*gkl*Vā *kṣatra*; *a*[1]Vā *kṣetra*.

[21] In *CGVa*[3]Mt *ath=ôtsādya*, *l*Mt *tath=ôt*°: *ce*Mt *ath=ôtpāṭya*, *a*[1]*a*[4]*b*Mt *tath=ôt*°. Bḍ *samuddhṛtya*. *Ca*[1]*a*[3]*bgkl*Vā *hṛtoddhṛtya* or *hṛtodvṛtya* or corruptions of these; other Vā *haroddhṛtya*; *e*Vā *athovṛtya*; *d*Vā *tato hatvā*. The correct reading may be *ath=ôtsādya*, or °*ôtpāṭya* or °*ôddhṛtya*.

[22] Vṣ *Paraśu-Rāma iv=âparaḥ*.

[23] So Mt genly (*ckn*Mt °*noditaḥ*): *b*Mt *bhavit-ârth*°; *j*Mt *bhavitorth*°. Vā genly, Bḍ *bhāvino 'rthasya vai balāt*; *l*Vā °*thasya mahābalāt* (with a syll. extra); *k*Vā °*tha-mahābalāt*; *a*[3]Vā °*thān mahābalān*: *e*Vā *Viśranāthasya vai balāt*. Vā, Bḍ have the same expression in *A*Vā *88*, 80, 95; *101*, 60; Bḍ iii, *63*, 79, 94; iv, *2*, 59.

[24] So Mt mostly: *fg*Mt *Sukulp*° or *Sukuly*°; *k*Mt *Sulul*°; *bln*Mt *Sumāly*°; *ce*Mt *Kuśal*°; *e*Vā *Sahaly-âdyāḥ*; *j*Mt †*Satulyā vai*: *a*[3]Vā *saṁhasrāt sa*, *f*Vā °*srātstat*, *m*Vā °*svāt* (one syll. short); *d*Vā *saṁhāsvās tat*: 3 MSS of *C*Vā *sahasvāt tat*, 3 MSS of *C*Vā and *a*[1]*a*[3]Vā °*srās tat* (which *A*Vā sdopts): *g*Vā *haṁsa-*

Mt, Vā, and *Bḍ.*

samā dvādaśa te nṛpāḥ [28]
Mahāpadmasya paryāye [30]
bhaviṣyanti nṛpāḥ kramāt [32]
uddhariṣyati tān sarvān
Kauṭilyo vai dvir aṣṭabhiḥ [35]
bhuktvā [37] mahīṁ [38] varṣa-śataṁ
tato [41] Mauryān gamiṣyati [42].

Bh (with *Vṣ*).

Sumālya-pramukhāḥ [29] sutāḥ
ya imām bhokṣyanti mahīṁ [31]
rājānaḥ sma [33] śataṁ [34] samāḥ
nava Nandān dvijaḥ kaścit
prapannān uddhariṣyati [36]
teṣām abhāve [39] jagatīm [40]
Mauryā bhokṣyanti [43] vai Kalau.

Mauryas.

Text—*A*Mt *272,* 23–26 ; *A*Vā *99,* 331–336 ; Bḍ iii, *74,* 144–149.

Corresp. passages—*C*Vṣ iv, *24,* 7–8 ; *G*Bh xii, *1,* 13–16[a].

This dynasty is given by all five Purāṇas, but the account of it has suffered more than that of any other dynasty [1]. Three versions exist here, the earliest in the

svās tat. Bḍ *tat-paścāt tat.*

[25] In *bfg*Mt *ṣutā* ; *e*Vā *satā.*

[26] *Hy* omitted in *j*Mt ; *b*Mt †*svaṁtyai,* corrected in margin to *hy aṣṭau* ; *g*Vā *hy ete.*

[27] In *d*Bh *tataś* c° ; cBh *yasya* c° ; *q*Bh *tasya tvāṣṭau, g*Bh *tasyāvā*°. Vṣ *tasy=âpy aṣṭau sutāḥ.*

[28] In *j*Mt *vai nṛpăḥ* ; *k*Mt *saṁsmṛtāḥ.*

[29] In *hkl*Vṣ *Sumāly-âdyāḥ* ; *ab*Vṣ *Sumāl-â*° ; Vṣ genly *Sumāty-â*° ; *fg*Vṣ *Sumaty-ā*°.

[30] In *g*Mt, *fm*Vā °*yāyo* : *d*Vā *payāye* altered to *dāyădā* ; *e*Vā *bhāryāyām.*

[31] In *d*Bh *pṛthivīṁ* ; *f*Bh *ye bhokṣyanti mahīm etāṁ* : v.r. in *G*Bh *mahīm bhokṣyanti ya imāṁ.*

[32] In *k*Mt *nṛp-ôttamāḥ.*

[33] *Ca* in *ars*Bh.

[34] In *k*Bh *taśaṁ.* Vṣ agrees—

Mahāpadmaḥ tat-putrāś ca ekaṁ varṣa-śatam avanī-patayo bhaviṣyanti.

[35] So Vā genly : *j*Vā *dvir aṣṭatiḥ* ; *e*Vā *dvi-ṣaṣṭibhiḥ* ; *a*[1]Vā *mahābalaḥ.* Bḍ agrees, but ends *dvija-ṛṣabhaḥ,* which may be the true reading (see Bh reading). Mt reads differently—

uddhariṣyati Kauṭilyaḥ samair dvādaśa-bhiḥ sutān :

where *b*Mt ends *sutāḥ* ; *cn*Mt *sa tān* ; *f*Mt *sa tā* ; *g*Mt *śatam* ; *j*Mt *samāt* ; *k*Mt *kramāt.* For *dvādaśabhiḥ* read perhaps *dvija-ṛṣabhaḥ.* After this line *bfgln*Mt insert the first line of the next dynasty.

[36] In *l*Bh *papannān uhariṣyati.* Vṣ says—

nav=aiva* tān Nandān† Kauṭilyo‡ brāhmaṇaḥ samuddhariṣyati :

where * *h*Vṣ *nava vai, j*Vṣ *navai, k*Vṣ *nav=aitā, a*Vṣ *tath=aiva* ; † *h*Vṣ *tān pyaśokaḥ, k*Vṣ *Nandavala* ; ‡ *jk*Vṣ *Koṭilyo.*

[37] In *fm*Vā *bhuktā.*

[38] In *n*Mt, *k*Vā *mahā-*. *Bhuktā mahī* would be better.

[39] In *f*Bh *abhāvāj.*

[40] In *d*Bh *pṛthivīm.*

[41] In *e*Vā *Nandair.*

[42] So *CGVa*[4]Mt, *e*Vā, *mahī* being understood : *f*Mt °*Mauryaṁ*° ; cMt °*gaur yāṁ*° ; *e*Mt °*gaur yaṁ*° ; *bg*Mt °*mokṣaṁ*° ; *l*Mt °*ekaḥ*° ; *a*[1]*a*[3]*k*Mt °*mokṣo bhaviṣyati* ; *j*Mt boldly paraphrases it, *prāpsyanti paramāṁ gatim.* Vā differently ; mostly *Nand-ênduḥ sa bhaviṣyati* (*d*Vā, *sambhav*°) : one MS of *C*Vā *Nandendaḥ*°, and so *d*Vā but altered to *nandanaḥ* ; *a*[3]*gl*Vā *Nandendhaḥ*° ; *a*[2]*f*Vā *Nandr-êndraḥ*°, so *m*Vā crp ; *b*Vā *Nandethā*° ; *k*Vā crp. The true reading is prob. *Nand-êndraḥ,* of which all the others are easy misreadings. Bḍ *narendraḥ*°.

[43] Similarly Vṣ—teṣām abhāve Mauryāś* ca pṛthivīm bhokṣyanti : where * *k*Vṣ *So[da]ryāḥ.*

[1] Because its great fame in Buddhism disgraced it in brahmanical eyes ?

Matsya, the second in *e*Vāyu, and the third in the Vāyu generally and the Brahmāṇḍa. They agree in general purport but have many differences. The second forms a stage of recension intermediate between the first and the third, and is the only copy that has preserved the names of all the kings. The Matsya version in all copies is incomplete and has one of its verses (v. 23) misplaced; thus, only 5 MSS mention Candragupta, the second king is always omitted, and the account generally begins with that verse 23, putting the last two kings first, and then mentions only four kings, Aśoka and his three successors. All three versions are important, but cannot be reconciled merely by criticism; and, as they cannot all be exhibited side by side, the Matsya version is given first, and the two other versions are printed side by side; but in the Matsya version verse 23 has been removed to its proper place after verses 24 and 25.

The Viṣṇu and Bhāgavata mention the kings in the same order as the Vāyu and Brahmāṇḍa with some differences in names, but the latter omits Daśaratha, and *bt*Bh want the whole.

In the Matsya version, *j*Mt omits lines 4, 5, 8, 9; *k*Mt l. 8, and inserts l. 9 after l. 12 of the following Suṅga dynasty; *hp*Mt want the whole. In the Vāyu version, *a*[4]Vā omits ll. 1–3; *k*Vā ll. 12, 13; *g*Vā has only ll. 1–5; *h*Vā wants the whole. In *e*Vā the account is omitted at first, and inserted long afterwards, out of place, after the first line about Viśvasphāṇi.

The versions vary in the number of the kings. Mt says 10, but names only 7; *e*Vā says 9 but gives 12; Vā and Bḍ say 9 and mention 9. Vṣ says 10 and names 10. Bh says 10 but gives only 9. The best attested number is 10, and the omissions can be particularized: but *e*Vā combines the Mt and Vā versions and has probably duplicated two kings in the middle.

All agree that the dynasty lasted 137 years. The regnal periods added together (excluding the Mt list which is incomplete) are 160 years in *e*Vā, and (Śāliśūka being omitted) 133 in Vā and Bḍ; or, if we add Śāliśūka's reign to the latter, the total is 146 years; and the total in *e*Vā would be reduced to about 145 years if we correct its duplication in the middle. This figure, 145 or 146, is compatible with the stated duration, 137 years, if (as is probable) the total of the several reigns is nominally raised above the true total by reckoning fractions of years as whole years.

Matsya.

Kauṭilyaś Candraguptaṁ tu tato rājye 'bhiṣekṣyati [1]
ṣaṭ-triṁśat tu samā rājā [2] bhavitā Aśoka [3] eva ca
saptānāṁ [4] daśa varṣāṇi tasya naptā bhaviṣyati (24)

[1] This line is found only in *bfgln*Mt where it is misplaced (see p. 26, note [35]); *b*Mt *Koṭiśaś Candraguptas*°; *n*Mt *Kauṭilyaś Candraguptasya tato rāṣṭe*°; and *l*Mt ends *rāṣṭre nivepsya*.

[2] But *cn*Mt °*samā rājā tu* (*n*, *ṣaḍiṁśat* = *ṣaṭ-triṁśat*); *b*Mt *ṣaṭ-triṁśati samān rājā*.

[3] So *dfgkm*Mt; *j*Mt °*Áśāka*: Mt genly °*Áśaka*; *ce*Mt °*Ákośa*; *l*Mt °*Áyoda v=eva ca*. Instead of the double expletive the true reading might be °*Áśokavardhanaḥ* as in Vṣ, Bh.

[4] So Mt genly; *d*Mt †*saptāno* (or °*nāṁ*); *l*Mt †*śatānāṁ*. Can the true reading be *Suyaśā*, who is named by Vṣ and Bh? Cf. *daśonaḥ sapta* in *e*Vā version, l. 7.

rājā Daśaratho [5] 'ṣṭau [6] tu tasya putro bhaviṣyati [7]
bhavitā nava varṣāṇi tasya putraś ca [8] Sampratiḥ [9] (25)
bhavitā Śatadhanvā [10] ca [11] tasya putras [12] tu ṣaṭ samāḥ [13]
Bṛhadrathas tu [14] varṣāṇi tasya putraś ca [15] saptatiḥ [16] (23)
ity ete daśa [17] Mauryās tu ye bhokṣyanti [18] vasundharām
sapta-triṁśac-chatam [19] pūrṇaṁ tebhyaḥ Śuṅgān [20] gamiṣyati [21] (26)

eVāyu.	*Vā genly and Bḍ.*
Candraguptaṁ nṛpaṁ rājye	Candraguptaṁ nṛpaṁ rājye
Koṭilyaḥ sthāpayiṣyati	Kauṭilyaḥ sthāpayiṣyati [22]
catur-viṁśat samā rājā	catur-viṁśat samā rājā
Candragupto bhaviṣyati	Candragupto bhaviṣyati
bhavitā Nandasāras [23] tu	bhavitā Bhadrasāras [24] tu
pañca-viṁśat samā nṛpaḥ	pañca-viṁśat samā nṛpaḥ
ṣaṭ-triṁśat tu samā rājā	ṣaṭ-triṁśat [25] tu [26] samā rājā [27]
bhavitā Âśoka eva ca	Aśoko bhavitā nṛṣu [28]
tasya putraḥ Kulālas [29] tu	tasya putraḥ Kunālas [30] tu
varṣāṇy aṣṭau bhaviṣyati	varṣāṇy aṣṭau bhaviṣyati

[5] In *c*Mt °*rath-âṣṭau*: see note [36].

[6] *Jyau* in *b*Mt; *d*Mt *au*.

[7] In a^3kMt *bhaviṣyanti ca tat-sutāḥ*.

[8] *Tu* in *bfgn*Mt.

[9] Mt genly †*saptatiḥ*; *dn*Mt °*ti*. Emended to *Sampratiḥ* as in *e*Vā; see note [36].

[10] In *n*Mt *Ṣaḍadh*°; *m*Mt *Sudh*°.

[11] *Tu* in *bcdefgjn*Mt.

[12] *Putrās* in a^1a^2bdMt.

[13] In *fg*Mt *tat-samaḥ*; *l*Mt *ṣaṣṭhamāḥ*; *m*Mt *padmapaḥ*.

[14] In *d*Mt °*rathasya*.

[15] In *dejn*Mt *tu*; *bf*Mt *putrasya*.

[16] So Mt genly, probably a misreading of *sapta vai* in Pkt form; see Vā, Bḍ, and Introdn. § 41: *e*Mt *viṁśatiḥ*.

[17] So all MSS, though they name only 6, or 7 at most.

[18] In *b*Mt *bhokṣyanti ca* as in Vā, Bḍ.

[19] In *cen*Mt *sapta-viṁśa-śatam*.

[20] In *d*Mt *Suṅgān*; *ce*Mt *Suṅgāṁ*; *k*Mt *svargaṁ*; *b*Mt *svargī*; *l*Mt *sarva*.

[21] *Vasundharā* being understood: see p. 26, note [42]; *Śuṅgas*, note [63].

[22] Vṣ says—*Kauṭilya eva Candraguptaṁ rājye 'bhiṣekṣyati*; where *k*Vṣ has *Kauṇḍilya*. Bh says—

sa eva Candraguptaṁ vai dvijo rājye 'bhiṣekṣyati.

[23] So *e*Vā, instead of *Vindusāras*.

[24] So Vā genly, Bḍ. Vṣ rightly *Vindusāra*. Bh *Vāris*°; *g*Bh *Vārīs*°; *em*Bh *Vārikāra*. Both add, 'son of Candragupta'; Vṣ *tasyāpi putro*, Bh *tat-suto*.

[25] *Ṣaḍ-viṁśat* in Ca^2a^4Vā only, which *A*Vā adopts.

[26] In *g*Vā *ca*; *fm*Vā *sa*.

[27] In *fm*Vā *mahā-rājā*.

[28] So Vā. Vṣ, Bh call him *Aśokavardhana*; *j*Vṣ *Asoka*°; *f*Bh *Aloka*°; *k*Vṣ *Ayośoka*°: see Appendix II, § 1. Bḍ *Aśokānāṁ ca tṛpti-daḥ*, perhaps a play on the name.

[29] An easy misreading of *Kunālas*.

[30] So *C*Vā here and in next line. But $a^{1-4}bdfgklm$Vā, Bḍ *Kuśālas*, *j*Vā *Kaśālas*, which all have *Kuśāla-* in next line, except *b*Vā *Nuśāla-* and lost in *g*Vā. Vṣ, Bh call Aśoka's successor *Suyaśas*; *ch*Vṣ *Svay*°; *g*Vṣ *Stuy*°; *b*Vṣ *Sudhaśāḥ*. Kunāla is so named and said to have been Aśoka's son in Buddhist books, e.g. Divyāvadana, pp. 403, 406 ff, 430.

e Vāyu.

Kulāla-tanayāś c=âṣṭau
bhoktāro Bandhupālitāḥ [32]
Daśonaḥ sapta [33] varṣāṇi
teṣāṁ naptā bhaviṣyati
rājā Daśarathas tv [35] aṣṭau
tasya putro bhaviṣyati
bhavitā nava varṣāṇi
tasya putras tu Sampratiḥ [36]
Śāliśūkaḥ [37] samā rājā
trayodaśa bhaviṣyati
sapta varṣāṇi [38] Devadharmā
bhaviṣyati narādhipaḥ
rājā Śataṁdhanuś c=âṣṭau
tasya putro bhaviṣyati
Vṛhadrathas tu varṣāṇi
saptâśītim [43] bhaviṣyati

Vā genly and Bḍ.

Kunāla-sūnur aṣṭau [31] ca
bhoktā vai Bandhupālitaḥ
Bandhupālita-dāyādo
daśa bhāv=Îndrapālitaḥ [34]

bhavitā sapta varṣāṇi
Devavarmā [39] narādhipaḥ
rājā Śatadhanuś [40] c=âṣṭau [41]
tasya putro bhaviṣyati
Bṛhadrathaś [42] ca varṣāṇi
sapta [44] vai bhavitā nṛpaḥ

[31] In *d*Vā *adau*, altered to *ādau*; *b*Vā *ādau*: *m*Vā °*sūnur* [*atrunur*] *aṣṭau*.

[32] Sic, showing that the preceding plurals are probably wrong, through misreading *aṣṭau* as applying to *tanaya* instead of as years. The line should probably be—

Kulāla-tanayaś c=âṣṭau bhoktā vai Bandhupālitaḥ.

[33] Compare l. 3 of Mt version. There seems to be some metathesis.

[34] *Ca*[3]*a*[4]*kl*Vā read *daśamānīndrapālitaḥ*; *a*[1]*a*[2]*fm*Vā *daśā*°; *bd*Vā *daśāmānind*° (altered in *d* to *daśānānind*°); *j*Vā *daśāmānandrapālitā*. Bḍ *bhavitā c=Êndrapālitaḥ*, which suggests that Vā reading should be *daśa bhāv=Îndrapālitaḥ*, and I have emended it so: but it might also be *daś-âbdān Indra*° as suggested in *C*Vā.

[35] Actually *carṣasamāsv*, no doubt for *Daśarathas tv* (see l. 4 of Mt), and I have emended it so, since Vṣ agrees in this name and places him after Suyaśas (see note [30]): *cd*Vṣ *Dāśaratha*; *b*Vṣ *Daśaratna*. Bh omits him. Three of his records are extant, see Lüders' List of Brāhmī Inscriptions, nos. 954–6, in Epig. Ind. x, Appendix.

[36] Cf. note [9]. *Samprati* is the Sanskrit form of Pali *Sampadī*. Sampadī was Kunāla's son (Divyāvadana, p. 430), and was established in the kingdom (*id.* p. 433, where his descendants are named). See SBE, xxii, 290 note, for Samprati. Vṣ, Bh place a king *Saṅgata* here, which is no doubt another reading of the same name; *d*Bh *Saṁyuta*, an easy misreading of *Samprata*. Bh adds 'son of Suyaśas', *Suyaśaḥsutāḥ*.

[37] First *Śāliyūkaḥ*, then corrected to °*śūkaḥ*. Vṣ, Bh corroborate. Bh, *cdk*Vṣ *Śāliśūka*; Vṣ genly, *s*Bh °*śuka*; *j*Vṣ °*śmūka*; *b*Vṣ °*śūlla*: *l*Vṣ *Śālaśūka*. Bh genly *Śāliśūkas tatas tasya*; *j*Bh °*kas tu Suyaśaḥ*, where *Suyaśaḥ* is meant for a genitive.

[38] Actually *varṇaṇi*; see Appendix I, § 1.

[39] In *b*Vā *Dacav*°. Vṣ, Bh *Somaśarman*.

[40] So Bḍ. Vṣ, Bh *Śatadhanvan*; *k*Bh *Sata*°; *h*Bh *Śāta*°; *de*Vṣ *Śaśa*°: *b*Vṣ *Śatadharman*; *q*Bh †*śatayitvā*. Vā *Śatadharaś*.

[41] So Vā. Bḍ merely *c=âpi*.

[42] So Bḍ. Vṣ, Bh agree; *c*Bh *Ūhad*°. Vā *Vṛhadaśvaś*, but has correct name *Bṛhadratha* in p. 31, l. 1: *m*Vā omits *ca*.

[43] Sic.

[44] In *d*Vā *sama*; *b*Vā *samu*.

eVāyu.

ity ete nava Mauryās [45] tu
ye bhokṣyanti vasundharām
sapta-triṁśac-chatam pūrṇaṁ
tebhyaḥ Śuṅgo [50] bhaviṣyati.

Vā genly and Bḍ.

ity ete nava [46] Mauryā vai [47]
bhokṣyanti ca [48] vasundharām
sapta-triṁśac-chatam pūrṇaṁ [49]
tebhyaḥ Śuṅgo [51] gamiṣyati [52].

Śuṅgas.

Text—*A*Mt *272*, 27–32^a; *A*Vā *99*, 337–343^a; Bḍ iii, *74*, 150–156^a.

Corresp. passages—*C*Vṣ iv, *24*, 9–11; *G*Bh xii, *1*, 16^b–19^a.

The Matsya, Vāyu, and Brahmāṇḍa give the whole; except that most copies of the Matsya omit l. 8, and all omit l. 3. The Viṣṇu gives a list of the kings, and the Bhāgavata all except the first.

As regards MSS, *ce*Mt invert lines 4, 5; *k*Mt omits ll. 1–6, 13 and inserts ll. 1, 2, 5, 6 at the end; *n*Mt omits ll. 4, 5: *g*Vā has only l. 2; *e*Vā omits this dynasty here and inserts it long afterwards, out of place, after the first line about Viśvasphāṇi: *hp*Mt, *h*Vā, and *bl*Bh want the whole.

The duration of the dynasty is stated by Vā and Bḍ, and by Vṣ generally, to be 112 years; by 7 MSS of Bh and one of Vṣ, 110; and by Bh generally 'over 100 years'. Mt reads 'hundreds two' wrongly for 'ten, two', and with this correction says 112 years. The duration therefore was 112 years. The aggregate of the reigns is 118 years. These virtually agree, if the total of the reigns was nominally raised above the true total by reckoning fractions of years as whole years.

Of the time of the Śuṅgas there are two records, nos. 687, 688 in Lüders' List of Brāhmī Inscriptions in Epig. Ind. x, Appendix. Another record assigned to their time, no. 905 in that list, mentions a king Bhāgavata, but he does not appear to be the Śuṅga king Bhāgavata, as the lineage is quite different.

[45] Actually *nara Mlauryyās* (an easy misreading of *nava*): but it has mentioned 12 kings.

[46] So Vā, Bḍ: *nava* may have been substituted since they name only 9 kings. Vṣ names and says 10—

evam Mauryā * daśa † bhūpatayo bhaviṣyanti abda†-śataṁ sapta-triṁśad‡-uttaram:

where **k*Vṣ *Soryyā*, *l*Vṣ *Mauryā*[*dayo*], see Appendix II, § 1: †*j*Vṣ *adda*, *h*Vṣ *aṣṭa*, *k*Vṣ *arū*: ‡*h*Vṣ *viṁśad*. Bh says 10, though it names only 9—

Mauryā hy ete* daśa nṛpāḥ sapta-triṁśac chat-ôttaram
samā bhokṣyanti pṛthivīṁ Kalau, Kuru-kul-ôdvaha:

where **jr*Bh *tv ete*, *a*Bh *te te*: *d*Bh reads the first line thus—

Maur[v]yā ete śata-nṛpāḥ sapta-triṁś-ôttaraṁ śatam.

[47] So Bḍ; a^4Vā *Mūrjā vai*; a^1a^3*bkl*Vā *Mūrtyā*°; *d*Vā *nava* [*Su*]*Mūrttyă*° (altered to *Naṁda-sambhūtā* wrongly): *fm*Vā *Mauryā ye*, *C*$ā^2$*g*Vā *bhūpā ye*; *j*Vā *yoyā* (or *yopā*) *yo*.

[48] In $a^1a^3a^4$*bd*Vā *ye bhokṣyanti*: *kl*Vā *yo*°.

[49] Similarly Vṣ, Bh; see note [46]: *d*Vā °*chataṁ* (altered to *chatăt*) *pūrṇāt*.

[50] Actually *Śuṅko*.

[51] So a^1*bdflm*Vā, Bḍ; *k*Vā *Śugo*; *C*Vā *tu gaur*: but a^{2-4}*j*Vā *Śuṅgān*, which *A*Vā adopts and seems preferable.

[52] *C*Vā *bhaviṣyati*. Vṣ says—

teṣām ante* pṛthivīṁ† Śuṅgā bhokṣyanti:

where **l*Vṣ *anvetāṁ*; †*abh*Vṣ add *daśa*: *j*Vṣ crp. Bh omits this statement.

Puṣyamitras [1] tu senānīr [2] uddhṛtya [3] sa [4] Bṛhadratham [5]

kārayiṣyati [6] vai rājyaṁ	kārayiṣyati vai rājyaṁ
ṣaṭ-triṁśati [7] samā nṛpaḥ	samāḥ ṣaṣṭiṁ [8] sad=aiva [9] tu

Agnimitraḥ sutaś c=âṣṭau bhaviṣyati samā nṛpaḥ [10]

bhavit=âpi Vasujyeṣṭhah [11]	bhavitā c=âpi Sujyeṣṭhaḥ [12]
sapta [13] varṣāṇi vai nṛpaḥ [14]	sapta varṣāṇi vai tataḥ

Vasumitraḥ [15] suto [16] bhāvyo daśa varṣāṇi pārthivaḥ [17]

tato 'ndhrakaḥ [18] same dve tu [19] tasya putro bhaviṣyati [20]

[1] So Mt genly, *l*Vṣ. Vā genly, *k*Mt, Bḍ, Vṣ *Puṣpa*°; *ce*Mt, *dfklm*Vā *Putra*° here, but *Puṣpa*° or *Puṣya*° in l. 3 (see note [10]); *k*Vṣ *Prakhya*° by an easy misreading: *n*Mt *Puṣpamitrasya* (omitting *tu*): *b*Vā *Putraḥ*. Bh omits him. Vṣ says—

tataḥ Puṣpamitraḥ senā-patiḥ svāminaṁ hatvā rājyaṁ kariṣyati.

[2] In *c*Mt *sa se*°; *b*Vā *su-se*°; *g*Mt *senāsanīr*; *e*Mt omits *tu*.

[3] In *bfj*Mt, *e*Vā, *uddhatya*; *ckn*Mt *samuddhṛtya* (omitting *sa*).

[4] So Mt, *e*Vā: *j*Mt *ca*. Vā genly *vai*: *bdfm*Vā, Bḍ *tu*.

[5] So Vā, Bḍ, *j*Mt. Mt genly °*thān*; *e*Vā °*thaḥ*: *cek*Mt *sadā gṛhāt*.

[6] So Mt: *j*Mt *kariṣyati sa*.

[7] So Mt genly; *n*Mt *ṣaḍiṁśati* (= *ṣaṭ-triṁśati*). *ACjk*Mt *ṣaṭ-triṁśat tu*.

[8] So Vā, Bḍ.

[9] So Vā. Bḍ *sa c=aiva*. These readings are no doubt corruptions of *ṣaṭ-triṁśad eva* in Pkt form.

[10] This line is only in Vā, Bḍ. Bḍ has—

Agnimitro nṛpaś c=âṣṭau bhaviṣyati samā nṛpaḥ;

where the first *nṛpaś* should no doubt be *sutaś*. Vā reads—

Puṣpamitra-sutāś c=âṣṭau bhaviṣyanti samā nṛpāḥ;

where singulars have obviously been wrongly converted into plurals through misapplying *aṣṭau* to *suta* instead of to *samā*. It should be—

Puṣpamitra-sutaś c=âṣṭau bhaviṣyati samā nṛpaḥ;

as *e*Vā shows by its reading—

tat-suto 'gnimitr=âṣṭau * bhaviṣyati samā nṛpāḥ †;

where read * °*mitro 'ṣṭau* and † *nṛpaḥ*. Vṣ and Bh name *Agnimitra*. Vṣ adds *asy=âtmajo*, 'son of Puṣyamitra'.

[11] So Mt genly: *gj*Mt *bhavitā vai Vasuśreṣṭhaḥ*; *f*Mt °*tā c=aiva Suś*°; *ce*Mt °*tā c* (cMt *v*)=*Âsurajyeṣṭaḥ*; *b*Mt °*tā c=âpi Sujyeṣṭhaḥ* (and *l*Mt crp), as in Vā, Bḍ.

[12] So a^2a^4*fkm*Vā, Bḍ. Vṣ genly and Bh agree. In *e*Vā *Sajy*°; *C*a^1a^3*l*Vā *taj-jy*°; *b*Vṣ *Sujeṣṭa*; *j*Vā *Sudyetaḥ*; *bd*Vā *Suṣaṣṭaḥ* (altered in *d* to *Suṣṭhaṣṭaḥ*); *k*Vṣ *Jyeṣṭha*; *hj*Vṣ crp. *Sutaḥ* added in *a*Bh.

[13] In *b*Mt *sama*.

[14] In *fgj*Mt *tataḥ*.

[15] So all; except *ce*Mt, a^{1-4}Vā °*mitra-*; *l*Mt *Vasuputras*; *j*Mt *Vāyumitrais*; *d*Mt *Sumitras tu*.

[16] So Vā genly, *ce*Mt. Bḍ, *e*Vā *tato*. Mt genly *tathā*.

[17] So Vā, Bḍ: *be*Mt *vai nṛpaḥ*. Mt genly *vai tataḥ*. After this king *k*Vṣ inserts a king *Vajramitra* besides the Vajramitra in l. 9.

[18] There is great variation in this name. Vā genly *'ndhrakaḥ*; *k*Mt, a^3Vā *'ndhakaḥ* (*k*Vā *teṣāṁdhakaḥ*): 4 MSS of *C*Vā *Dhrukaḥ*; *fm*Vā *Dhrakaḥ*; 2 MSS of *C*Vā *Vṛkaḥ*: Mt genly *'ntakaḥ*; *e*Mt *Taka*; *j*Mt *Nukaḥ*; *l*Mt *'ṣṭakaḥ*. All these should prob. be read with avagraha. Vṣ genly *Ārdraka*; *bh*Vṣ *Odruka*. Bḍ *Bhadraḥ*; *e*Vā *Madraḥ*. Bh genly *Bhadraka*; *g*Bh *Bhaḍ*°. *Andhraka* seems most probable.

[19] So Mt genly, *bdefkm*Vā, Bḍ. Vā genly *samā*°; *d*Mt *sama*°; *ce*Mt *samā dvau tu*: but a^1*n*Mt *samāḥ sapta*; *k*Mt *samohaṁtus*.

[20] So Mt; *j*Mt *putrau bhaviṣyataḥ*. This half line is in a^3a^4*kl*Vā *bhaviṣyati suto 'sya vai*; *b*Vā °*sutaisya*°; *defm*Vā °*sutasya*° (altered in *d* to °*sutaiḥ sa*°); *C*a^1a^2Vā °*sutaś ca*°. Bḍ °*nṛpaś ca vai*.

bhaviṣyati [21] samās [22] tasmāt [23]
triṇy evaṁ [27] sa Pulindakaḥ [28]
bhaviṣyati ca Yomeghas [31]
trīṇi varṣāṇi vai tataḥ
bhavitā Vajramitras tu [34]
samā rājā punar nava [37]
dvā-triṁśat tu [39] Samābhāgaḥ [40]
Samābhāgāt tato [42] nṛpaḥ [43]

bhaviṣyati [24] samās [25] tasmāt [26]
tisra eva [29] Pulindakaḥ [30]
rājā Ghoṣaḥ sutaś [32] c=âpi
varṣāṇi bhavitā trayaḥ [33]
sapta [35] vai Vajramitras [36] tu
samā rājā tataḥ punaḥ [38]
dvā-triṁśad bhavitā c=âpi [41]
samā Bhāgavato [44] nṛpaḥ

bhaviṣyati sutas tasya Devabhūmiḥ [45] samā daśa [46]

[21] So Mt: cMt °*ṣyanti*.
[22] *Samas* in *C*Mt.
[23] In *b*Mt *tasyās*.
[24] So *bdem*Vā, Bḍ. Vā genly °*ṣyanti*.
[25] In *l*Vā *sutās*: *acdfyhjklnqr*Bh say *sutaḥ*.
[26] In *e*Vā *tasya*.
[27] So Mt genly: *bn*Mt °*eva*; *k*Mt *trīṇi vai*; *dfgjm*Mt *tisro vai*. See Appendix I, § iii.
[28] So Mt mostly: *b*Mt *sa Pulandakaḥ*: *m*Mt °*Nunandanaḥ*, *j*Mt *Madhunan*°; *fg*Mt *Marunan*°; *d*Mt *Medhunandakaḥ*: *k*Mt merely *nṛpaḥ*: *ce*Mt read this half line *trīṇi varṣāṇi vai tataḥ*, giving no name.
[29] In *e*Vā *tripuśrava* or *triyu*°.
[30] So *m*Vā. Bḍ and other Vā read the plural °*kāḥ* wrongly: *e*Vā *Mulindakaḥ*. Vṣ genly *Pulindaka*; *l*Vṣ *Puḷ*°; *k*Vṣ *Pralingaka*. Bh *Pulinda*.
[31] This line is only in *dfgjm*Mt. So *dfg*Mt, but *fg* omit *ca*: *m*Mt °*va Yomekha*; *j*Mt °*sa Momeghas*. *Yome* may be a misreading of *Ghoṣa*, see note [32].
[32] Vā genly *Ghoṣa* (*m*Vā *Dhoṣa*) *sutaś*, for *Ghoṣaḥ sutaś*, as Bh has. Bḍ and *d*Vā *Ghoṣas tataḥ*. Vṣ genly *Ghoṣavasu*; *b*Vṣ *Ghoṣaka*; *k*Vṣ *Yoṣavasu*; *h*Vṣ by inversion *Soghavamu*; cBh *Ghopa*: *e*Vā has a different line—

trīṇi varṣāṇi bhavitā rājā Ghoṣavasur nṛpaḥ.

[33] So Vā and Bḍ. See Appendix I, § iii.
[34] So Mt genly, *e*Vā; *e*Mt *Vajamitras*; *k*Mt *Yajñam*°: *fg*Mt *bhaviṣyate Vajramitraḥ*; *j*Mt *Vajramitraś ca bhavitā*.
[35] So Bḍ. Vā *tato*.
[36] So Bḍ. Bh and Vṣ genly agree: *h*Bh *Vajamitra*; *c*Bh *Vajrā*°; *ek*Bh *Vraja*°; *n*Bh *Vañna*°; *fg*Vṣ *Vakṣa*°; *c*Vṣ *Vadrā*°; *p*Bh *Vajramindra*. Vā genly *Vikramitras*; *d*Vā *Vikṛ*°.
[37] So cMt; *dfgjkn*Mt *navaḥ*; *em*Mt *navā*: other Mt *bharaḥ*.
[38] So Vā, Bḍ; *e*Vā *catur-daśa*.
[39] So Mt genly; *cen*Mt *ca* for *tu*; *d*Mt omits *tu*; *bfg*Mt *dvā-triṁśati*; *j*Mt *sa dvā-triṁśat*.
[40] *Samabh*° in cMt; *e*Mt *Samaṁbh*°.
[41] So Vā. Bḍ *v=âpi*.
[42] So Mt genly; *bc*Mt *Samabh*°; *k*Mt *samā bhoktā*°; *j*Mt *Samābhāg-ânugo*.
[43] *Vṛṣaḥ* in *b*Mt, adding an extra king.
[44] So Vā, Bḍ. Bh and Vṣ genly agree; *cem*Bh *Bhagavato*.
[45] So Mt, *e*Vā, Bḍ. Vā *Kṣemabhūmiḥ* here but *Deva*° in the next list (l. 2). Vṣ *Devabhūti*. Bh *Devabhūtir iti śrutaḥ*; *g*Bh °*bhūr iti viś*°, but °*bhūti* afterwards.
[46] In eMt *vaśuḥ*.
[47] So *dfgmn*Mt, *d*Vā, Bḍ, and 2 MSS of *C*Vā: a^1a^3*kl*Vā and 4 MSS of *C*Vā *Śṛṅga*; *b*Vā *Ścuṅga*. Vā genly *tuṅga*: *e*Vā *Śaṅka*; cMt *Śuddha*; *e*Mt *Śruddha*. Mt genly *kṣudra*: *j*Mt *trayodaś=Āṅga*; *k*Mt has this half line, *ity ete daśa Mauryās tu* [*me*]. Vṣ says—

ity ete daśa* Śuṅgā dvādaś†-ôttaraṁ varṣa-śatam pṛthivīm bhokṣyanti; tataḥ Kaṇvān‡ eṣā§ bhūr yāsyati:

where **l*Vṣ *dvādaśa*; †*a*Vṣ *daś-*; ‡*l*Vṣ *Kāṇvān*; §*k*Vṣ *eyān*. Bh has—

Śuṅgā* daś=aite bhokṣyanti bhūmiṁ† varṣa-śat-âdhikam
tataḥ Kaṇvān iyam bhūmir yāsyaty alpa-guṇān, nṛpa:

where **de*Bh *Suṅgā*, *h*Bh *Sumbhā*; †*cehjklm*Bh *daśa* (marg. correction *bhūmiṁ* in *j*Bh).

daś=aite Śuṅga[47]-rājāno bhokṣyant=īmāṁ [48] vasundharām
śatam pūrṇaṁ [49] daśa dve ca [50] tataḥ [51] Kaṇvān [52] gamiṣyati [53].

Kāṇvāyanas (Śuṅgabhṛtyas).

Text—*A*Mt *272*, 32[b]-37 ; *A*Vā *99*, 343[b]-347 ; Bḍ iii, *74*, 156[b]-160[a].
Corresp. passages—*C*Vṣ iv, *24*, 12 ; *G*Bh xii, *1*, 19[b]-21.

The Matsya, Vāyu, and Brahmāṇḍa give the whole ; but they all differ in the last part, where the Matsya version is placed on the left, the Vāyu on the right, and the Brahmāṇḍa in the notes along with the concluding parts of the Viṣṇu and Bhāgavata. The names Kaṇva, Kāṇva, and Kāṇvāyana are often sadly corrupted, and many of the variations are mentioned in the notes to show how simple and well-known names can be corrupted.

As regards MSS, *bdfgjlm*Mt omit line 6 ; *g*Vā has only the last line ; *e*Vā omits the whole here and inserts it long afterwards, out of place, after the first line about Viśvasphāṇi : *hp*Mt, *h*Vā, *h*Vṣ, and *bt*Bh want the whole.

The duration of the dynasty is stated to be 45 years and agrees with the aggregate of the reigns.

Amātyo Vasudevas [1] tu bālyād vyasaninaṁ nṛpam [2]

[48] In *d*Mt °*ṣyante tāṁ* ; *b*Mt °*ṣyanty eva* ; *j*Mt *bhojyante te*.

[49] In *b*Mt *śara-pūrṇa-*.

[50] So Vā, Bḍ : *fm*Vā *darā dve ca* ; *b*Vā †*daśarddava*. Mt *śate dve ca* : *j*Mt reads this line—

aṣṭā-triṁś-âdhikā samyag varṣāṇāṁ śata-pañcakam.

[51] So Mt. Vā, Bḍ *tebhyaḥ*.

[52] Bḍ *Kaṇvaṁ* ; *e*Vā *Kaṇṭho* ; *m*Vā *Kaṁga* ; *bf*Vā *Kaṁvā* ; *d*Vā *Kaṁvo*. Vā genly *kiṁ vā* : a^3a^4Vā *Śaikaṁ*. Mt genly *Śuṅgān* ; *n*Mt *Śuṅgaṁ* ; *ce*Mt *tuṅgo* ; *d*Mt *Śuṅgād gāna* : a^1*bl*Mt *svargaṁ*, °*gī*, °*ga* ; *fg*Mt boldly read this half line, *tatas te svarga-gāminaḥ*. *Kaṇvān* seems the correct word, if we read *gamiṣyati*.

[53] *Mahī* being understood, see p. 28, note [21]. But *bl*Mt, *e*Vā *bhaviṣyati* ; *cen*Mt *haniṣyati*, which would be good, if we read *tataḥ Śuṅgān haniṣyati*.

[1] So Mt genly, *e*Vā, Bḍ : *dm*Mt *Vās*° ; *b*Mt *Vasudevasya* (omitting *tu*). Vā genly *apārthivasudevas* ; *C*Vā °*devam* ; *d*Vā °*vaḥ Sudevas*. Vṣ says—

Devabhūtiṁ tu Śuṅga-rājānaṁ vyasaninaṁ*
tasy=aiv=âmātyaḥ Kaṇvo† Vasudeva-nāmā
nipātya ‡ svayam avanim bhoktā :

where * *k*Vṣ *vyavaśinaṁ* ; † *l*Vṣ *Kāṇvo*, *k*Vṣ *Kāśvā* ; ‡ *l*Vṣ *Vāsudeva-nām=âpatya*. Bh has—

Śuṅgaṁ hatvā Devabhūtiṁ * Kaṇvo
'mātyas† tu ‡ kāminam
svayaṁ kariṣyate rājyaṁ§ Vasudevo
mahā-matiḥ :

where * *h*Bh °*bhṛtiṁ*, *l*Bh °*hūtiṁ* ; † *d*Bh *Kaṇv-âmātyas* ; ‡ *k*Bh *śu* ; § *d*Bh *ca bhokṣyate rājyaṁ*, *q*Bh *kariṣye rājyaṁ ca*. See p. 32, note [45].

[2] So Vā genly, Bḍ : *f*Vā *bālya-vy*° ; *e*Vā *balad vyesaninaṁ nṛpaḥ* ; *l*Vā *balyāṁd vasati nṛpam*. But $a^1a^3a^4$*cefgkln*Mt *prasahya* (*cen*, °*hyā*) *vyasanī* (*n*, °*nīr* ; *l*, °*nā*) *nṛpam* (*l*, °*paḥ* ; $a^1a^3a^4$*cek*, °*pa*) ; where the true reading should be *prasahya vyasaniṁ nṛpam*, see Appendix I, § ii. *CGVb*Mt corrupt it to *prasahya hy avanīṁ nṛpaḥ* ;

Devabhūmim ath:ôtsādya [3] | Devabhūmiṁ [4] tath:ôtpāṭya [5]
Śauṅgas [6] tu [7] bhavitā nṛpaḥ | Śuṅgeṣu [8] bhavitā nṛpaḥ
bhaviṣyati samā [9] rājā nava [10] Kāṇvāyano [11] dvijaḥ [12]
Bhūmimitraḥ [13] sutas tasya [14] caturdaśa [15] bhaviṣyati
Nārāyaṇaḥ [16] sutas tasya [17] | bhavitā dvādaśa samās [18]
bhavitā dvādaś:aiva tu | tasmān Nārāyaṇo nṛpaḥ
Suśarmā [19] tat-sutaś [20] c:âpi bhaviṣyati daś:aiva tu [21]
ity [22] ete Śuṅga-bhṛtyās [23] tu | catvāras [24] Tuṅga-kṛtyās [25] te
smṛtāḥ [26] Kāṇvāyanā [27] nṛpāḥ | nṛpāḥ Kaṇvāyanā [28] dvijāḥ

and *a²djm*Mt amend it to *prasahya vyasan-âturam*. The expression *vyasanī nṛpaḥ* occurs in *A*Vā *88*, 122.

[3] So Mt genly: *ce*Mt Pkt *ath:ôchādya*; *fy*Mt *tat:ôtsādya*.

[4] So Bḍ. Vā °*bhūmis* wrongly: *b*Vā *Deva-bhūmi[samādeśādeśete]s*. See p. 32, note [45].

[5] So *a¹a³a⁴*Vā; *flm*Vā *tat:ôtpāṭya*; *k*Vā †*tathānpāṭya*; *d*Vā *tathonyadya*, *b*Vā °*nya-dhā*; Vā genly *tato 'nyaś ca*. But *e*Vā *ath:ôddhṛtya* or °*dhatya*. Bḍ *tato hatvā*.

[6] So *ACdm*Mt: *j*Mt *Soṅgas*; *k*Mt *Śuṅgaḥ*; *cfg*Mt *Suṅgaḥ*; *el*Mt *Sugaḥ*; *e*Vā *Śubhaḥ*; *b*Mt *Sauraḥ*: *n*Mt *Śuṅgaṁ*.

[7] In *beekn*Mt, *e*Vā *sa*; *fy*Mt *saṁ-*.

[8] So *a⁴m*Vā, Bḍ. Vā genly *Śṛṅ*°; *f*Vā *Muṅ*°.

[9] Altered in *d*Vā to *haniṣyati sa vai*. This line occurs previously in Mt, see p. 21, note [24]: *j*Mt there *daśa ṣaṭ ca samā*, here *dvijo daśa samā*; *k*Mt there has this half line, *catvāriṁśat samā rājyaṁ*.

[10] So Mt, Vā: *b*Mt *aṁva* here, but *nava* earlier. Bḍ *pañca*.

[11] So Mt genly here and in the earlier passage. Bḍ, *n*Mt *Kaṇ*°. Corruptions are many, as *e*Mt *Kaṁvāyata*; *k*Mt *Kampāyana*, *Kaṇṭhā*°; *l*Mt *Kaṇṭhāyana*, *Kanmā*°; *fgj*Mt *Kāṣṭhāyana*, *Kāṣṭā*°; *d*Mt *Kāsvāyate*; *b*Mt *Kācāyate*. Vā genly, *ck*Mt *Kaṇṭhāyana*; *d*Vā *Kaṇṭa*°; *b*Vā *Kaṁtapanu*; *e*Vā *Kaṇṭhā-mana*; *k*Vā *Kañcayana*; *fm*Vā and 2 MSS of *C*Vā *Kăṅgăyana*; &c. Vṣ, Bh *Kaṇva*, see note [1].

[12] So *a¹a³cejkl*Mt; *bdfg*Mt *dvijāḥ*: other Mt *nṛpaḥ* redundantly, and so all Mt in earlier passage. Vā, Bḍ *tu saḥ*. Vṣ, Bh *svayam*.

[13] So Mt genly, Bḍ, Vṣ. This line occurs previously in Mt, see p. 21, note [24]; where *c*Mt *Bhūmiputraḥ*, *e*Mt °*putraṁ*. Vā, *m*Mt *Bhūtimitraḥ*. Bh, *ab*Vṣ *Bhūmitra*; *c*Bh *Bhūrm*°: *l*Vṣ *Bhūmiputra*.

[14] In *n*Mt *sutasya*; *m*Mt *tatasya*. Vṣ adds *tat-putro*; Bh *tasya putras*.

[15] So Mt. Vā, Bḍ *catur-viṁśad*.

[16] *C*Mt *Nārāthanaḥ*; *n*Mt *Nārāyaṇa-*. Vṣ, Bh agree; *g*Bh *Pārāy*°.

[17] So Bh *tasya sutaḥ*.

[18] So *bdfm*Vā, Bḍ. Vā genly Pkt *samā*.

[19] So Mt genly, Vā, Bḍ. Vṣ agrees: *cj*Vṣ *Susarman*; *d*Vā *Suśaṁmatiḥ*; *e*Vā *Sudharmā*. Bh omits him, but *g*Bh has preserved him thus (also mentioned as v.r. in *G*Bh)—

Pārāyaṇasya bhavitā Suśarmā nāma viśrutaḥ.

[20] In *l*Vṣ *tasy:âtmajaḥ*; *k*Vṣ *Nārāyaṇasy:ânujaḥ*.

[21] So Mt. Vā *samā daśa*. Bḍ *catuḥ-samāḥ*.

[22] In *b*Mt *ya*.

[23] So Mt genly: *k*Mt *Śṛṅ*°; *cfy*Mt *Suṅ*°; *l*Mt *Suga*°; *j*Mt *Cāṅga*° or *c:Âṅga*° (see p. 32, note [47]); *b*Mt *Muṅganṛtyās*; *e*Mt *Bhuṁgavatyās* (omitting *tu*).

[24] So *e*Vā. Vā genly *caturas*: see Appendix I, § iv.

[25] So Vā genly; *b*Vā °*kṛ[tvā]tyās*; *d*Vā °*lāṁtyās*: *e*Vā nearly correctly *Śuṅga-vṛtyās*: see Appendix II, § iii. For Bḍ, Vṣ, Bh see note [43].

[26] In *e*Mt *smutuḥ*; *m*Mt *sthitāḥ*.

[27] With variations (see note [11]), as *e*Mt *Kaṁjāy*°; *l*Mt *Kagvoyata*.

[28] Amended. Vā *Kaṇṭhāyanā* with vv. rr.

catvāras tu [29] dvijā hy ete [30]
Kaṇvā [31] bhokṣyanti vai [32] mahīm
catvāriṁśat pañca [33] c=aiva [34]
bhokṣyant=īmāṁ vasundharām
ete [35] praṇata-sāmantā
bhaviṣyā dhārmikāś ca ye
yeṣām [36] paryāya[37]-kāle tu [38]
bhumir Āndhrān gamiṣyati [40].

bhāvyāḥ praṇata-sāmantāś
catvāriṁśac ca pañca ca

teṣām paryāya-kāle tu [39]
bhūr Andhrāṇām [41] bhaviṣyati [42].

Andhras.

Text—*A*Mt *273*, 1–17ᵃ; *A*Vā *99*, 348–358ᵃ; Bḍ iii, *74*, 160ᵇ–170.

Corresp. passages—*C*Vṣ iv, *24*, 12–13; *G*Bh xii, *1*, 22–28.

This dynasty is given in full by the Matsya, while the accounts in the Vāyu and Brahmāṇḍa are far from perfect. The Bhāgavata and Viṣṇu give a list of the kings though not completely, with some details at the beginning and end.

The defects in the MSS will appear from the following notices of the kings; but *e*Vā, which stands midway between the Matsya and Vāyu, has misplaced the first portion down to Svāti, inserting it long afterwards, out of place, after the first line about Viśvasphāṇi: *hp*Mt have nothing; *h*Vā omits ll. 1–21.

[29] So *j*Mt. Mt genly *catvāriṁśad*; *bdn*Mt °*śa*: see Appendix I, § iv.

[30] But *j*Mt omits *hy*; *n*Mt omits *hy ete*: *b*Mt *cite* (for *c=aite*).

[31] So Mt genly: *Cfgm*Mt *Kāṇvā*; *n*Mt *Kaṇvo*; *e*Mt *Kāvo*; *l*Mt *Kagvo.*

[32] In *l*Mt crp: *j*Mt reads this half line, *bhokṣyante pṛthivīṁ imām.*

[33] So Mt genly: *b*Mt °*riṁśa naghaṁ* (or *nadyaṁ*).

[34] In *j*Mt *c=aite.*

[35] So Mt genly: *j*Mt *gate.*

[36] In *bcdefgjkn*Mt *teṣām.*

[37] In *l*Mt *payoja.*

[38] So Mt genly: *e*Mt *kāleṣu.*

[39] So Vā genly: *Cl*Vā *kāleṣu*, *bd*Vā *kal*°.

[40] So Mt genly; *f*Mt *An*°: *g*Mt *Andhrāṁ*, *c*Mt °*rā*. This half line is in a^2*bn*Mt *bhūmir* (*n*, *mūmir*) *iddhā bhaviṣyati*; *l*Mt *munir i bh*° (short); *j*Mt *bhūmiḥ sāṁdrā* (for *s-Āndhrā*?) *bh*°.

[41] All Vā readings are crp, and this is an emendation. *Bhūr* is represented thus, a^3a^4Vā *tur*; *C*a^2*gjkl*Vā *tar*; a^1Vā *ter*; *fm*Vā *star*; *bd*Vā *ster* (altered to *ter* in *d*). *Andhrāṇām*, or rather its Pkt form *Andhrāṇa*, is represented thus, a^1*fgm*Vā *Andhrā nu*; a^3a^4*bd*Vā *Andhā nu*; *C*a^2*jkl*Vā *Andhā tu*. But *e*Vā has Mt reading crp, *bhumiv=Antān gamiṣyati.*

[42] Bḍ and Bh have not got the concluding lines (5 in Mt, 3 in Vā). Bḍ has—

Kaṇvāyanās tu catvāraś catvāriṁśac ca pañca ca
samā bhokṣyanti pṛthivīm punar Andhrān gamiṣyati.

Bh similarly—

Kāṇvāyanā* ime bhumiṁ catvāriṁśac ca pañca ca
śatāni trīṇi bhokṣyanti varṣāṇāṁ† ca Kalau yuge:

where **jl*Bh *Kaṇ*°; †*q*Bh *varṣāṇi.* Vṣ says—

ete Kāṇvāyanāś* catvāraḥ pañca-catvāriṁśad-varṣāṇi bhūpatayo bhaviṣyanti:

where **e*Vṣ *Kaṇv*°, *k*Vṣ *Kāśv*°.

The Vāyu, Brahmāṇḍa, Bhāgavata, and Viṣṇu all say there were 30 kings, though they do not give 30 names. The Vā MSS name only 17, 18, or 19, and *e*Vā which is the fullest names only 25; Brahmāṇḍa only 17; Bhāgavata 23; and Viṣṇu 24, or 22 and 23 in two MSS. The Matsya says there were 19 kings, but 3 MSS (*dgn*) actually name 30, and the others vary from 28 to 21. Before noticing the differences in them and the other authorities, it will be convenient to set out the list of the kings, of whom 30 are clearly named; and 30 is no doubt the correct number.

1 Simuka
2 Kṛṣṇa
3 Śrī-Śātakarṇi (Śrī-Mallak°)
4 Pūrṇotsaṅga
5 Ṣkandhastambhi
6 Śātakarṇi
7 Lambodara
8 Āpīlaka (Divilaka)
9 Meghasvāti
10 Svāti
11 Skandasvāti
12 Mṛgendra
13 Kuntala
14 Svātivarṇa
15 Pulomāvi (Padumān)
16 Ariṣṭakarṇa
17 Hāla
18 Mantalaka or Pattalaka
19 Purīndrasena
20 Sundara Śātakarṇi
21 Çakora
22 Śivasvāti
23 Gautamīputra
24 Pulomā
[24*a* Śātakarṇi]
25 Śivaśrī
26 Śivaskandha
27 Yajñaśrī
28 Vijaya
29 Caṇḍaśrī
30 Pulomāvi

The lists in the MSS stand thus, omitting at present no. 24*a* who is mentioned only in *e*Vā. Mt MSS name the following (*fgm*Mt calling no. 15 Pulomāvi a second Meghasvāti), the numbers within brackets denoting those who are omitted:— *CGV* have 27 kings (nos. 2, 5, 15 omitted); $a^1a^2a^3a^4$ 28 (5, 15); *b* 27 (9, 20, 22); *c* 27 (2, 5, 20); *e* 25 (2, 5, 20, 23, 24); *f* 27 (24, 25, 29); *j* 24 (5, 7, 8, 18, 19, 29); *k* 21 (5, 9–11, 20–23, 29); *l* 20 (2, 5, 9, 12, 13, 20–24); *m* 27 (1, 2, 5); *n* 29 (20); *d* 30, and repeats 6–10; *g* 30, and repeats 10–14 and 15 (with correct name Pulomāvi): *hp*Mt have nothing. All Vā MSS, other than *eh*Vā, name nos. 1–3, 6–8, 15–23, 27–30; except that Ca^2a^3f omit no. 21; *k* no. 8; *l* 8, 21; *m* 21, 30: *h* has lost the first part and begins with no. 19: a^1a^4 apparently insert no. 8 twice; *m* repeats 3, 6 after no. 8. All these Vā name no. 20 Sundara merely as Śātakarṇi.

But *e*Vā is peculiar and its list is broken up into three sets. It begins thus, nos. 11, 18, 19, 20 (calling him Sundara), 21; then reverting mentions 12–15, 24*a*, 25–30; and long afterwards (see p. 35) names 1–4, 6–10 (corrupting no. 9's name). It thus omits 5, 16, 17, 22–24, yet makes its total 25 by including 24*a*, who is considered further on.

Bd names 1–3, 6, 8, 15–20, 22, 23, 27–30. Vṣ mentions 1–4, 6–9, 15–30; but *b*Vṣ omits 4, 6; *k*Vṣ no. 21; *l*Vṣ, 28, 29. Bh names 1–4, 7–9, 15–20; but *bt*Bh have nothing.

All the authorities keep the order of the kings as in the above list, except that 5 Mt MSS show three discrepancies. Two are small, namely, (1) *d*Mt mentions 6–10 and immediately repeats them; (2) *n*Mt inverts nos. 5 and 6, and mentions no. 19 twice, first after no. 13 and again in his proper place. The third discrepancy concerns nos. 10–15: *g*Mt names these in their place and repeats them after no. 29; and *bl*Mt omit them from their place and insert them (*l* omitting 12, 13) after no. 29. These discrepancies appear to be mere mistakes due to carelessness, or to lacunae or disarrangements of leaves in the MSS copied.

Every king in the list (except 24*a*) is mentioned by most of the MSS of at least two Purāṇas, except nos. 5, 10–14. No. 5 occurs only in Mt, but 5 MSS name him. Nos. 10–14 are mentioned only by Mt and *e*Vā; but no. 14 appears in them all; nos. 10, 11 in all except *k*Mt; and nos. 12, 13 in all except *l*Mt. They seem to be genuine, and help to constitute the total number 30. The general consensus then establishes the number, names, and order in the above list.

No. 24*a*, Śātakarṇi, mentioned only in *e*Vā, is not no. 20, who is called Śātakarṇi merely in all other Vā MSS and in Bḍ, for Mt, Vā, Bḍ, and *e*Vā agree that the latter reigned only one year (p. 41, l. 23), while the description of the former in *e*Vā is l. 28 on p. 42, and assigns 29 years to him. There is no line like it except l. 32 about Yajñaśrī, but he is not apparently Yajñaśrī whom *e*Vā mentions in his proper place. According to the *e*Vā list he should come presumably either immediately after no. 15, or immediately before no. 25 Śivaśrī. The only indication I can find bearing upon this puzzle occurs in *l*Vṣ, which regards Śātakarṇi Śivaśrī as two, (1) Śātakarṇi, (2) Śivaśrī (see p. 42, note [1]), and so places a Śātakarṇi exactly in one of the two positions required by *e*Vā. If this Śātakarṇi then be real, his place would be 24*a*. A line found in only one MS should not be rejected straight away (see Introdn. § 31), hence I have included him in the list in that position by l. 28; but, since his existence is vouched for by no other authority and he would raise the number of the kings to 31, that line is enclosed in brackets. If he is genuine, we may suppose that the total 30 is a round number.

Many of the kings bore the name Śātakarṇi, and it is spelt in many ways, the first part as *Śāti*, *Śānta*, *Śānti*, *Śita* (with *s* often instead of *ś* in these forms), and the latter part as *karṇi*, *karṇa*, *koṇa*, *varṇa*, &c. It is needless to state all such variations in the text and notes, and the form *Śātakarṇi* is adopted because it agrees best with the Pkt form *Sātakaṇi* generally found on coins. The names *Svātikarṇa* and *Svātivarṇa* occur sometimes and seem to be merely variants of it (see notes [57, 61, 65]). All these forms may obviously be Sanskritizations of that one Pkt name.

Prof. Rapson's 'Indian Coins, Andhras, &c.' elucidate this dynasty partially. I have not attempted, as it is not my function here, to identify the names in this list with those mentioned in inscriptions and on coins, except those of the first three kings who seem clear. The first king, whose correct name was Simuka Sātavāhana, is mentioned in Lüders' List of Brāhmī Inscriptions, no. 1113 (Epig. Ind. x, Appendix); the second Kṛṣṇa or Kanha in *id.* no. 1144; and the third Śrī-Śātakarṇi in *id.* nos. 346, 1114. In other inscriptions the following kings are mentioned—Gotamīputa Siri Sātakaṇi, nos. 1123, 1125; Siri Sivamaka Sada, no. 1279; Sati (= Śakti ?) Sirimata, no. 1112; Vāsiṭhīputa Siri Puḷumāvi, nos. 1106, 1124 (and probably 1100); Siri Pulumāvi, no. 1248; Vāsiṭhiputa Siri Puḷumāyi, nos. 1122–3; Vāsaṭhiputa Catarapana Satakani, no. 1120; Gotamīputa Siri Sātakaṇi, no. 1123, and Sadakaṇi, no. 1125; Sivakhada (or Sadakhada) Nāga siri, no. 1186; Gotamīputa Siri Yaña, nos. 987, 1024, 1146, 1340; Vasiṭhīputa Caḍasāta, no. 1341; and Māḍhariputa Sirivira Purisadata of the Ikhākus, nos. 1202–4 (see note [78]).

It may be noted that one line in certain Mt MSS differs from all the others in its expression, namely, l. 30 about Yajñaśrī (see note thereto). He is spoken of there in the present tense, *kurute*: see Introdn. § 21, note.

The total of the individual reigns (excluding no. 24*a*) is only 442½ years, even if we take the longest periods wherever there is a difference; but the whole duration is said to have been 460 years in Mt, 411 in Vā, and 456 in Bḍ, Vṣ, and Bh. The addition of no. 24*a* would increase the first total.

Kāṇvāyanāṁs [1] tato bhṛtyāḥ [2]	Kaṇvāyanam [3] ath=ôddhṛtya [4]
Suśarmāṇaḥ [5] prasahya [6] tam [7]	Suśarmāṇam prasahya tam [8]
Śuṅgānāṁ [9] c=aiva yac cheṣaṁ [10]	Śuṅgānāṁ [11] c=âpi yac chiṣṭaṁ [12]
kṣapitvā tu [13] balīyasaḥ [14]	kṣapayitvā [15] balaṁ tadā [16]
Śiśuko 'ndhraḥ [17] sa-jātīyaḥ [18]	Sindhuko hy Andhra-jātīyaḥ [19]
prāpsyat=îmāṁ vasundharām	prāpsyat=îmāṁ vasundharām

trayo-viṁśat [20] samā rājā Simukas [21] tu bhaviṣyati [22]

[1] This line is in Mt. This name is often corrupted as in p. 34, note [11]; and first vowel is long or short. In *n*Mt °*yanāṁs*; *f*Mt °*yanī*; Mt genly °*yanās*, which should be °*yanāṁs*, as the accus. is required.

[2] So *dfgk*Mt; *b*Mt *tadā*°: *j*Mt *tato bhṛtyān*. Mt genly *tato bhūpāḥ*. But *e*Mt *tadodhṛtya*; *c*Mt *tad=ôddhṛtya*; so *n*Mt crp. *Bhṛtyāḥ* is prob. correct, cf. Vṣ, Bh; the plural here may refer to 'Simuka and his fellow-tribesmen' in l. 3. Vṣ says—

Suśarmāṇaṁ Kaṇvaṁ* ca bhṛtyo† balāt‡ Śipraka§-nāmā hatvā‖ Andhra¶-jātīyo vasudhām bhokṣyati:

where * *kl*Vṣ *Kāṇvaṁ*, *b*Vṣ *Kāṇvāyanaṁ*; † *al*Vṣ *sa-bhṛtyaṁ*, *j*Vṣ *sva-bhṛtyo*, *b*Vṣ *sad-bhṛtya-*, *k*Vṣ *sa bhūtyaṁ*; ‡ *a*Vṣ *balat*, *b*Vṣ *balaṁ*, *l*Vṣ *vali*, *j*Vṣ *balavān*, *k*Vṣ *valākṣi*; § *b*Vṣ *Chiptaka*, *a*Vṣ *Śivika*, *k*Vṣ *Pulaka*, *l*Vṣ *Pucchaka*; ‖ *b*Vṣ *hatva-r*; ¶ *l*Vṣ *Āndha*, *b*Vṣ *Aṁ[ptyaṁ]pra*, *k*Vṣ *hy Andha*, *j*Vṣ *Śudhra*. Bh says—

hatvā Kāṇvaṁ* Suśarmāṇaṁ tad-bhṛtyo† vṛṣalo balī‡
gāṁ bhokṣyaty Andhra§-jātīyaḥ kañcit‖ kālam a-sattamaḥ:

where * *r*Bh *Kaṇvaṁ*; † *k*Bh *tadvatyo*; ‡ *fl*Bh *vṛṣabho*° (*f* strictly *vṛṣabhordhalī*, cf. p. 25, note [7]); § *d*Bh *Andhri*, *f*Bh *anya*; ‖ *c*Bh *kiñcit*.

[3] This line in Vā, Bḍ. Bḍ *Kaṇv*°. Vā genly *Kaṇṭh*°: other variations similar to those in p. 34, note [11]. Bḍ, *Ca²a⁴e*Vā °*yanam*; *a¹a³bdfgklm*Vā °*yanān*.

[4] So *Ca²a³e*Vā, Bḍ: *a¹a⁴kl*Vā *at=ôd*° or *at=ôdvṛtya*; *fgm*Vā *ato dhṛtya*; *d*Vā *tat=ôdhṛtya* (Pkt).

[5] In *j*Mt °*ṇeḥ*; *bcn*Mt °*ṇaṁ*; *l*Mt °*ṇa*; *g*Mt °*sarmāṇaṁ*.

[6] In *a²n*Mt *pragṛhya*.

[7] *Cbdj*Mt *tāṁ*; *g*Mt *tān*; *f*Mt *tvān*.

[8] In *e*Vā *Sudharmāṁsaṁ prasahyataḥ*.

[9] So Mt; *b*Mt *Suṁnānāṁ*; *cekn*Mt *sutā*°; *j*Mt *Aṁgārā*.

[10] In *e*Mt *c=aiva ḍheṣaṁ*; *f*Mt *c=aiva sarveṣāṁ*.

[11] This line is in Vā, not in Bḍ. *Ca¹a²*Vā *Śṛṅg*°.

[12] In *e*Vā *yac cheṣaḥ*; *fm*Vā defective.

[13] So Mt mostly: *d*Mt *kṣayitvā sa*; *ce*Mt *kṣipitvā sa*; *l*Mt *jṛyitvā tu*: *fyn*Mt *kṣapayitvā*, *j*Mt *kṣep*°, *b*Mt *kṛp*°.

[14] In *e*Mt *balāyasaḥ*; *j*Mt *mahīyasām*.

[15] *C*Vā *kṣayayitvā*.

[16] In *e*Vā *balī tathā*, *d*Vā °*tadā*.

[17] So Mt genly; *d*Mt °'*dhraḥ*; *j*Mt °'*ddhra*; *n*Mt °'*dhra*; *k*Mt °*va*; *b*Mt °*yaḥ*: *d*Mt *Śiśurko*° here, *Śiśukas* in next line; *e*Mt *Śiśruk-Āndhraḥ*; *fy*Mt *Śikhukas tu*; *l*Mt *Kiṁśukrodhaḥ*. The correct name is *Simuka* (Rapson, 'Indian Coins, Andhras, &c.' pp. xviii, xlvi). It was misread as *Sisuka*, and then Sktzd (1) as *Śiśuka*, and (2) as *Śiṣuka* whence *Śikhuka*, by dialectical variation of *ṣ* and *kh*. *Śimuka* could be misread as *Śipraka* which Vṣ has, see note [2].

[18] In *k*Mt *śa-jāt*°.

[19] So Vā, Bḍ: *e*Vā *Chismako hy a-jātīyaḥ*.

[20] So *Cdfgj*Mt, Vā, Bḍ. Mt genly °*viṁśa*: *e*Vā reads this line—

sa trayo-viṁśati rājā bhavitā Chismakaḥ samāḥ

[21] I put the correct name here to combine Mt, Vā, Bḍ, which read it as above: *e*Mt *Śiśrukas*; *c*Mt *Śiṁśukaḥ*.

[22] So Mt. Vā, Bḍ *bhavitā tv atha*; *d*Vā omits *tv*; *m*Vā °*tv a[rka]thaṁ*; *g*Vā *bhavitā[s] tathā*.

Kṛṣṇo [23] bhrātā yavīyāṁs tu [24] | Kṛṣṇo [25] bhrāt=âsya [26] varṣāṇi
aṣṭādaśa [27] bhaviṣyati | so 'smād daśa [28] bhaviṣyati
Śrī-Śātakarṇir [29] bhavitā tasya putras [30] tu vai daśa [31]
Pūrṇotsaṅgas [32] tato [33] rājā varṣāṇy [34] aṣṭādaś=aiva tu
Skandhastambhis [35] tathā [36] rājā varṣāṇy [37] aṣṭādaś=aiva tu
pañcāśataṁ [38] samāḥ ṣaṭ ca [39] Śātakarṇir [40] bhaviṣyati
daśa c=âṣṭau ca [41] varṣāṇi tasya [42] Lambodaraḥ [43] sutaḥ [44]
Āpīlako [45] daśa dve ca [46] tasya putro bhaviṣyati

[23] Mt genly the Pkt nomin. form *Kṛṣṇa*; *j*Mt *Kṛṣṇā*. Vṣ says—*Kṛṣṇa-nāmā tad-bhrātā*. Bh says—

Kṛṣṇa-nām=âtha tad-bhrātā bhavitā pṛthi-vī-patiḥ.

See Rapson, *op. cit.*, pp. xix, xlvi.

[24] In *fg*Mt *ca*.

[25] So *a*[1]*a*[3]*a*[4]*dg*Vā, Bḍ: *e*Vā *Kṛṣṇā*; *b*Vā *klptau*: *a*[2]Vā *Tvaṣṭo*; *fm*Vā *Tvaṣṭro*; *Cjkl*Vā *aṣṭau*.

[26] So *bde*Vā, Bḍ: *a*[1-4]*fgkm*Vā, 3 MSS of *C*Vā *bhrātasya*; *l*Vā, 2 MSS of *C*Vā *bhrātaś ca*; 1 MS of *C*Vā *smāta=ya*.

[27] So all Mt; but *n*Mt *aṣṭāṁ daśa*, see Introdn. § 40.

[28] So *a*[2-4]*bdfgkm*Vā, Bḍ: *l*Vā *so smā d*°; *e*Vā *so 'ṣṭād*°; *Ca*[1]*j*Vā *tasmād d*°; see Introdn. § 40.

[29] This name is spelt variously, see p. 37. Vā genly °*Śātakarṇir*. Bḍ, Vṣ °*Śāntakarṇir*. But *bcde*Mt °*Mālakarṇī*, *n*Mt °*kaṇī* (easy misreadings); Mt genly °*Mallakarṇi*; *j*Mt °*Śālakarṇir*, *k*Mt °*parṇi*. Bh °*Śāntakarṇa*, *f*Bh °*varṇa*.

[30] Bh, *l*Vṣ agree, *tasya putras*: *fgj*Mt *putrās*.

[31] So Mt genly; *bcekn*Mt *samāḥ*. Vā, Bḍ *mahān*.

[32] This line is only in Mt, *e*Vā. So Mt genly; *f*Mt *Pūrṇotsarga*; *c*Mt *Pūrṇāsaṅgas*, *e*Mt °*sagas*: *e*Vā reads this line—

Pūrṇosantu ca varṣāṇi bhavit=âṣṭādaś=aiva tu.

Vṣ *Pūrṇotsaṅga*; *j*Vṣ °*saṁ[mṛ]ga*; *h*Vṣ *Pūrṇeśaṅga*; *l*Vṣ *Vasukarṇṇotsaṅga*. Bh *Paurṇamāsa*, and adds *tat-sutaḥ*.

[33] *Tu vai* in *bcen*Mt.

[34] *Samā* in *n*Mt.

[35] This line is only in *bdfgn*Mt. So *fg*Mt; *d*Mt °*stabhis*; *b*Mt *Svīrasvanis* (an easy misreading); *n*Mt *Śovastuti*, and inverts him and the next king.

[36] *Tapā* in *n*Mt.

[37] *Samā* in *n*Mt.

[38] So Vā, *Ccdemn*Mt; *j*Mt °*śatāḥ*. Bḍ, *bfg*Mt °*śat tu*; *Akl*Mt °*śac ca*.

[39] *Saṭ kar* in *e*Vā; *e*Mt *ṣaḍu*; *n*Mt omits *ca*.

[40] No marked variations in this name: *n*Mt inverts him and the preceding king; *m*Vā repeating the line reads *tasya putro*. Bh omits him.

[41] *Daśa vāsaiva* in *b*Mt.

[42] In *e*Vā [*bhavitā*] *tasmāl*.

[43] This line only in Mt and *e*Vā. Bh and Vṣ agree in the name.

[44] Bh agrees, *tat-putras*: *e*Vā *nṛpaḥ*.

[45] Mt genly *Āpītako*; *cfg*Mt *Apīt*°; *e*Mt *Apit*°; *n*Mt *Apīt*° or *Apīl*°; *b*Mt †*Aryāṁtako*: *e*Vā *Āpīlako*. But *g*Vā *Āpīlavā*; *f*Vā, 3 MSS of *C*Vā *Āpol*°; *j*Vā *Āpol*°; 1 MS of *C*Vā *Apal*°; *m*Vā *Ārpāl*° or *Āryāl*°; *a*[1-4]Vā, 2 MSS of *C*Vā *Āpādaba-*; *bd*Vā *Āpīstavā*. Bḍ *Āpolavo*. *Āpīlaka* seems the best form: the third syll. *ta* in Mt names may be a misreading of *la*, and may be read either way in *n*Mt. Vṣ genly reads *tasmād* before this name, and it was apptly often read as Pkt *tasmā* with the final *d* applied to the name; thus *l*Vṣ *Dāpīlaka* (though it interposes *ca*), and *cdek*Vṣ (*tasmādivīlakaḥ*) *Ivīl*° or *Divīl*°; hence *afg*Vṣ *Divīl*°, *C*Vṣ *Divil*°: *h*Vṣ *Divīla*; *j*Vṣ *Vilaka*; *b*Vṣ *Divānīka*. Bh genly (reading *d* in Gupta script as *c*) *Civīlaka* or *Cibil*°, *aqs*Bh °*lika*; *f*Bh *Cilibaka*, *d*Bh °*bika*; *e*Bh *Cibilika*, *Vicilaka*; *r*Bh *Vivilaka*, *h*Bh *Yil*° or *Ghil*° and *Civil*°. *B*Bh *Vikala* apptly.

[46] So Mt; *cen*Mt *tu*. Vā genly, Bḍ *dvādaśa vai*, which is equally good: *a*[1-4]Vā, 2 MSS of *C*Vā †*-ddhodaśa*°.

daśa c=âṣṭau ca varṣāṇi Meghasvātir[47] bhaviṣyati

Svātiś ca bhavitā[48] rājā[49] samās[50] tv aṣṭādaś=aiva[51] tu
Ātir bhaviṣyati nṛpo varṣāṇi dvādaś=aiva tu[52]
Skandasvātis[53] tathā rājā sapt=aiva tu[54] bhaviṣyati
Skandasvātiḥ samās tasmāt sapta[55] rājyaṁ kariṣyati

Mṛgendraḥ[56] Svātikarṇas[57] tu[58] bhaviṣyati samās trayaḥ[59]
Kuntalaḥ[60] Svātikarṇas[61] tu[62] bhavit=âṣṭau samā[63] nṛpaḥ
eka-saṁvatsaraṁ[64] rājā Svātivarṇo[65] bhaviṣyati

ṣaṭ-triṁśad[66] eva[67] varṣāṇi Pulomāvir[69] bhaviṣyati
catur-viṁśat[68] tu varṣāṇi Pulomāvir[69] bhaviṣyati

bhavit=Âriṣṭakarṇas[70] tu varṣāṇām pañca-viṁśatiḥ[71]

47 This line only in Mt, *e*Vā. So Mt genly; *j*Mt °*svāmī*; *C*Mt *Medhasvātir*; *n*Mt *Saṁghasvāṇi*, an easy misreading; *ce*Mt *Saṁghaś c=âpi*. Vṣ, Bh *Meghasvāti*, *j*Vṣ *Maghas*°; *k*Vṣ *Meghaghāti*. The name has been corrupted in *e*Vā which reads—

daśa c=âṣṭau ca bhavitā so 'ṣṭādaśa bhaviṣyati.

48 This line only in Mt: *bl*Mt *Svātir bhaviṣyate*, *n*Mt *Svāmī bh*°; *g*Mt, in repeating the line, *Svāmi bh*°: *ce*Mt *sa eva bhokṣyate.*

49 In *b*Mt *ramyā.*

50 In *celn*Mt *samā*: *b*Mt *manās*, so *g*Mt in repeating.

51 In *cen*Mt *aṣṭau daś=aiva* (omitting *tu*).

52 This line is in *e*Vā only. Introdn. § 40.

53 So Mt, mostly. *C*Mt °*svātis* misprinted as °*racātis*: *bcen*Mt and *g*Mt (in repeating) *Skandhasvātis*, *d*Mt °*svāmis*; *l*Mt *Skaṁvastrāṇis* (an easy misreading).

54 Misread as *sam=aiva tva* in *g*Mt (repeated), °*tvaṁ* in *b*Mt; *cen*Mt *sapta c=aiva.*

55 This line in *e*Vā only; thus, *Skandansvātiḥ samāt tasmā samā*, where *samā* is misreading for *sapta.*

56 This line only in Mt, *e*Vā: *b*Mt *Bhagendraḥ*; *e*Vā *Mahen*°; *j*Mt *naren*°.

57 So Mt genly: *fg*Mt °*varṇas*, but *g*Mt repeats as in text; *n*Mt *Śātikarṇas*; *e*Vā *Sātakarṇis.*

58 In *e*Mt *mu*: after this *n*Mt adds by mistake and superfluously *varṣāṇi pañca-viṁśati* (from l. 19).

59 In *e*Vā *samā-trayam.*

60 This line only in Mt, *e*Vā: *b*Mt *Kuśalaḥ*; *j*Mt *Kṣettulaḥ.*

61 In *n*Mt *Śāntik*°; *e*Vā *Śātakarṇis.*

62 *Ca* in *cef*Mt, and *g*Mt in repeating.

63 In *j*Mt °*âṣṭā samo.*

64 But *bcjln*Mt °*saṁvatsaro*, *e*Mt °*śe v*°, *g*Mt (in repeating) *śakasaṁv*°.

65 This line only in Mt, *e*Vā. So *ACbdl*Mt: *cej*Mt °*karṇo*; *fgm*Mt °*koṇo*, *g*Mt (in repeating) °*varṇo*; *d*Mt °*keṇo*; *e*Vā °*ṣeṇo*; *k*Mt *Syātiseno*; *n*Mt *Śātikarṇo.*

66 This line is in Mt, except *AC*Mt: *lm*Mt *ṣaḍ-triṁśad*; *g*Mt (in repeating) *ṣaḍ-viṁśad*; *n*Mt *ṣaḍgiṁśa* (= *ṣaḍ-viṁśa*).

67 So *dm*Mt and *g*Mt (in repeating): *l*Mt *deva*; *jk*Mt *c=aiva*; *cen*Mt *tv eva*; *bfg*Mt *dve ca.*

68 So Vā, Bḍ: *e*Vā °*triṁśat.*

69 This name has been greatly corrupted. So *bdkln*Mt; *g*Mt (in repeating) °*vi*: *ce*Mt *Pulomāvid*; *j*Mt *Sulomānir* (an easy misreading). In Vā: *dgk*Vā *Padumāvir* (or, as it may be read in *dg*Vā, *Yadu*°; and so *a*²*a*⁴*l*Vā and 3 MSS of *C*Vā): then by easy misreadings, *b*Vā *Paṭu*° (or *Ya*°); *e*Vā *Patramātir* (or *Ya*°); *f*Vā *Ṣaṭumāvir*; 4 MSS of *C*Vā *Ṣaḍu*°; *m*Vā *Ṣaṭu*° or *Ṣaḍu*°; *j*Vā *Ṣadrarmāvi*; *a*¹Vā and 2 MSS of *C*Vā *ṣaṭ samā vai* (by attempt at emendment). By regarding the final *vi* (in Pkt) as an expletive (= *vai* or *api*), *hj*Vṣ *Padumān* or *Paṭu*°; *abcdegkl*Vṣ *Paṭu*°; Bḍ *Paṭumāṁś ca*; other Vṣ *Padhumān.* Then *ar*Bh *Vaṭamāna*; Bh genly *Aṭa*°; *n*Bh *Aṭha*°; *m*Bh *Aṁḍa*°; *d*Bh *Ara*°; *s*Bh *Raca*°. For this name *fm*Mt substitute (a second) *Meghasvātir*; and *g*Mt *Bhegha*°.

70 There is great variation in this name

tataḥ saṁvatsarān pañca [72] Hālo [73] rājā bhaviṣyati

pañca Mantalako [74] rājā [75]
bhaviṣyati samā nṛpaḥ [77]
Purīndraseno [79] bhavitā
tasmāt saumyo bhaviṣyati [81]
Sundaraḥ [83] Śātakarṇis [84] tu
abdam [86] ekam bhaviṣyati

pañca Pattalako [74] rājā [76]
bhaviṣyati mahābalaḥ [78]
bhāvyaḥ Purikaṣeṇas [80] tu
samāḥ so 'py eka-viṁśatim [82]
Śātakarṇir [85] varṣam ekam
bhaviṣyati narādhipaḥ

Cakoraḥ [87] Śātakarṇis [88] tu ṣaṇ māsān [89] vai bhaviṣyati [90]

Vā genly *bhavitā Nemikṛṣṇas*; *d*Vā °*Nemikasmas*; *m*Mt °*Nauvikṛṣṇas*; *d*Mt °*Naurik*°; *j*Mt °*Nārik*°; *k*Mt °*Saurik*°; *fg*Mt °*ṣṭauvik*°; *e*Mt °*Gaurak*°; *c*Mt °*Gaurakṛtsvas*. *AC*Mt *bhavit=Âriktavarṇas*; *bl*Mt °*Âriktakarṇas*; *n*Mt °*Âriṣṭakarṇis*. Vṣ *Ariṣṭakarmā*; so *a*Bh. Bḍ *bhavit=Âniṣṭakarmā*. Bh *Aniṣṭakarmā*. It is impossible to extract the correct name out of this confusion, and I have adopted *Ariṣṭakarṇa* as the most central form.

[71] So $a^{1}a^{2}a^{4}$*bdfg*Vā: Vā genly, *b*Mt, Bḍ °*tìm*. Mt *varṣāṇi . . . tiḥ*; *j*Mt reads this half line, *ṣaṇ-māsān vai bhaviṣyati*.

[72] So Mt. Vā, Bḍ *saṁvatsaram pūrṇam*.

[73] So all, except *l*Vṣ *Hala*; Bh *Hāleya*; *r*Bh *Hālela* or *Hālena*; *c*Bh *Hālaya*.

[74] There is great variation in this name. *ACb*Mt *Mandulako*; *c*Mt *Mantalako*, *e*Mt °*laṁko*; *l*Mt *Menulake*; *fgkn*Mt *Maṇḍalako*; *d*Mt *Maṇḍako*; *m*Mt *Kuṇḍalako*. Then *k*Vṣ *Pantalaka* or *Patt*°; Vṣ genly *Patt*°; *l*Vṣ *Pitt*°; *de*Vṣ *Putt*°; *j*Vṣ *Pakṣal*°; *a*Vṣ *Prabhul*° (or *Prattal*°?). Bḍ *Pattallaka*. Bh, losing the first syll., *Talaka* (see Appendix II, § vi); *a*Bh *Tanaka*; *h*Bh *Halaka*; *d*Bh *Śūl*°. Vā, by losing the third syllable, *Saptaka*; *f*Vā *Saptaṁka*; *bd*Vā *Masaka* (misreading of *Maptaka*?): *e*Vā reads this half line, *pañc=aivabhā . . ko rajā*. *Mantalaka* or *Pattalaka* seems the most likely form, from which the other readings might have been derived by misreadings. Bh says, *tasya c=âtmajaḥ*.

[75] So Mt, *e*Vā: *b*Mt *rākṣo*.

[76] Vā, to compensate for the lost syllable in *Saptaka*, and by the meaning of *sapta*, reads *rājāno* and turns the two following words into plurals: *m*Vā *rānā[maṁ]no*. Bḍ *nāma*. The correct reading must be *rājā*.

[77] So Mt, *e*Vā, where *nṛpaḥ* is redundant, cf. line 26.

[78] So Bḍ. Vā °*ṣyanti mahābalāḥ*.

[79] This line is in Mt. So Mt genly; *C*Mt °*seno* or °*senī*; *n*Mt *Purīndraseno* and *Purīdra*°; *b*Mt *Purāṇḍa*°: *h*Vṣ *Pulindrāsana* (for °*drasena*); *abk*Vṣ °*dasena*; *l*Vṣ *Pullas*°; Vṣ genly, *e*Vā *Pravillas*°; *de*Vṣ *Pravilas*°; *j*Mt *Pravilis*°; where *pra* may be a misreading of *pu*.

[80] This line is in Vā, Bḍ. So a^{1-4}*fglm*Vā; *bd*Vā *Purīkasenas*; *k*Vā *Purikāṣaṇas*; *j*Vā *Purīkheṇus*; *C*Vā *Putrikaṣeṇas*. Then *d*Bh *Purīṣaseru* (where *s* and *bh* are much alike); *ars*Bh °*bheru*; *eghjklmnpq*Bh °*bhoru*; other Bh, Bḍ °*bhīru*. These variations suggest the name *Puruṣasena*. A king *Purisadata* of the Ikhākus is mentioned, see p. 37.

[81] So Mt genly: *b*Mt *sāmyo*°; *n*Mt *saimyo*°, °*yau*°; *d*Mt *seno*°. *Saumyo* cannot well be a king, though the line says so on its face, because in this dynasty two kings are never put together in a single line without any mention of their reigns. *Saumyo bhaviṣyati* is probably a corruption, see Appendix II, § iii.

[82] So Ca^{2}*fjkm*Vā, Bḍ; $a^{1}a^{3}a^{4}$*bdhl*Vā °*tiḥ*; *g*Vā °*ti*: *e*Vā reads this half line *samā dvādaśa bhū-tale*.

[83] This line is in Mt, *e*Vā. Vṣ *Sundara*: *fg*Mt *Sundharaḥ*. Bh, *l*Vṣ *Sunandana*.

[84] Usual variations, see p. 37.

[85] So Vā, Bḍ, with variations, but no personal name: 1 MS of *C*Vā *Śāntakīrttir*.

[86] In *e*Vā *varṣam*; *j*Mt . . *tam*.

[87] So Mt genly, *e*Vā. Vā genly *Cakāra*. Vṣ, Bh *Cakora*; *gp*Bh *Cakara*; *h*Vṣ *Cā[kā]kāra*. But *ce*Mt *Rājāda*; *n*Mt *rājā vai*: *b*Mt reads this half line *rājā vaṁśyo vikarṇaś ca*: *l*Vṣ merely *Śātakarṇi*.

aṣṭā-viṁśati [91] varṣāṇi Śivasvātir [92] bhaviṣyati
rājā ca Gautamīputra [93] eka-viṁśat tato [94] nṛpaḥ [95]
aṣṭā-viṁśaḥ [96] sutas [97] tasya Pulomā vai [98] bhaviṣyati
[ek-ôna-triṁśatim bhāvyaḥ Śātakarṇis tatho nṛpaḥ] [99]
Śivaśrīr [1] vai Pulomā tu [2] sapt≈aiva [3] bhavitā nṛpaḥ [4]
Śivaskandhaḥ [5] Śātakarṇir [6] bhavit≈âsy≈âtmajaḥ samāḥ [7]

nava-viṁśati [8] varṣāṇi	ek-ôna-viṁśatiṁ [9] rājā
Yajñaśrīḥ [10] Śātakarṇikaḥ [11]	Yajñaśrīḥ [12] Śātakarṇy atha [13]

88 So Vā, *cdefgjn*Mt, Vṣ, with variations. Mt genly *Svātikarṇas*. Instead of this name Bh genly *vaṭako yatra*; *r*Bh *vaṭṭikā*°; *n*Bh (and *B*Bh?) *navamo*°; *j*Bh *cavako*° altered to *vaṭako*°; *Gg*Bh *bahavo*°; *d*Bh *baṭako* (or *ṣaṭako*) *yasya*. Read *vaṭuko yasya*?

89 In *bde*Mt *māso*; *e*Vā *ṣaṭ samān*.

90 So Mt. Vā genly *vai narādhipaḥ*; *e*Vā *bhavitā nṛpaḥ*; *k*Vā *vi[ta] narādhipaḥ*.

91 So Mt, *bm*Vā, Bḍ. Vā genly, *j*Mt °*viṁśat tu*.

92 So Mt, *d*Vā, Bḍ. Vṣ, Bh agree: *l*Vṣ °*svātiḥ*; *a*Vṣ *Śivaḥ Svātiḥ*; *fg*Mt *Śikhasvātir*; *k*Bh *Śiras*°; *j*Mt *Śiraḥs*°. *Ca*¹*djl*Vā *Śivasvāmī*; *a*²⁻⁴*bfghk*Vā °*svāmir*; *m*Vā °*svāmīr*. Bh calls him *arindamaḥ*.

93 In *bc*Mt, *b*Vṣ *Gotamīp*°. Vṣ, Bh *Gomatīp*°; *l*Vṣ *Gomati*. Mt adds *hy*.

94 So *dfgj*Mt, *a*³Vā; *cn*Mt °*viṁśa*°. *Am*Mt *eka-viṁśaty ato*; *C*Mt *aka-v*° by misprint: *b*Mt, *a*¹*a*²*a*⁴*bdfghklm*Vā *eka-viṁśattamo*; *Cj*Vā, Bḍ °*viṁśat samā*. *Eka-viṁśattamo*, '21st king', can hardly be right, because he is not 21st in any list except *A*Mt where two preceding kings are omitted; and he can only be made 21st by omissions.

95 So Mt, *bdfghlm*Vā, Bḍ, though it is redundant. *Ajk*Vā *nṛṣu*.

96 This line only in Mt: *dg*Mt °*śa*; *bj*Mt °*śat*; *C*Mt °*śati*.

97 In *n*Mt *tutas*; *j*Mt *tatas*; *b*Mt *samas*.

98 *Cb*Mt *Sulomā vai*; but *be*Mt *Pulomā tu* in next line. Vṣ *Pulimān*; *l*Vṣ *Pul*°; *a*Vṣ *Kul*°. Bh *Purīmān*; *k*Bh *Puri*°; *f*Bh *Putrī*°. The name should no doubt be *Pulomāvir*. Vṣ adds, *tat-putraḥ*.

99 This line only in *e*Vā: see p. 37.

1 This line only in Mt, *e*Vā. So Mt genly: *ce*Mt °*śrī*; *n*Mt °*śvā*; *b*Mt *Sivaśir*; *j*Mt *Śirogrīvaḥ* (omitting *vai*). Vṣ *Śātakarṇī Śivaśrīḥ*; *l*Vṣ makes this two kings, *tasy≈âpi Śātakarṇiḥ tataś Śivaśrīḥ* (see p. 37): *d*Bh *Sacaśirā*; *n*Bh *Midaśirāḥ*; Bh genly *Medaś*°; *k*Bh *Medāś*°; *f*Bh *Medaśś*°. This half line in *e*Vā is, *Śirasi putra Āvis tu*.

2 So Mt genly; *c*Mt °*māḥ tu*; *bg*Mt °*māsu*. But *j*Mt °*māt tu*; *C*Mt *Sulomāt tu*.

3 In *b*Mt *samaiva*; *e*Vā *catasro*.

4 In *e*Vā *samāḥ*.

5 This line only in Mt, *e*Vā. So Mt genly. Vṣ, *afmnr*Bh agree: *c*Bh °*skadhra*: *dfg*Mt, Bh genly, *hl*Vṣ °*skandaḥ* (altered in *s*Bh to °*skandha*); *b*Vṣ °*svanda*; *k*Vṣ °*sunda*: *j*Mt *Śiraskandho*, *e*Vā °*skandaḥ*.

6 So *cdefgmn*Mt, *e*Vā; *b*Mt *Sāmak*°. *ACl*Mt *Śātikarṇād*; *k*Mt *Śalaiḥkarṇikā*; *j*Mt *Nṛpaskando*.

7 So *cdejn*Mt; *b*Mt defective *vin≈âsy*°; *fg*Mt *bhāvī tasy*°. *ACklm*Mt *bhavitā hy āt*°: *e*Vā *bhaviṣyati samā nṛpaḥ*. No number is mentioned. Perhaps Mt should read, *bhāvī tasmāt trayo samāḥ* (see Appendix I, § iii), and *e*Vā *bhaviṣyati samās trayaḥ*.

8 So Mt: *j*Mt °*viṁśat tu*; *fg*Mt °*śivāt tu*: *bceln*Mt read this line—

nava varṣāṇi Yajñaśrīḥ* kurute† Śātakarṇikaḥ‡:

where **b*Mt °*ṣnīḥ*; †*b*Mt *kurune*, *n*Mt *kusate*; ‡*ce*Mt °*karṇinā*, *l*Mt *Sātavarṇitā*, *b*Mt *Śaḥsakarnikaḥ*.

9 So Vā, Bḍ: *bdgh*Vā °*triṁśataṁ*; *k*Vā *trikonatriśataṁ*.

10 Mat genly *Yajñaśrīḥ*; *dl*Mt °*śrī*; *j*Mt *Yajñaḥ Śrī-*.

11 In *k*Mt *Śātakarṇinā*.

12 So *Ca*¹*ej*Vā; *m*Vā *Yajñaḥ Śrīḥ*. Bḍ *Yajñaḥ Śrī-*: *a*¹*a*²*a*⁴*bfgl*Vā *Yajuḥśrī-ḥ*; *dhk*Vā *Yajuśrī-ḥ*. Vṣ, Bh *Yajñaśrīḥ* with

ṣaḍ eva [14] bhavitā [15] tasmād [16] Vijayas [17] tu samā nṛpaḥ [18]

Caṇḍaśrīḥ [19] Śātakarṇis [20] tu [21]	Daṇḍaśrīḥ [22] Śātakarṇī ca
tasya putraḥ samā daśa	tasya putraḥ samās trayaḥ [23]

Pulomāviḥ [24] samāḥ sapta [25] anyas teṣām [26] bhaviṣyati 34

ek-ôna-viṁśatir hy ete [27]	ity ete vai nṛpās triṁśad [28]
Āndhrā [29] bhokṣyanti vai mahīm	Andhrā [30] bhokṣyanti ye [31] mahīm
teṣāṁ varṣa-śatāni syuś	samāḥ śatāni catvāri
catvāri ṣaṣṭir [32] eva ca.	pañca ṣaḍ vai tath≈aiva ca [33].

marg. alteration °*sāra* in *a*Bh; *s*Bh °*śīla*, altered to °*śrī*: *k*Vṣ *Suṅgaśrīs*. Bh adds *tat-sutas*.

[13] In *e*Vā °*api*: 2 MSS of *C*Vā *Sāmakarṇy atha*.

[14] In *e*Vā *ete*.

[15] In *j*Mt *nacidā* (misreading of *bhavitā* in old Bengali script?).

[16] In *bcen*Mt *yasmād*; *e*Vā *vastu*.

[17] So all: but *de*Vṣ *Vījaya*; *b*Mt, *j*Vṣ *Vijas*; *e*Vā *dvijaḥ yaśu* (omitting *tu*); *b*Vṣ *Dviyajña*; *l*Bh *Vinaya*. Bh says, *tat-suto*.

[18] So Vā, Bḍ. Mt genly *samās tataḥ*; *bcn*Mt *samaṁ*°; *fgj*Mt [*sa*] *samā daśa*.

[19] So Mt genly; cMt *Caḍaśrīḥ*; *eg*Mt *Vaṇḍa*°; *b*Mt *Candratīḥ*. Vṣ genly *Candraśrīḥ*; *c*Vṣ *Cadra*°: *d*Bh *Candraṣīja*, *fr*Bh °*vīja*, *as*Bh °*vīrya*, Bh genly °*vijñaḥ*.

[20] Mt genly *Śāntikarṇas*, with variations; *bg*Mt *Śamakarṇis*.

[21] So Mt, *e*Vā. Vā, Bḍ *ca*.

[22] So Vā. Bḍ *Daṇḍa-Śrī-*.

[23] In *e*Vā *samās trayam*; *a*[1]Vā *samāśrayaḥ*.

[24] So *e*Vā, *a*Vṣ; *l*Vṣ °*māvī*. Bḍ °*māriḥ*. Vṣ genly °*māciḥ*; *cdefjk*Vṣ °*mārciḥ*; *h*Vṣ °*mādi*; *b*Vṣ *Anulomāviḥ*. Bh genly *Salomadhiḥ*; *m*Bh *Sul*°; *k*Bh *Mal*° (all easy misreadings).

[25] Mt genly *Pulomā sapta varṣāṇi*; *Cbdm*Mt *Sul*°; where the last syll. of the name has been probably regarded as a particle and ousted by the change of Pkt *varṣā* to Skt *varṣāṇi*. Vā genly *Pulov≈âpi*.

[26] So Mt, Vā genly: *e*Mt *antyes*°, *n*Mt *antas*°, cMt *aṁnyas*°; all mistakes for *antyas teṣām*, probably the true reading, cf. p. 12, l. 22; p. 18, note [7]. *Ca*[2]*f*Vā †*anyeṣāṁ ca* (*f* omits *ca*). Bḍ *tataś c≈aiṣām*; *e*Vā *san tasmād*.

[27] So Mt, genly: *fg*Mt °*śati*°; *d*Mt °*śatiś c≈ête*; *j*Mt °*śad ete ca*; *n*Mt *ek-ônā-navatiṁ hy ete*, *ce*Mt †*ekānā-n*°.

[28] So Vā, Bḍ: *m*Vā omits this line.

[29] So Mt genly: *cfjn*Mt *Andhrā*; *d*Mt *Andhrān*; *b*Mt *nṛpā*.

[30] In *e*Vā *akṣā*.

[31] So Vā. Bḍ, *g*Vā *vai*.

[32] So Mt: *n*Mt *ṣaṣṭīr*, *b*Mt *ṣaṣṭim*: *j*Mt reads this line—

dvādaś-âdhikam eteṣāṁ rājyaṁ śata-catuṣṭayam.

[33] This line is in Vā, Bḍ: not in *m*Vā. So Vā genly: *h*Vā *pañca ṣaḍ va*°: *bdfgk*Vā °*ṣaṭ ca*°; *e*Vā °*ṣaṭ sapta c≈aiva hi*. Bḍ *pañcāśat ṣaṭ tath≈aiva ca*. Vṣ says—

evam ete triṁśat* catvāry abda†-śatāni ṣaṭ-pañcāśad‡-adhikāni pṛthivīm bhokṣyanti:

where *kVṣ omits *triṁśat*; †*h*Vṣ *aṣṭa*; ‡*l*Vṣ *ṣaś pañcā*[*da*]*śad*. Bh says—

ete triṁśan* nṛpatayaś catvāry abda†-śatāni ca
ṣaṭ pañcāśac ca pṛthivīm bhokṣyanti, Kuru-nandana:

where **a*Bh has *viṁśan* written above; †*g*Bh *aṣṭa*.

Various Local Dynasties.

Text—*A*Mt *273*, 17b–24; *A*Vā *99*, 358b–365; Bḍ iii, *74*, 171–179a.

Corresp. passages—*C*Vṣ iv, *24*, 13–16; *G*Bh xii, *1*, 29–32b.

The account of these dynasties consists of three parts, the first of which summarizes the number of kings in each dynasty and the second states its duration, while the third adds certain subsequent kings. In the first part the Matsya, Vāyu, and Brahmāṇḍa agree generally, but in the second the Matsya has one version and the two others another. Here the dynastic matter in the Matsya ends, and the third part is found only in the two others. The Bhāgavata gives the first part in verses which are much like the texts of those Purāṇas, only the concluding portion of the second, and a very brief notice of the third. In the first part therefore the two versions are printed side by side. In the second part the Matsya version and that of the Vāyu and Brahmāṇḍa are compared side by side, but in the third there is only the text common to those two. The Bhāgavata statements in both these parts are given in the notes. The Viṣṇu in prose agrees closely with the Bhāgavata.

The Vā and Bḍ mention the dynasties in the second part in the same order that all three Purāṇas observe in the first part, but the Mt verses are disarranged in the second part, and are re-arranged here in that order for convenience. This involves no tampering with its text, because each line is complete in itself and independent, except ll. 12, 13 which compose a couplet forming verse 22 and which remain undisturbed; hence the Mt verses are placed here thus, 23b, 24a, 20b, 21b, 20a, 21a, 22ab, 23a, 24b.

The Mt is generally complete; but *e*Mt omits ll. 12–14; *f*Mt l. 8; *g*Mt repeats ll. 3, 4 after l. 10; *k*Mt omits ll. 4, 5; *hp*Mt have nothing. *AC*Vā omit ll. 7, 8, but *A*Vā mentions them in a note; most other copies give them; *a*⁴Vā omits ll. 7 (second half)–9 (first half); *m*Vā ll. 1–3, but they are added in the margin. Of Bh versions *j* omits ll. 1–5, but they are added in the margin; *bt* have nothing.

These local dynasties are all classed together as more or less contemporaneous. The number of years assigned to them must be considered according to the remarks in Introdn. §§ 42 ff., and with reference to the middle of the 3rd century A.D. when the account was first compiled as preserved in the Mt, for the revised versions in Vā and Bḍ did not revise the periods[1]. If those remarks be sound, the Śrīparvatīya Andhrabhṛtyas had at that time reigned 52 years, or (if we read *dviḥ pañcāśatam*) possibly 100 roundly, according to Mt; while the Vā and Bḍ reading is no doubt corrupt and should perhaps be 112 or 102 years. The Ābhīras had then reigned 67 years, the Gardabhilas 72 years, the Śakas 183 years, the Yavanas 87 or 82 years, and the Tuṣāras 7,000 or 500 according to the proper construction of the sentences but perhaps 107 or 105 is really meant. The 13 Guruṇḍas or Muruṇḍas had then reigned half of the quadruple of 100 years, that is 200, according to Mt, or 350 according to Vā and Bḍ, but the latter is probably a corruption of the former

[1] Except in l. 6, if Mt reading *dvi-pañcāśatam* is right, and if we emend Vā and Bḍ to *daśa dve ca śataṁ ca vai*; see Introdn. § 41.

reading, for Vṣ and Bh say precisely 199 years. The 11 Hūṇas or Maunas had then lasted 103 years.

Mention of these races is found in the inscriptions; thus Ābhīras in Lüders' List of Brāhmī Inscriptions, nos. 963, 1137 (Epig. Ind. x, Appendix) and Fleet's Gupta Inscriptions, p. 14; Śakas, Lüders' list, nos. 1123, 1135, 1137, 1148, 1149, 1162, and perhaps 1001–2, and FGI p. 14; Yavanas, Lüders' list, nos. 669, 965, 1093, 1123, 1140, 1154, 1156; Muruṇḍas in FGI, p. 14, and Muruṇḍadevī, *id.*, pp. 128, 132, 138; Hūṇas, FGI, pp. 56, 148, 206. A Vākāṭaka prince Vindhyaśakti is mentioned in Kielhorn's Inscriptions of Northern India, no. 622 (Epig. Ind. v, Appendix).

Mt, Vā, Bḍ.	*Bh* (with *Vṣ*).
Andhrāṇāṁ [1] saṁsthite rājye [2]	
teṣām bhṛty-ânvayā [3] nṛpāḥ [4]	Sapt=Âbhīrā Āndhrabhṛtyā [5]
sapt=aiv=Ândhrā [6] bhaviṣyanti	
daś=Âbhīrās [7] tathā nṛpāḥ [8]	
sapta Gardabhinaś [9] c=âpi	daśa [10] Gardabhino [11] nṛpāḥ
Śakāś c=âṣṭādaś=aiva tu [12]	Śakāḥ [13] ṣoḍaśa [14] bhūpālā
	bhaviṣyanty ati-lolupāḥ [15]
Yavan=âṣṭau [16] bhaviṣyanti	tato 'ṣṭau Yavanā [17] bhāvyāś
Tuṣārās [18] tu [19] caturdaśa	caturdaśa ca Tuṣkarāḥ [20]

1 So *cdfn*Mt, Vā, Bḍ. Mt genly *Āndh°*; *j*Mt *sandh°*: *e*Vā *Arthānāṁ*.

2 So *cdefgkn*Mt; *j*Mt *sāsthite°*; *b*Mt *saṁśrite°*; other Mt *saṁsthitā°*: *e*Vā *saṁsthite vaṁśe*. Vā, Bḍ *saṁsthitāḥ pañca*; so *m*Vā (defective).

3 So *dfgk*Mt, *e*Vā; *l*Mt *-atrayā*; *j*Mt †*dady-ânvayā*. Mt genly *bhṛty-ânvaye*: *b*Mt *-adyaso*. But *fm*Vā *vaṁśāḥ svayāḥ* (for *vaṁś-ânvayāḥ*?), Vā genly *°samāḥ*. Bḍ *vaṁśyāś ca ye*.

4 So Mt: *fm*Vā *punāḥ*. Vā, Bḍ *punaḥ*.

5 Bh genly *Āvabhṛtyā*; *e*Bh *Āv°*; *a*Bh *°c=Âv°*; *f*Bh *Āvabhṛthyā*. Vṣ rightly *Andhra-bhṛtyāḥ sapt=Âbhīrā*; *l*Vṣ *Āndh°*.

6 So Mt; *e*Vā *sapta c=Ândhrā*. Vā, Bḍ *sapt=aiva tu*; *h*Vā *°nu*.

7 So Mt, Vā, genly, Bḍ: *d*Vā *°Âbhārās*; *e*Vā *dār-Âbhīrās*, *d*Mt *var-°*; *j*Mt *var-Âdhīrā*; *b*Mt *nāv-Âmīrās*; *l*Mt *naiv=Âbhīrā*: *m*Mt, *kl*Vā defective; *fg*Mt *Ābhīrāś ca*.

8 So Mt mostly: Vā, Bḍ *tato°*: *dn*Mt *nṛpās tathā*, *e*Mt *bhṛtās°*, *c*Mt *mṛtās°*, *fg*Mt *vṛṣās°*: *j*Mt *nṛpās tadā*.

9 So Vā, *bckn*Mt, Bḍ: *e*Mt *Mard°*, but when repeated *Gardabhilāś* as in Mt genly: *l*Mt *Kardabhilā*; *j*Mt *Gatabhṛtāś*.

10 Vṣ agrees.

11 So Bh genly, *al*Vṣ: *k*Vṣ *°nā*; *p*Bh *Garbhattino*. Vṣ genly *Gardabhilāḥ bhūbhujo*, *h*Vṣ *°bhikā°*: *q*Bh †*daśarddagabhino*; *j*Vṣ, *e*Bh crp.

12 So Mt genly; *j*Mt *Śakāśāṣṭ°*: *b*Mt *Śakāś c=aiva daś°*, *cen*Mt *Śākyāś°*, but *e*Mt in repeating reads as in text: *l*Mt †*Kośaiva daś°*. But *e*Vā *tath=âṣṭādaśa vai Śakāḥ*; Vā, Bḍ *tato 'tha daś°*: *k*Vā has *Thakāḥ*.

13 So Vṣ. Bh *Kaṅkāḥ*; *c*Bh *Kāṅ°*.

14 Vṣ agrees.

15 So Bh mostly: *cefgjklnq*Bh *ca lol°*; *h*Bh *na lol°*.

16 By double sandhi (= *Yavanāḥ aṣṭau*); *fm*Vā *Yāv°*: *fgm*Mt *Yavanāś ca*. This half line is in *j*Mt *aṣṭau tu Yavanā dhīrās*, in *e*Vā *tath=aiva Yavanā aṣṭau*.

17 Vṣ agrees: *j*Bh *Javanā*.

18 In *j*Mt *Tuḥkhārāś*; *c*Mt *Tuṣāgāś*.

19 So Vā, *e*Mt, Bḍ. Mt *ca*; *j*Mt omits.

20 So *Baeghjlmpq*Bh: *ds*Bh *°Tuḥkharāḥ*, *r*Bh *°Tuṣśarāḥ*, *n*Bh and v.r. in *G*Bh *°Puṣka-*

Mt, Vā, Bḍ.

trayodaśa {Guruṇḍāś / Muruṇḍāś}[21] ca
{Hūṇā[24] hy ek-ôna-viṁśatiḥ[25]. / Maunā[24] hy ekādaś≠aiva tu[26].}

Bh (with *Vṣ*).

trayodaśa[22] Guruṇḍāś[23] ca
Maunā[27] ekādaś≠aiva[28] tu.

Mat.

Āndhrāḥ[29] Śrīparvatīyāś[30] ca
te dvi-pañcāśataṁ[32] samāḥ
sapta-ṣaṣṭis[35] tu varṣāṇi[36]
daś≠Âbhīrās[38] tath≠aiva ca[39]
sapta Gardabhilā[41] bhūyo[42]
bhokṣyant≠īmāṁ vasundharām[45]
śatāni trīṇy aśītiṁ ca[47]
Śakā hy[49] aṣṭādaś[50]≠aiva tu

Vā, Bḍ.

Andhrā[31] bhokṣyanti vasudhāṁ
śate[33] dve ca śataṁ[34] ca vai
sapta-ṣaṣṭiṁ ca varṣāṇi[37]
daś≠Âbhīrās tato[40] nṛpāḥ
sapta Gardabhinaś[43] c≠aiva[44]
bhokṣyant≠īmāṁ dvi-saptatiḥ[46]
śatāni trīṇy aśītiṁ ca[48]
bhokṣyanti[51] vasudhāṁ Śakāḥ

sāḥ. *Gbfkt*Bh *Turuṣkakāḥ*, *c*Bh °*karāḥ*. *C*Vṣ *caturdaśa Tukhārāḥ*, *bcdefghj*Vṣ °*Tuṣārā*, *a*Vṣ °*Tukhāvā*, *l*Vṣ °*Kharā*.

[21] Both forms are well supported. Mt genly, Bḍ *Guruṇḍāś*; *n*Mt *Gar*°. Vā genly, *j*Mt *Mar*°; *j*Vā, *m*Mt *Mur*°; *f*Vā *Mer*°. Others, *fg*Mt *Pur*°; *cd*Mt *Puranḍāś*; *e*Mt *Purañjāś*: 4 MSS of *C*Vā *Mananṭāś*, which *AC*Vā adopt; *e*Vā *Ranḍās* with *tu* for *ca*. *Guruṇḍa* occurs in Bhaviṣya iii, *5*, 32, where it is said Vraja-bhāṣā, Mahārāṣṭrī, Yāvanī, and Guruṇḍikā are the four Mleccha bhāṣās. For Muruṇḍa see p. 45. Cf. notes [65, 68].

[22] So Vṣ, *dfgm*Bh and v.r. in *G*Bh. Bh genly *bhūyo daśa*, an easy misreading; *j*Vṣ omits.

[23] So Bh genly; *d*Bh *Sur*°: *a*Bh *Surāṇḍāś*, *s*Bh *Subā*°. Vṣ *Muṇḍāś*, prob. error for *Muruṇḍāś*, which *l*Vṣ has.

[24] Both names are well supported. Mt genly *Hūṇā*; *j*Mt *Hūnā*; *l*Mt *Janā*; *e*Vā *Yaunā*; Vā, Bḍ, *b*Mt *Maunā*: *n*Mt *smṛtā*. See note [76].

[25] So Mt; *d*Mt *c≠êk*°: *ce*Mt omit *hy*.

[26] So *e*Vā, Bḍ. Vā *hy aṣṭādaś*°.

[27] So Bh, Vṣ: *h*Bh *Monā*; *a*Bh *Maulā*.

[28] Vṣ agrees.

[29] In *g*Mt *An*°; *df*Mt *Andhā*: *j*Mt *yuktā*; *b*Mt reads this half line *Andhākṣāḥ parvatīyāś ca*.

[30] So *cdfgjkmn*Mt; *l*Mt omits *Śrī*. *AC*Mt *Śrīpār*°; *e*Mt °*parvatāyāś*.

[31] In *e*Vā *Randhrā*.

[32] So *ACbhkl*Mt: *cefgmn*Mt *te dve pañca śataṁ*, *d*Mt *dve pañca ca śataṁ*: *j*Mt *ta dve pañca daś≠âpi ca* for this half line.

[33] In *fm*Vā *śataṁ*; *k*Vā *śato*. Read probably *daśa*; see Introdn. § 41.

[34] In *k*Vā *dva ca*°; *e*Vā *dve 'rddha-śataś*.

[35] In *ce*Mt °*ṭi*; *n*Mt °*ṭī*.

[36] In *cen*Mt *sahasrāṇi*.

[37] This line is in a^{1-3}*bdefghklm*Vā, Bḍ; first half in a^{4}Vā, *sapta-ṣaṣṭi śatān≠îha*. Not in *ACj*Vā, but mentioned in note to *A*Vā: a^{1-3}*bl*Vā °*ṣaṣṭi*°; *e*Vā *tu* for *ca*.

[38] In *fm*Vā *daśabhīrās*, *j*Mt °*bhī . . s*: *k*Mt *Darbharomā*.

[39] In *bcen*Mt *tatas tu vai*.

[40] In *e*Vā *tatho*.

[41] In *bcen*Mt °*bhino*; *j*Mt °*bhṛto*.

[42] But better *bcegn*Mt *bhūpā*.

[43] This line is in a^{1-3}*bdefghklm*Vā, Bḍ. Not in *ACj*Vā, but in note to *A*Vā.

[44] In *ek*Vā *c≠âpi*.

[45] Sic: read *dvi-saptatim*?

[46] In *e*Vā, Bḍ °*tim*.

[47] In *bgj*Mt *aśītiś ca*; *cen*Mt *trīṇi ca tathā*.

[48] In *bdg*Vā °*aśītiś ca*; *fm*Vā *trīṇi 'śītiś ca*; *e*Vā *trīṇi varṣāṇām*: a^{4}Vā omits this half line, see note [37].

[49] Mt genly *śatāny*, *j*Mt *tathā hy*, no doubt corruptions of *Śakā hy*, and I have

Mat.

Yavan-âṣṭau bhaviṣyanti [52]
 sapt-âśītim [54] mahīm imām
sapta varṣa[55]-sahasrāṇi [56]
 Tuṣārāṇāṁ [58] mahī smṛtā
śatāny ardha[60]-catuṣkāni [61]
 bhavitavyās [62] trayodaśa [63]
Guruṇḍā [65] Vṛṣalaiḥ [66] sārdham [67]
 bhokṣyante[69] Mleccha[70]-sambhavāḥ[71]
śatāni trīṇi bhokṣyante [73]
 Hūṇā hy [74] ekādaś-aiva tu [75]

Vā, Bḍ.

aśīti dve ca [53] varṣāṇi
 bhoktāro Yavanā mahīm
pañca varṣa-śatān-îha [57]
 Tuṣārāṇām [59] mahī smṛtā
śatāny ardha-caturthāni
 bhavitāras trayodaśa [64]
Muruṇḍā [68] Vṛṣalaiḥ [66] sārdham
 bhāvy-ânyā [72] Mleccha-jātayaḥ
śatāni trīṇi bhokṣyante [73]
 Maunā [76] ekādaś-aiva tu [77]

emended it so: *bcln*Mt †*nava*; *e*Mt †*naca*.

[50] So Mt genly: *bcen*Mt *c-âṣṭau*°; *l*Mt *v-âṣṭau*°; *j*Mt *Andhā*°.

[51] In *a*[1-3]*defgm*Vā °*te*.

[52] Sic: better *ca bhokṣyanti*.

[53] So *beh*Vā; *a*[3]*gl*Vā *aśītir*°: *m*Vā *āśīti*°; *d*Vā, Bḍ *āśūī*°; *f*Vā *āśītir*°. *Ca*[1]*a*[2]*a*[4]*ck*Vā *aśītiṁ c-aiva*.

[54] So *Alm*Mt; *Cb*Mt °*ti*: but *cemn*Mt *sam-âśīti-ṁ*, *d*Mt °*âśītiṁ*; see Introdn. § 40. Others, *g*Mt *saṁśāsyanti*; *f*Mt *saṁsās*°; *k*Mt *śaṁsās*°; *j*Mt *praśās*° (see p. 16, note [78]).

[55] In *b*Mt *varṣasyātu*; *l*Mt *varṣāṇāṁ* (one syll. short).

[56] So all Mt: read *śatān-îha*?

[57] In *e*Vā *śatānīkaṁ*.

[58] In *j*Mt *Tuḥkhār*°.

[59] In *e*Vā *Tuṣāṇāṁ tu*.

[60] *Cc*Mt °*ardhaṁ*: *b*Mt *śatam ardha-*; *k*Mt *śat-ârdha-*.

[61] In *bcjkn*Mt *caturthāni*.

[62] In *c*Mt °*vyaṁ*; *j*Mt *samaṁtāś ca*.

[63] In *m*Mt *trayo nṛpāḥ*; *bn*Mt *caturdaśa*. This line and the next go together.

[64] See note [52]. This line and the next go together.

[65] *ACb*Mt *Guruṇḍā*; *n*Mt *Gar*°; *g*Mt *Kur*°; *m*Mt *Mur*°; *f*Mt *Muc*°; *l*Mt *Puru-[ṣā]ṇḍā*; *ck*Mt *Puruḍā*; *d*Mt *Su[dvi]ruṇḍā*; *j*Mt *Sudaṇḍā*.

[66] In *n*Mt *dṛś*°; *ej*Vā *pṛś*°; *bl*Mt *vṛṣabhaiḥ*.

[67] In *c*Mt *sarvair*.

[68] Bḍ, *ghkl*Vā *Guruṇḍā*; *a*[2]*dfm*Vā *Mur*°; *Ca*[1]*a*[3]*b*Vā *Mar*°; *a*[4]Vā *Pur*°: *j*Vā *Munujā*; *e*Vā *Aṣaṇḍā*. Regarding these Vṣ says—

ete pṛthivīṁ trayodaśa* varṣa-śatāni† nava‡-navaty-adhikāni bhokṣyanti:

where * this means the 13 Guruṇḍas, and so *l*Vṣ *ete trayodaśa pṛthivīṁ*; yet it has affected *śatāni*; but *d*Vṣ *ete pṛthivīm Ābhīr-âdyā Maun-ântā ek-ôn-âśītir āttā* [sic] *ṣoḍaśa*: † *k*Vṣ *śata-varṣāṇi*: ‡ *dhjl*Vṣ omit *nava*. Bh, in consequence of the misreading *bhūyo daśa* (see note [22]), says 10, and applies it wrongly to the period instead of to the kings—

ete bhokṣyanti pṛthivīṁ daśa varṣa-śatāni ca
nav-âdhikāṁ ca navatim*:

where * *c*Bh omits this half line.

[69] In *fg*Mt *ślaukṣyante*.

[70] In *l*Mt *muru*; *j*Mt *vṛṣa*.

[71] In *fg*Mt *saṁyuvāḥ*; *c*Mt *jātayaḥ*; *l*Mt *jantavaḥ*.

[72] So *Aflm*Vā by double sandhi for *bhāvyāḥ anyāḥ*: *j*Vā *bhāvy-ânnā*; *g*Vā °*ânye*; *bh*Vā °*ārtya*; *d*Vā *bhāryās te*; *k*Vā *bhāvyā[nye]s te*, showing influence of both readings: *e*Vā *tath-ânye*. Bḍ *bhokṣyante*.

[73] In *bcgn*Mt, *Ca*[4]Vā, °*ti*.

[74] All Mt *varṣāṇy* with no name: no doubt a corruption of *Hūṇā hy* (see l. 5), and I have emended it so.

[75] In *b*Mt †*ekādaśāni ca*; *fg*Mt *aṣṭādaś-aiva tu*: see l. 5.

[76] So Bḍ, see l. 5: *e*Vā *Yaunās tv*. Vā genly *Mlecchā*. *C*Vā *Snecchā* by misprint.

[77] Vṣ says—tataś ca Paurā* ekādaśa bhūpatayo 'bda†-śatāni trīṇi mahīm bhokṣyanti:

Mat.	*Vā, Bḍ.*
teṣ=ûtsanneṣu[78] kālena[79]	tac-channena ca[80] kālena[79]
tataḥ Kilakilā nṛpāḥ[81].	tataḥ Kolikilā vṛṣāḥ[82].

Vā and *Bḍ.*

tataḥ Kolikilebhyaś[83] ca Vindhyaśaktir[84] bhaviṣyati
samāḥ ṣaṇ-ṇavatiṁ[85] jñātvā[86] pṛthivīṁ tu[87] sameṣyati[88].

Dynasties of Vidiśā, &c.

Text—Mt nil; *A*Vā *99*, 366–372; Bḍ iii, *74*, 179[b]–185.

Corresp. passages—*C*Vṣ iv, *24*, 17; *G*Bh xii, *1*, 32[b], 33.

The Vāyu gives the whole, and the Brahmāṇḍa all except line 7. The Viṣṇu is concise but not clear, and the Bhāgavata has only three obscure lines: they mention no names except where stated in the notes. Among MSS *a²fm*Vā omit l. 7; *e*Vā l. 11; *k*Vā and *bt*Bh have nothing.

There are references to the people of Vidiśā, Vediśa, in Kielhorn's 'Inscriptions of Northern India' (Epig. Ind. v, Appendix), namely, Sāñchi inscriptions, nos. 187–524 *passim*; Bharaut inscriptions, nos. 712–885 *passim*. For Vindhyaśakti see p. 45; and as regards Pravīra, a successor of Vindhyaśakti, named Pravarasena, is mentioned with his five successors, *op. cit.*, no. 622. As regards Nakhavān, king

where **hl*Vṣ *Maunā*, *k*Vṣ *Pauravā*; †*h*Vṣ *aṣṭa*. Bh says—

Maunā* ekādaśa kṣitim
bhokṣyanty abda†-śatāny aṅga‡ trīṇi:

where **a*Bh *Maulā*, *c*Bh omits this half line; †*g*Bh *aṣṭa*; ‡*h*Bh *aṁtra*, altered in *d*Bh by later hand to *śatān pañca*; *f*Bh omits this line.

[78] So Mt genly; *b*Mt †*naiṣu chatreṣu*: *cdj*Mt *teṣ=ûtpanneṣu*; *g*Mt *teṣ=ûcchinneṣu*; *f*Mt *teṣu cch°*: *k*Mt *teṣ=ûtsaveṣu*.

[79] In *bcdefgn*Mt *kāleṣu*; *e*Vā *sarveṣu*.

[80] So Vā genly; *d*Vā †*tachāsanaś ca*: *e*Vā *teṣ=ûtsanneṣu*. Bḍ *teṣu cchinneṣu*.

[81] So Mt, *e*Vā: *l*Mt *Kilāk°*; *fg*Mt *Kilik°*: *d*Mt *Kilakalā*, *jm*Mt *°kilau*.

[82] So Vā genly; *b*Vā *Ko[li]lākikā°*, but *Kolikilebhyaś* in next line. Bḍ *Kilakilo nṛpaḥ*. Vṣ says (*h*Vṣ omits)—

teṣu channeṣu* Kailakilā† Yavanā bhūpatayo bhaviṣyanti:

where **de*Vṣ *cchinneṣu*, *b*Vṣ *putreṣu*, *j*Vṣ *kṣetreṣu*, *fgk*Vṣ *teṣ=ûcchanneṣu*, *l*Vṣ° *ûtsanneṣu*; *bl*Vṣ add *punaḥ*, *k*Vṣ *puraḥ*: †*ak*Vṣ *Kelik°*, *l*Vṣ *Kaikilā*, *b*Vṣ *Kaiśilānā*. Bh says—

taiḥ saṁsthite* tataḥ
Kilikilāyāṁ† nṛpatayo:

where **e*Bh *°taiḥ*, *q*Bh *°taṁ*, *f*Bh omits this line: †*aps*Bh *Kilak°*, *em*Bh *Kalik°*, *l*Bh *Kaliṁk°*, *hj*Bh *Kiṁliṁk°*, *f*Bh *Kiṅkilāyāṁ*.

[83] So Vā: *e*Vā *Kel°*; Bḍ *Kilak°*: *k*Vā *Pholikolabhyaś*.

[84] Vṣ agrees,—*mūrdh*-âbhiṣiktas teṣāṁ Vindhyaśaktiḥ*†: where **l*Vṣ *a-mūrdh°*; †*l*Vṣ *Viṇḍa°*. Bh omits.

[85] In *b*Vā *samā yayāvati*; *k*Vā *samān parṇamatiṁ*.

[86] In *e*Vā *bhūtvā*. Bḍ *c=aiva*.

[87] So *dfghkm*Vā, Bḍ; *b*Vā *nu*. Vā genly *ca*.

[88] But 2 MSS of *C*Vā *sa bhokṣyati*; *k*Vā merely *saḥ*, but adds *moṭāṁpāṁnāṁ* (for *Maunānāṁ*?) *samāpti*: *e*Vā reads this half line *pṛthivī tu gamiṣyati*.

Nahapāna (see note [11]) is mentioned, *id.* nos. 1099, 1131–5, 1174; Purikā in nos. 782, 812, 837–9, and JRAS, 1910, p. 445. Bhogin may perhaps bear some allusion to Bhogavardhana, nos. 264, 266, 373, 572, 797. For Nahapāna see JRAS, 1910, p. 820; 1912, p. 785.

Nṛpān [1] Vaidiśakāṁś [2] c=âpi [3] bhaviṣyāṁs tu [4] nibodhata
Śeṣasya Nāga-rājasya putraḥ para-purañ-jayaḥ [5]
Bhogī bhaviṣyate rājā [6] nṛpo Nāga[7]-kul-ôdvahaḥ [8]
Sadācandras [9] tu Candrāṁśo [10] dvitīyo Nakhavāṁs tathā [11]
Dhanadharmā [12] tataś c=âpi caturtho [13] Vaṅgaraḥ [14] smṛtaḥ
Bhūtinandas [15] tataś c=âpi Vaidiśe tu [16] bhaviṣyati
Śuṅgānāṁ [17] tu kulasy=ânte [18] Śiśunandir [19] bhaviṣyati
tasya bhrātā [20] yavīyāṁs tu namnā Nandiyaśāḥ [21] kila
tasy=ânvaye bhaviṣyanti [22] rājānas te trayas [23] tu vai
dauhitraḥ [24] Śiśuko [25] nāma Purikāyāṁ [26] nṛpo 'bhavat [27]

[1] So Bḍ, *a*[1–3]*bdefgh*Vā and 1 MS of *C*Vā: other Vā *vṛṣān*.
[2] *Vaidiśik°* in *e*Vā; *a*[1]Vā *Vaideśik°*: *g*Vā *ca diśak°*.
[3] Bḍ *c=âtha*; *e*Vā *c=aiva*.
[4] So *bdfh*Vā, Bḍ, *m*Vā crp. Vā genly *ca*.
[5] So *a*[1]*a*[3]*bdeghl*Vā, 2 MSS of *C*Vā: other Vā *svara-pur°*. Bḍ *sura-pur°*. Vṣ *tataḥ Purañjayaḥ*, i.e., after Vindhyaśakti: *l*Vṣ *tataḥ paraṁ Pur°*; *abk*Vṣ *°Para-pur°*; *h*Vṣ *Puraṁpur°*.
[6] In *e*Vā *°ṣyati nṛpo*, *a*[3]Vā *°tato*.
[7] In *bdh*Vā *Nāma*.
[8] This half line in *e*Vā is *Nāga-loka-samudbhavaḥ*.
[9] In *a*[1]Vā *putraś C°*: *e*Vā *Dāmadhandras*. Vṣ *Rāmacandra*; *bh*Vṣ *Vāma°*.
[10] So Vā genly. Bḍ *°āṁśur*; *j*Vā *°āso*; *e*Vā *°ābho*: *d*Vā *Vaṁdāṁśo*.
[11] In *bdh*Vā *tataḥ*; *g*Vā *tu saḥ*: *e*Vā *Nakhapāna-jaḥ* (see above), which may be the true reading.
[12] In *e*Vā *Vakhampīta*. Vṣ *Dharmaḥ*; *l*Vṣ *Dharmavarmā*.
[13] In *bghj*Vā *°the*; *d*Vā *°thaṁ* or *°tho*.
[14] Vā genly *Viṁśajaḥ*; *j*Vā *viṁśaḥ bhūmī* (with excess syll.). Bḍ, *l*Vā *vaṁśajaḥ*: *e*Vā, *c*Vṣ *Vaṅgavaḥ*: *bfgj*Vṣ *Vaṅgara*; *l*Vṣ *°garā*; *a*Vṣ *°gāra*; *d*Bh *°gari*; *r*Bh *°gira*; Bh genly *°giri*; *a*Bh *°kiri*: *m*Bh (misreading *v* as *tr*) *Traṅgiri*, *e*Bh (*Va*)*Tuṁgiri*; *c*Bh *Bhṛṁgiri*: *h*Vṣ *Vagara*; *k*Bh *Vāgiri*. Vṣ genly *Varāṅga*: *k*Vṣ *Urddara* (or *Dur°*). *Vaṅgara* seems the most central form.
[15] So Vā, Bḍ: *e*Vā *Bhūmi°*. Bh genly *Bhūtananda* (inverting him and Vaṅgara), *l*Vṣ *°nandi*, *p*Bh *°manda*: *q*Bh *Bhṛthananda*: *k*Vṣ *Kṛtanandi*, Vṣ genly *°nandana*.
[16] So Bḍ. Vā genly *vai deśe tu* (*b*Vā *nu*): *a*[3]Vā *vaṁśe sa tu*; *e*Vā †*vaiśogaiśo* or *vaiśig°*.
[17] So *a*[1]*a*[3]*a*[4]*ghl*Vā: *e*Vā *Śuṅkā°*; *bd*Vā *Śṛṅgā°*. Vā genly *Aṅgā°* (see p. 32, note [47]).
[18] So *e*Vā. Vā genly *nakulasy=ânte*: *Cj*Vā *nandanasy°*, which *A*Vā adopts.
[19] So *e*Vā; *ak*Vṣ, Bh agree: *c*Vṣ *Śuṣi°*; *g*Vṣ *Śuṣir°*. Vṣ genly *Suṣi°*; *l*Vṣ *Suṣu°*; *bh*Vṣ *Sukhi°*. Vā *Madhu°*.
[20] So *bhkl*Vṣ, Bh, *tad-bhrātā*.
[21] So Vā, Bḍ, Vṣ genly: *fm*Vā *Mandiy°*; *d*Vṣ *Nandriy°*; *h*Vṣ *Randiy°*; *b*Vṣ [*Ra*]*Nandiy°*: *j*Vṣ *Nandipāśāḥ*. Bh *Yaśonandi*; *h*Bh *Yaśi°*.
[22] In *e*Vā *tasy=ânvavāye bhavitā*.
[23] In *m*Vā *taṁ trayas*; *bd*Vā *tatra yas*; *h*Vā *tan-nayas*.
[24] In *bd*Vā *dauhitryaḥ*: *C*Vā *dohitraḥ*, *f*Vā *daih°*.
[25] So Vā; Vṣ agrees. Bḍ *Śiśiko*; *j*Vṣ *Śibhuka*; *k*Vṣ *Śuśika*; *l*Vṣ *Śukra*.
[26] So Vā genly: *d*Vā *°kāyā*, *e*Vā *°kāyo*. Bḍ *Pūrikāyāṁ*; *g*Vā *Ripuk°*: see above.
[27] In *d*Vā *bhavet*.

Vindhyaśakti[28]-sutaś c=âpi Pravīro[29] nāma vīryavān[30]
bhokṣyate[31] ca samāḥ ṣaṣṭim[32] purīṁ Kāñcanakāṁ ca vai[33]
yakṣyate[34] vājapeyaiś[35] ca samāpta-vara[36]-dakṣiṇaiḥ.
tasya putrās tu[37] catvāro bhaviṣyanti narādhipāḥ[38].

Dynasties of the Third Century, A.D.

Text—Mt nil; *A*Vā *99*, 373–382[a]; Bḍ iii, *74*, 186–193.

Corresp. passages—*C*Vṣ iv, *24*, 17, 18; *G*Bh xii, *1*, 34–37[b].

The Vāyu gives the whole, and the Brahmāṇḍa all except the last three lines. The Viṣṇu and Bhāgavata are condensed and not clear; but they are fuller about Viśvasphūrji, and the Bhāgavata version is placed on the right side by side with the Vāyu and Brahmāṇḍa version in ll. 10–14.

Among MSS *a²fm*Vā want ll. 17–19; *e*Vā gives ll. 1–10, then inserts the last part of the *Early Contemporary Dynasties* (p. 23), all the Nandas, Mauryas, Śuṅgas, Kāṇvāyanas and the first 12 lines of the Andhras, by reason of a large displacement, and then gives ll. 12–19 here, omitting l. 11: *k*Vā and *bt*Bh have nothing.

Bāhlikas are mentioned in Fleet's *Gupta Inscriptions*, p. 141; Puṣyamitras, *id.* p. 55; Măhiṣatī (=Māhiṣmatī), pp. 375, 497–8, 501, and JRAS, 1910, pp. 444, 867. For other geographical information my Translation of the Mārkaṇḍeya Purāṇa (Index) may be consulted.

Vindhyakānāṁ[1] kule 'tīte[2] nṛpā vai Bāhlikās[3] trayaḥ[4]
Supratīko[5] Nabhīraś[6] ca[7] samā bhokṣyanti[8] triṁśatim[9]

[28] *Viṁdhiś* in *g*Vā; see p. 45.

[29] So Vā, Bḍ. Vṣ says *Śiśuka-Pravīrau ca*; *l*Vṣ *Śukra-Pravīraś ca.* Bh merely *Pravīrakaḥ.* See p. 48.

[30] Vṣ adds—ete * varṣa-śataṁ ṣaḍ † varṣāṇi bhaviṣyanti:
where * *l*Vṣ *etasmād*; † *l*Vṣ *ṣaś pañca.* Bh says—
ity ete vai ‡ varṣa-śatam bhaviṣyanty adhikāni ṣaṭ:
where ‡ *c*Bh *ity evaṁ te* [*ya*], *ar*Bh *bhokṣyanty ete*, v.r. in *G*Bh *yuktā ete.*

[31] So *bdfghm*Vā, Bḍ. Vā genly *bhokṣyanti*, *e*Vā °*te*, which may apply to Śiśuka and Pravīra; plural instead of dual, cf. next dynasties, l. 2.

[32] In *bdg*Vā *ṣaṣṭiḥ.*

[33] In *bdm*Vā *purī*°; *m*Vā ends *nau*: *e*Vā *Pulakāṁś Calakāṁś ca vai.*

[34] So Bḍ. *C*Vā °*ti.* Vā genly *yakṣyante*, *a⁴j*Vā °*ti.* The sing. is clearly right, but see note [31].

[35] In *e*Vā *vājimedhaiś.*

[36] In *e*Vā *samāpte bahu-.*

[37] In *e*Vā *ca*; see p. 48.

[38] In *e*Vā *su-mūrtayaḥ.* Vṣ *tataḥ tat-putrāḥ trayodaś=aiva* (*l*Vṣ *=aite*). Bh *teṣāṁ trayodaśa sutāḥ.*

[1] In *e*Vā *Karmakānāṁ.*

[2] So Vā genly: *f*Vā *kulīnīte*; *m*Vā *kulīnātena.* Bḍ *kulān=âṁte*, Pkt for *kulānām ante.*

[3] So *Ceghm*Vā. Bh, *l*Vṣ agree: *k*Bh *Vah*°. Vṣ genly *Bāhlīkās*: *cjl*Bh *Bālhikāḥ*; *dk*Vṣ *Vālhīkāḥ.* *Abdjl*Vā *Vāhnikās*; *f*Vā *Vāhri*°; Bḍ *Vāhi*°: *h*Bh *Vāhṇi*°.

[4] Vṣ agrees.

[5] In *h*Vā °*tāko*; *d*Vā *Suprako.*

Śakyamān-âbhavad[10] rājā Mahiṣīṇām[11] mahī-patiḥ
Puṣyamitrā[12] bhaviṣyanti Paṭumitrās[13] trayodaśa[14]
Mekalāyāṁ[15] nṛpāḥ sapta[16] bhaviṣyant-îha saptatim[17]
Kośalāyāṁ[18] tu[19] rājāno bhaviṣyanti mahābalāḥ[20]
Meghā iti[21] samākhyātā[22] buddhimanto nav-aiva tu
Naiṣadhāḥ[23] pārthivāḥ sarve bhaviṣyanty ā-Manu-kṣayāt[24]
Nala-vaṁśa-prasūtās te vīryavanto mahābalāḥ[25]

[6] In *bdVā Nabhāraś* (altered in *d* to *Nabha°*); *eVā Nnaratīvaś*. Bḍ *Gabhīraś*.

[7] So *bdefghm*Vā, Bḍ. Other Vā *tu*.

[8] *C*Vā, Bḍ *bhokṣyati*.

[9] So *Ca*[1]*jl*Vā, Bḍ: *a*[2–4]*fgm*Vā *°tīḥ*; *bdh*Vā *°tiḥ* (altered in *d* to *viṁśatiḥ*): *e*Vā *viṁśatim*.

[10] In *a*[1–4]*j*Vā and 3 MSS of *C*Vā *Śakyamā nāma vai*: other MSS divide it into two. For first part, *flm*Vā *Śakyamānā*, *gh*Vā *Śakyā°*, *d*Vā *Śākyā°*, *b*Vā *Śikyā°*; 3 MSS of *C*Vā *Śakyamīmā*; *e*Vā *Sākṣonāmān*: Bḍ *Śaṅkamāno*. For second part, Bḍ, *e*Vā *bhavad*; *ghlm*Vā and 3 MSS of *C*Vā *bhavo*; *b*Vā *bhavī*; *f*Vā *savo* or *tavo*; *d*Vā *vīya*. From all these variations I have adopted *Śakyamān-âbhavad*.

[11] Bḍ, *a*[1]Vā and 3 MSS of *C*Vā *Māh°*; *l*Vā *Mahīṣ°*; *e*Vā *Mahiṣyāṇām*.

[12] Vā genly, Bḍ *Puṣpa°*; *a*[4]Vā *Putra°*: *e*Vā *Pundramindrā*.

[13] *Ca*[3]*l*Vā *Paṭṭa°*; *a*[2]Vā *Paṭu°*; *g*Vā *Paṭu°* or *Paḍu°*; *h*Vā *Yadu°*; *a*[1]Vā *Puṭa°*; *b*Vā *Paḍa°*; *fm*Vā *Ṣaṭū°*; *e*Vā *Padumindrās*. Bḍ *ṣaṭ Strimitrās*. Others short, *d*Vā *Yāmitrās*, *a*[4]Vā *ṣaṇ m°*, *j*Vā *Sadamīs*. *Paṭumitrās* seems the most central form.

[14] In *g*Vā *tath-aiva ca*. Vṣ says—

tataḥ* Puṣpamitra†-Paṭumitrās‡ trayodaśa§:

where **b*Vṣ adds *castrayaḥ*; †*l*Vṣ *Puṣya°*, *a*Vṣ *Puṣā°*; ‡*kl*Vṣ *Paṭa°*, *bj*Vṣ *Yadu°*, *h*Vṣ *Pahu°*, *a*Vṣ *Paṭumitr-âdyās*, *C*Vṣ *Paḍhumitra-Padmamitrās*; §*h*Vṣ *sarva-varṇeṣu balavān jayo bhaviṣyati trayodaśa*, as if *trayodaśa* belongs to the following words. Bh says—

Puṣpamitro* 'tha rājanyo Durmitro† 'sya‡ tath-aiva ca:

where **df*Bh *Puṣya°*; †*d*Bh *Damitro*; ‡*ah*Bh *'tha*.

[15] In *g*Vā *Mekalāyā*, *bd*Vā *Mik°*; *h*Vā *Mikalayā*.

[16] Vṣ says—Mekalāś* ca sapta† Kośalāyāṁ‡ tu nav-aiva§ bhūpatayo bhaviṣyanti: where **d*Vṣ *Mekalyaś*, *h*Vṣ *Meka[kā]lāḥ*; †*l*Vṣ *sapt-Ândhrāḥ*, *h*Vṣ *°Ândhra*, *k*Vṣ *°âtra*, and *hkl*Vṣ add *tataś ca*; ‡*l*Vṣ *sapta Kauśalāḥ*; §*l*Vṣ *nava*, *h*Vṣ *tath-aiva*, *k*Vṣ *tayeva*. Bh says, agreeing with some of these readings—

eka-kālā ime bhūpāḥ* sapt-Ândhrāḥ† sapta Kauśalāḥ‡:

where **d*Bh *bhūmeḥ*; †*cm*Bh *Âmbhrāḥ*, *k*Bh *Âmprā*; ‡*ars*Bh *Koś°*, *f*Bh *Kaus°*, *d*Bh *Kos°*. Cf. *eka-kālā* here with the error *Mekakālāḥ* in *h*Vṣ.

[17] So *e*Vā; Bḍ *°ṣyanti ca saptatiḥ*. But *a*[1–4]*bdghl*Vā *°ṣyant-îti santatiḥ*; *fm*Vā *°ṣyanti santatiḥ* (short); *Cj*Vā *°ṣyanti ca sattamāḥ*, and *C*Vā mentions *santatiḥ*.

[18] So *e*Vā; *d*Vā *Kos°*. Vṣ, Bh agree, see note [16]. Vā genly, Bḍ *Kom°*.

[19] *Ca* in *e*Vā.

[20] In *g*Vā *narādhipāḥ*.

[21] In *h*Vā *Medyā*; *e*Vā either; *a*[4]Vā *Medhātithi-*.

[22] In *e*Vā *°khyāto*.

[23] Vṣ says—Naiṣadhās* tu tāvanta† eva‡ bhūpatayo bhaviṣyanti:

where **k*Vṣ *Śaiṣarās*; †*l*Vṣ *tata*; ‡*bkl*Vṣ stop here: *h*Vṣ omits the whole. Bh says—

Vaidūra*-patayo bhāvyā Naiṣadhās† tata eva hi:

where **cj*Bh *Vaidūrya*, *G*Bh *Vidūra*; †*G*Bh *Niṣadhās*. See p. 50.

[24] In *e*Vā *°ṣyanti manuṣyayāt*.

[25] In *g*Vā *mahāyaśāḥ*, Pkt plural.

Māgadhānām[26] maha-vīryo	Māgadhānāṁ tu[27] bhavitā
Viśvasphāṇir[28] bhaviṣyati	Viśvasphūrjiḥ[29] purañ-jayaḥ[30]
utsādya pārthivān sarvān	
so 'nyān varṇān[31] kariṣyati	kariṣyaty aparān[32] varṇān
Kaivartān[33] Pañcakāṁś[34] c=aiva	Pulinda-Yadu[35]-Madrakān[36]
Pulindān brāhmaṇāṁs tathā	
sthāpayiṣyati[37] rājāno[38]	prajāś c=âbrahma[39]-bhūyiṣṭhāḥ[40]
nānā[41]-deśeṣu te janā[42]	sthāpayiṣyati[43] durmatiḥ[44]
Viśvasphāṇir[45] mahā-sattvo	vīryavān kṣatram[46] utsādya[47]
yuddhe Viṣṇu-samo balī[48]	Padmavatyāṁ[49] sa vai puri

Viśvasphāṇir[50] nara-patiḥ klīv-âkṛtir iv=ocyate[51]

[26] In *bdfghm*Vā *Mag°*; *e*Vā *Magadhāyān.*

[27] In *ad*Bh *ca.*

[28] So $a^{2}a^{3}$*fylm*Vā, Bḍ. Vā genly *°sphānir* here, but *°sphāṇir* in l. 14; *bh*Vā *°sphīṇir*; *e*Vā *°sphācir*; *j*Vā *Viṣyaphāṇī.*

[29] So Bh genly: *g*Bh *°sphūrjhiḥ*; *r*Bh *°sphurjriḥ*; *ah*Bh *°sphūrtti*; cBh *°skurtsīḥ*; *n*Bh *Viśva[va]spharjji.* Vṣ says—

Māgadhāyāṁ* Viśvasphaṭika-sañjño 'nyān varṇān kariṣyati:

where **acfghjk*Vṣ *Mag°.*

[30] In *d*Bh *paran-tapaḥ.*

[31] Defective in *d*Vā, *pārthivān sāsvarṇān*, altered to *pārthivān so va kīrṇān.*

[32] So *dekmpqs*Bh; *Gaf*Bh *aparo*: *ghjlnr*Bh *°ti paro*; cBh *°ti puro.* For Vṣ see note [29].

[33] In *h*Vā *°varttyān*; *f*Vā *°vattyān.*

[34] So Vā; *j*Vā *Nañc°.* Bḍ *Madrakāṁś*: *e*Vā *Yapumāṁś* (or *Papu°*).

[35] In cBh *Yadra*; *k*Bh *Yadru* (or *Padru*): *h*Bh *Pulindāyavu.*

[36] Vṣ says—Kaivarta-Yadu*-Pulinda-brāhmaṇān† rājye sthāpayiṣyaty utsādy=âkhila‡-kṣatra-jātim:

where **bfh*Vṣ *Yadu* or *Padu*, *g*Vṣ *Yadu* or *Paṭu*, *de*Vṣ *Paṭu*, *k*Vṣ *Paṭṭā*, *l*Vṣ *Vaṭuḥ*, *a*Vṣ *Kaṭu*, *C*Vṣ *Kaḍku*: †*Caf*Vṣ *brāhmaṇyān*, *b*Vṣ *Pulind-âbrāhmaṇān*: ‡*k*Vṣ *uchādyośeṣa.*

[37] So *e*Vā. Vā genly, Bḍ *°ṣyanti.* The sing. is required by the sense and is corroborated by Vṣ and Bh; the plural is prob. a mistake through misunderstanding *rājāno.*

[38] So Vā, Bḍ: *e*Vā *rājā tu.* Hence *rājāno* is obviously not a nomin., but the Pkt accus. plural and = *rājñaḥ* (see Pischel's Prakrit Grammar, § 399), because Viśvasphāṇi had, as said above, overthrown all kings and it was he who created these miscellaneous kings. *Rājāno* should have been Sanskritized as *rājñaḥ* with some expletive for the lost syllable, but was mistaken for the nomin. and so remained unchanged.

[39] *C=âdharma* in *d*Bh.

[40] *Bhūmiṣṭhā* in *a*Bh.

[41] *Nānā* wanting in *e*Vā.

[42] So *bdhj*Vā (altered in *d* to *°janāḥ*). Here *te janā* are obviously not the nomin. but the Pkt accus. plural and = *tān janān* (Pischel's Prakrit Grammar, §§ 363, 425), because they refer to the Kaivartas, &c. Not being fully understood they appear Sanskritized as *te janān* in Bḍ; while they were mistaken for the nomin. and were Sanskritized as *te janāḥ* in a^{1-4}*dfylm*Vā. *Ce*Vā read *tejasā* (an attempted emendation?) which *A*Vā adopts.

[43] But *q*Bh *°ṣyanti.*

[44] *Bhūpatiḥ* in *f*Bh.

[45] *Vimvasphāṭir* in *e*Vā.

[46] *Kṣetram* in *a*Bh; *d*Bh *akṛm.*

[47] But *as*Bh *utsārya*; *f*Bh *utpāṭya.*

[48] Bḍ *°sama-prabhaḥ*; *fj*Vā *°prabho*; *m*Vā *°prabhā.* After this line *d*Vā inserts—

Viśvasphīti Kaivartyānāṁ Chakāṁś c=aiva Pulindakān.

[49] *Padmāv°* in cBh: see p. 53, notes [1, 2].

[50] So Bḍ, *b*Vā. Vā genly *°sphānir*; *e*Vā *°sphāṭir.*

[51] So Vā genly, Bḍ; a^{1}Vā *ih=ĉcyate*; *e*Vā *ath=ôc°*: *g*Vā †*klīvāvikṛtirocyate*; *h*Vā †*klī-*

utsādayitvā kṣatraṁ tu [62] kṣatram anyat kariṣyati
devān pitṝṁś ca viprāṁś ca tarpayitvā sakṛt punaḥ [53]
Jāhnavī-tīram āsādya [54] śarīraṁ yaṁsyate [55] balī
sannyasya [56] sva-śarīraṁ tu [57] Śakra-lokaṁ gamiṣyati.

Contemporary Dynasties of the Early Fourth Century.

Text—Mt nil; *A*Vā *99*, 382b–388a; Bḍ iii, *74*, 194–200a.

Corresp. passages—*C*Vṣ iv, *24*, 18; *G*Bh xii, *1*, 37c–40.

The Vāyu and Brahmāṇḍa give the whole of this passage except ll. 12–15. The Viṣṇu gives the whole fully in prose. The Bhāgavata has ll. 3, 4 (condensed into one) and 12–17, and agrees closely with the Viṣṇu. Ll. 12–15 are taken from it and placed on the right, to supplement the account given by the Vāyu and Brahmāṇḍa; and they appear to be old ślokas because they agree closely with the older prose account of the Viṣṇu. Among MSS *e*Vā has only ll. 1–6; *k*Vā and *bt*Bh have nothing.

As regards Naiṣadhas and Kosalas see p. 51; and for other peoples and countries my translation of the Mārkaṇḍeya Purāṇa may be consulted.

Nava Nākās [1] tu bhokṣyanti purīṁ Campāvatīṁ [2] nṛpāḥ
Mathurāṁ ca purīṁ ramyāṁ Nāgā [3] bhokṣyanti sapta vai [4]
anu-Gaṅgā [5] Prayāgaṁ ca Sāketam [6] Magadhāṁs [7] tathā
etān janapadān sarvān bhokṣyante Gupta-vaṁśa-jāḥ [8]

vāttatīrorācyate; *b*Vā †*klivāmratirācyate* (short); *d*Vā *klīvāsantatir ucyate.*

[62] *Ucoādayitvā tat kṣatraṁ* in *e*Vā: see note [53].

[53] *Satsut punaḥ* in *h*Vā; *b*Vā *sasat°*; *d*Vā *sat°*; *e*Vā *yathākramam.*

[54] But *d*Vā *Jāhnavā-tīre prāsādya.*

[55] Vā genly *yasyate*: *a*[3]Vā *nyasate*; *e*Vā *nyasya vai*; *d*Vā *yāsyu*, altered to *yasmajveta*; *g*Vā *tyakṣate*: *tyakṣyate* is suggested in *C*Vā but it anticipates the next line. *Yaṁsyate* seems the best emendation.

[56] So Vā genly: *bd*Vā *sa ny°*; *h*Vā *samy°*; *g*Vā *sa y°*; *e*Vā *niḥkṣipya*: *l*Vā reads this half line *sasya sva-śarīraṁ rūpaṁ.*

[57] In *h*Vā *nu.*

[1] So Vā. Bḍ *Nāgās*; *e*Vā *Rāndhās.*

[2] *Padmāvatīṁ* in *e*Vā: see l. 8. This line and the next refer to different cities and dynasties, but Vṣ, reading Nāgas in both, condenses the two lines and the preceding mention of Padmavatī (p. 52, l. 14) into one statement—

nava Nāgāḥ Padmāvatyāṁ* Kāntipuryām† Mathurāyām‡:

where * *l*Vṣ *Padmav° nāma puryāṁ*, *j*Vṣ *Pasāṁvanyāṁ*; *c*Vṣ *Kātip°*, *ajk*Vṣ *Kāntāp°*, *bh*Vṣ *Kāntyām*; ‡ *h*Vṣ *Medhurāyām.* Bh nil.

[3] But *d*Vā *Nākā*; *h*Vā *Nāmā*; *b*Vā *Nānā*; *e*Vā *Yaunā.*

[4] In *b*Vā *sapta vi*; *d*Vā *saptatim.*

[5] So *a*[1–4]*bdefghlm*Vā, Bḍ. *Cj*Vā *°Gaṅgam.*

[6] So *a*[3]*d*Vā, Bḍ. *Cbfghm*Vā *°tum*; *a*[1]*a*[2]*a*[4]*jl*Vā *°tu*; *e*Vā *Sāketa.*

[7] In *b*Vā *Madhyagās*; *e*Vā *Makhagās.*

[8] So Vā genly: *e*Vā *Gupa°*; *b*Vā *Guhya°.* Bḍ *sapta*; *l*Vā *Maṇidhānya-jāḥ.* Vṣ says—

Naiṣadhān [9] Yadukāṁś [10] c=aiva Śaiśītān [11] Kālatoyakān [12]
etān janapadān sarvān bhokṣyante [13] Maṇidhānya-jāḥ [14]
Kośalāṁś [15] c=Āndhra-Pauṇḍrāṁś [16] ca Tāmraliptān sa-sāgarān [17]
Campāṁ c=aiva [18] purīṁ ramyām bhokṣyante [19] Devarakṣitāḥ [20]
Kaliṅgā Mahiṣāś c=aiva Mahendra-nilayāś ca ye [21]
etān janapadān sarvān pālayiṣyati vai Guhaḥ [22]
Strīrāṣṭram [23] Bhokṣyakāṁś [24] c=aiva bhokṣyate Kanak-âhvayaḥ [25]
Saurāṣṭr-Āvanty-Ābhīrāś [26] ca
Śūdrā [27] Arbuda-Mālavāḥ [28]

anu-Gaṅgā Prayāgam Māgadhā* Guptāś† ca‡ bhokṣyanti:
where * *hlVṣ Māgadhān, kVṣ Mādgadhā, jVṣ Magadhā Suhmā*; † *lVṣ Guptāṁś, aVṣ* omits *Guptāś ca*; ‡ here *bVṣ* adds *Māgadhān, klVṣ Magadhā*. Bh says—

anu-Gaṅgām ā-Prayāgaṁ guptām* bhokṣyati† medinīm‡:

where * *fBh goptā*; † *hjBh bhokṣyanti* correctly; *fBh vai mahīm*.

[9] *Niṣadhān* in *Ca²djVā*.

[10] In *dghVā Yudakāṁś* or *Pud°*; *eVā Yadumāṁś*.

[11] In *bdVā Śaiśijān*; *gVā Śaiśikān*; *eVā Śeśikān*; *hVā Śauśītān*.

[12] *AVā °topakān* (misreading *y* as *p*).

[13] *Ca²jVā bhokṣyanti*.

[14] So Vā; *mVā °ja*; Bḍ *°jān*: *eVā Māladhānyagaḥ*. Vṣ similarly—

Naiṣāda*-Naimiṣika†-Kālatoyān‡ janapadān§ Maṇidhāra‖-vaṁśā bhokṣyanti¶:

where * *bhlVṣ Naiṣadha, kVṣ Śaiṣara* (see p. 51, note [23]); † *hVṣ Naimika*; ‡ *abhVṣ °yakān, lVṣ °yakā*; § *lVṣ °padā*; ‖ *kVṣ °dhāraka, deVṣ °dhāna, lVṣ °dhānya, aVṣ °dhānaṅka, bVṣ °dhānavaka, cVṣ °dhā, hVṣ Maṇadhanyaka*; ¶ *acfkVṣ vaṁśyā°, lVṣ vaṁśo bhokṣyati*. Bh, *jVṣ* omit this.

[15] In *fVā Kos°*; *dgVā Kośalāś*; *bhVā Chośalāś*.

[16] So *ClVā*, Bḍ: *a¹a²a⁴jVā Pauḍ°*; *dVā Poṇḍāś*; *a³Vā Pāṇḍyāś*: *hVā c=Ādhra-Podrāś*, *bVā °Poṭāś*: *mVā c=Ādha-Pauḍrāṁś*, *fVā °Pauṇḍrāś*: *gVā c=ānupādāś*.

[17] In *fmVā Tāma°*: *dVā Tāmralipt-ânusāgarān*, *bghVā Tāma°*, *lVā Nāma°*.

[18] In *bhVā* [*Paṁ*]*Caṁpāṁ cica*; *dVā Paṁcapāṁci*.

[19] *Ca³a⁴fjVā °ṣyanti*; *hVā °ṣyate*.

[20] So *a¹a²glmVā*; *bdVā Daiva°*. *Ca³a⁴fjVā Devarakṣitām*, *hVā Daiva°*. Vṣ similarly—

Kośal*-Auḍra†-Puṇḍraka‡-Tāmraliptān§ samudrataṭa-purīṁ ca Devarakṣito rakṣiṣyati‖:

where * *hVṣ Kośalam, cgVṣ Koyāl-, lVṣ Kaulpa*; † *hVṣ Udra, jVṣ Ēdra, kVṣ Ōtra, lVṣ Loddhra*; ‡ *lVṣ Puṇdra, bcVṣ Puḍraka*, wanting only in *dejVṣ*; § *acgjklVṣ Tāma°*; ‖ *lVṣ rakṣati*. Bh nil.

[21] In *gVā tathā*.

[22] Vṣ similarly—

Kaliṅga*-Mahiṣika†-Māhendrabhaumā‡ Guhāṁ§ bhokṣyanti:

where * *bVṣ* puts *nakṣatra* before *Kaliṅga*; † *defjkVṣ °ṣaka, lVṣ °ṣa, hVṣ Māheya-Kaccha*; ‡ *hVṣ °drān°, lVṣ °drabhaumān* correctly, *jkVṣ °drabhaumāṁ*; § *blVṣ Guhā* correctly, *jVṣ Guhān, hVṣ* omits. Bh nil.

[23] So *Ca³jVā*; Bḍ *°ṣtra-*: *a¹a²a⁴bdfghlmVā Strīrājyam*. *AVā Srī* by misprint.

[24] So *bdfhmVā*; *gVā Bhokhya°*; *lVā Bhokṣa°*; *ACjVā Bhakṣya°*: Bḍ *Bhoja°*.

[25] In *jVā °āhvaye*. Vṣ says—

Strīrājya*-Trairāja†-Mūṣika‡-janapadān Kanak-âhvayā bhokṣyanti§:

where * *alVṣ* omit; † so *CgkVṣ*, but *bhlVṣ, °rājya, aVṣ Tepirājya, cfVṣ* omit; ‡ *cVṣ Mūṣivā, hVṣ Mūkhika, lVṣ Muṣita, akVṣ Mṛṣika*; § *lVṣ °āsvayo bhokṣyati*. Bh, *dejVṣ* omit this.

[26] So Bh. Vṣ similarly—

Saurāṣṭr-Āvanti*-Śūdrān† Arbuda-Marubhūmi‡-viṣayāṁś ca vrāty-âdvij§-Ābhīra‖-śūdr-âdyā bhokṣyanti:

where * *hVṣ Surāṣtr-Āvaśca*; † *fVṣ Śūdra, abVṣ Śūdr-*(*aVṣ Śūr-*)*Ābhīrān, hVṣ Bhadr-Ābhīrā, kVṣ Sur-Ābhīr-Ārb°*; ‡ *hVṣ °bhū, bVṣ Maru, kVṣ Mevabhūmi*; § or *vrātyā dvij-, bhVṣ vrātya dvij-, aVṣ vrajñe°, kVṣ*

vrāty-âdvijā [29] bhaviṣyanti
   śūdra-prāyā janādhipāḥ
Sindhos taṭaṁ Candrabhāgāṁ [30]
   Kauntīṁ [31] Kāśmīra-maṇḍalam
bhokṣyanti śūdrā vrāty-âdyā [32]
   Mlecchāś c-âbrahma[33]-varcasaḥ
tulya-kālā ime [35] rājan
   Mleccha[36]-prāyāś ca bhūbhṛtaḥ [37]
ete [39] 'dharm-ânṛta-parāḥ [40]
   phalgu-dās tīvra-manyavaḥ.

tulya[34]-kālam bhaviṣyanti
   sarve hy ete mahīkṣitaḥ
alpa-prasādā hy anṛtā [38]
   mahā-krodhā hy adhārmikāḥ.

Evils of the Kali Age.

Text—*A*Mt *273*, 25-34 ; *A*Vā *99*, 388ᵇ–412 ; Bḍ iii, *74*, 200ᵇ–224.

Corresp. passages—*C*Vṣ iv, *24*, 18–29 ; *G*Bh xii, *1*, 41–*2*, 23.

After having thus brought the dynasties down to the early part of the 4th century A.D., these Purāṇas launch out into a prophetic description of the future evils of the Kali age, and the Vāyu and Brahmāṇḍa deal with them at great length. It is unnecessary to set out these passages, because they merely embody gloomy brahmanic forecasts, which were no doubt based on actual calamities, but which have no historic value except in so far as they may portray, more or less really, miseries which the country underwent in lawless times. But the first portion of the description appears to depict the unsettled condition of the country in the early part of the 4th century, and this alone is presented here. The references for it are—*A*Mt *273*, 25, 26ᵃ ; *A*Vā *99*, 388ᵇ–393ᵃ ; Bḍ. iii, *74*, 200ᵇ–203 ; *C*Vṣ iv, *24*, 18, 19;

rājye 'bhiṣikt- ; ‖ *j*Vṣ *Â[ū]bhīra*, *a*Vṣ *Âtira*. But *l*Vṣ has only *Saurāṣṭrā* ; *de*Vṣ nil.

[37] So Bh, except *Gcr*Bh *Śūrā*.

[38] In *f*Bh *Abhyuda-Pālavāḥ*.

[29] Or *vrātyā dvijā*.

[30] So Bh. Vṣ similarly (*l*Vṣ omits)—
   Sindhutaṭa-Dārvīkorvī*-Candrabhāgā-Kāśmīra†-viṣayān‡ vrātyā§ Mlecch‖-âdayaḥ sūdrā bhokṣyanti:
where * *f*Vṣ *Dārvikorvī*, *c*Vṣ °*kovī*, *j*Vṣ °*kevī*, *g*Vṣ °*kocaṁ*; *a*Vṣ *Dāvikorvī*, *k*Vṣ *Davi*°, *b*Vṣ *Deva*° ; *h*Vṣ *Davakorthā* : † *k*Vṣ *Raśmīva* : ‡ *fhjk*Vṣ *viṣayaṁ ca*, *c*Vṣ *viṣaya* : § *abcfhj*Vṣ *vrātya-*, *k*Vṣ *rājyā* : ‖ *bh*Vṣ *Mleccha-śūdr*, *k*Vṣ *Mlekṣa-śūdr*.

[31] In *glnr*Bh °*tī* : *c*Bh *Kautc* ; *d*Bh *Kaucīṁ* ; *f*Bh *Kāṁñcī*.

[32] In *e*Bh *vrātyās te*, *cf*Bh °*ca* : *d*Bh *śūdrāś c-ântyā* (one syll. short).

[33] In *afrs*Bh *Mlecchā abr*°.

[34] So Vā, Bḍ : *l*Vā *kalpa*.

[35] Vṣ similarly—
   ete ca tulya-kālāḥ sarve pṛthivyām bhūbhṛto bhaviṣyanti*:
where * *l*Vṣ *bhokṣyanti*.

[36] *Mlekṣa* in *c*Bh.

[37] In *r*Bh *bhūpateḥ*.

[38] In *d*Vā *a-nṛpā* ; *b*Vā *hi nṛpāḥ*.

[39] In *f*Bh *nṛpā*.

[40] So Bh ; so *j*Bh, altered from *dharmā nṛpatayaḥ* : *f*Bh *dharmaparāḥ*. Vṣ says—
   alpa-prasādā vṛhat-kopāḥ sarva*-kālam anṛt-âdharma-rucayaḥ :
where * *ej*Vṣ *sarve*.

*G*Bh xii, *1*, 41–43. Of this account the Matsya contains only lines 1, 10; the Brahmāṇḍa omits ll. 4–6. The Vāyu contains the whole, but *f*Vā omits ll. 4–6; *fjk*Mt omit l. 10; *hp*Mt, *k*Vā have nothing. Vṣ has nothing corresponding to ll. 1–3.

A further description of the evils is given afterwards, see p. 57.

Bhaviṣyant=îha[1] Yavanā dharmataḥ kāmato 'rthataḥ
n=aiva mūrdh-âbhiṣiktās te[2] bhaviṣyanti narādhipāḥ
yuga-doṣa-durācārā[3] bhaviṣyanti nṛpās tu te
strīṇām bāla[4]-vadhen=aiva hatvā c=aiva parasparam
bhokṣyanti Kali-śeṣe[5] tu vasudhām pārthivās tathā[6]
udit-ôdita-vaṁśās[7] tu[8] udit-âstamitās[9] tathā
bhaviṣyant=îha[10] paryāye kālena[11] pṛthivīkṣitaḥ
vihīnās tu[12] bhaviṣyanti dharmataḥ kāmato 'rthataḥ
tair vimiśrā janapadā[13] Āryā Mlecchāś ca[14] sarvaśaḥ[15]
viparyayeṇa vartante[16] kṣayam eṣyanti[17] vai prajāḥ.

[1] In *dehj*Vā °*ṣyanti ha*.

[2] In *e*Vā *tu*.

[3] In *e*Vā °*doṣā durātmāno*.

[4] In *Ca*³Vā *bala*: *e*Vā *strī-bāla-go-vadhaṁ kṛtvā*, *d*Vā °*bāla-bandhanaiś c=aiva*. Vṣ similarly—

strī-bāla-go-vadha-kartāraḥ* para-sv-
âdāna†-rucayo‡ 'lpa-sārāḥ:

where * *k*Vṣ °*bālāmāradha-rucayo*; † *h*Vṣ °*âdātāro*, *k*Vṣ *parabhyādānaka*, *j*Vṣ *paras-para-dāma*; ‡ *h*Vṣ *'śucayo*. Bh says—

strī-bāla-go-dvija-ghnāś ca para-dāra-
dhan-âdṛtāḥ*:

where * *dhl*Bh °*âhṛtāḥ*, *e*Bh °*âvṛtāḥ*.

[5] In *e*Vā *bhaviṣyanti Kali-śeṣaṁ*.

[6] In *g*Vā *tadā*.

[7] In *e*Vā *uditiditi-vaṁsyās*. Vṣ says—

udit-âstamita-prāyāḥ sv-alp-âyuṣo mahe-
cchā aty-alpa*-dharmāś ca† bhaviṣyanti:

where * *ef*Vṣ °*ch=âty-alpa*, *hj*Vṣ °*ch=âlpa*, *l*Vṣ °*chāś c=âlpa*; † *j*Vṣ inserts *na*. Bh says—

udit-âstamita-prāyā alpa-sattv=âlpak-
âyuṣaḥ
a-saṁskṛtāḥ kriyā-hīnā rajasā tamas=
âvṛtāḥ.

[8] *Ca*²*jl*Vā *te*.

[9] In *e*Vā *uditv=âst*°.

[10] In *bdhj*Vā °*ṣyanti ha*.

[11] In *f*Vā *kālaṁ na*.

[12] In *e*Vā *vihitās te*; *d*Vā *vihatās tu*.

[13] In *l*Mt *samādānu*.

[14] So Mt genly; *bf*Mt, *e*Vā *Ārya-M*°; *l*Mt *varṣā M*°; *a*¹Mt *Mleccha-prāyāś ca*; *j*Mt *ā-Mlecchāś c=aiva*. Vā genly, Bḍ *Mlecch-âcārāś ca*, *f*Vā °*âvārāś*°, *d*Vā °*âvāṇaś*°. *C*Vā *Snecch*° (misprint). Vṣ says—

taiś ca vimiśrā* janapadās tac-chīla-
vartino† rāj-âśraya-śuṣmiṇo Mlecchāś c=
Âryāś‡ ca viparyayeṇa vartamānāḥ prajāḥ
kṣapayiṣyanti:

where * *l*Vṣ *vimiśritā*; † *l*Vṣ *chīl-ânuvart*°; ‡ *k*Vṣ *Mlecch-âcāryāś*, *l*Vṣ °*âcārāś*; *h*Vṣ omits all after *Mlecchāś*. Bh says—

prajās te bhakṣayiṣyanti Mlecchā rājanya-
rūpiṇaḥ
tan-nāthās te janapadās tac-chīl-âcāra-
vādinaḥ
anyonyato rājabhiś ca kṣayaṁ yāsyanti
pīḍitāḥ.

[15] In *a*¹*bgjk*Mt *sarvataḥ*.

[16] In *c*Mt °*ta*; *gn*Mt, *dg*Vā °*taḥ*: *e*Vā reads this half line, *paryāyai vartamānānāṁ*.

[17] So Mt: *g*Mt *kṣapayiṣyanti*. Vā, Bḍ *nāśayiṣyanti*.

Chronological and Astronomical Particulars.

Text—*A*Mt *273*, 35–52[a]; *A*Vā *99*, 413–430; Bḍ iii, *74*, 225–243.

Corresp. passages—*C*Vṣ iv, *24*, 30–42; *G*Bh xii, *2*, 24–34.

Concluding passages containing chronological and astronomical particulars about the Kali age are found, more or less full, in all the five Purāṇas. Here the Viṣṇu relinquishes its prose, and both it and the Bhāgavata adhere to an old śloka version (which the Viṣṇu introduces with the phrase *atr=ôcyate*), similar to the version of the Matsya, Vāyu, and Brahmāṇḍa, but containing some verses not found in those three Purāṇas. Hence it is convenient to divide this subject into three parts.

The first part contains matter which is common to those three Purāṇas, and which the Viṣṇu and Bhāgavata give partially. The passages are these—*A*Mt *273*, 35–45[a]; *A*Vā *99*, 413–423; Bḍ iii, *74*, 225–236[a]; *C*Vṣ iv, *24*, 30–33; *G*Bh xii, *2*, 24–28[a]. The Vāyu and Brahmāṇḍa give the whole, the Matsya all except the first two lines, and the Viṣṇu and Bhāgavata have ll. 1, 2, 4–6, 18–20, 22.

Then those three Purāṇas insert 8 or 9 lines alluding to the evils of the age, which may be omitted, and *e*Vāyu omits most of them. The Viṣṇu and Bhāgavata offer instead other verses giving further particulars, and these constitute the second part, namely—*C*Vṣ iv, *24*, 34–39; *G*Bh xii, *2*, 28[b]–32. The verses in the Bh have been slightly re-arranged to correspond to the Vṣ.

The Purāṇas all unite again in the old śloka version and this forms the third part. The passages are—*A*Mt *273*, 49[b]–52[a]; *A*Vā *99*, 428[b]–430; Bḍ iii, *74*, 241–243; *C*Vṣ iv, *24*, 40–42; *G*Bh xii, *2*, 33–34. All give the whole, except that the Bhāgavata omits ll. 39, 40; but as there is considerable divergence, the Mt version and that of Vā and Bḍ are printed side by side, and the Vṣ and Bh versions are given in the notes.

As regards MSS *c*Mt omits ll. 21–23; *e*Mt ll. 21–23, 39 (second half)–41 (first half); *j*Mt ll. 15–17, 19; *k*Mt ll. 6–9, 18; *l*Mt ll. 12–15; *n*Mt ll. 13, 14; *a*[2]Vā ll. 11–14; *e*Vā l. 16; *h*Vā ll. 1, 2 (first half); *m*Vā ll. 11, 13, 15, and places 12 after 14; *hp*Mt, *k*Vā, and *t*Bh have nothing.

It is no part of the scope of this edition to discuss these chronological and astronomical particulars, beyond what is noticed in the Introdn. § 25, and in the notes to the translation of this passage, *infra*.

Yadā candraś[1] ca sūryaś ca tathā[2] Tiṣya[3]-Bṛhaspatī
eka-rāśau[4] sameṣyanti[5] tadā Kṛta-yugam bhavet[6]

[1] In *m*Vā *vaṁśa vaṁśaś*.
[2] In *j*Vṣ *yathā*; *b*Vṣ, *f*Bh *yadā*.
[3] *Śukra* in *h*Vṣ.
[4] *Ca*[2–4]*bfghjl*Vā *rātre*; *m*Vā *rāve*: *k*Vṣ *etair aṁśeṣu*.
[5] So *e*Vā, Vṣ, Bh; *l*Vṣ *sah=êṣyanti*. Vā genly, Bḍ *bhaviṣyanti*; *C*Vā *bhariṣyanti* (misprint).
[6] So Vā, Bḍ: *e*Vā, Vṣ, *ar*Bh *bhaviṣyati tadā* (*bdefgj*Vṣ *tataḥ*) *Kṛtam*; *h*Vṣ gives the line twice and ends first *kṣayam* and then *Kaliḥ*. Bh *tadā bhavati tat Kṛtam*.

eṣa [7] vaṁśa[8]-kramaḥ kṛtsnaḥ [9] kīrtito yo [10] yathā-kramam [11]
atītā vartamānāś ca tath=aiv=ânāgatāś [12] ca ye [13]
Mahāpadm[14]-âbhiṣekāt tu [15] | yāvat Parikṣito [16] janma
yāvaj janma [17] Parīkṣitaḥ | yāvan Nand-âbhiṣecanam
evaṁ [18] varṣa[19]-sahasraṁ tu jñeyam [20] pañcāśad-uttaram [21]
Pulomās tu [22] tath=Ândhrās tu [23] | pramāṇaṁ vai tathā vaktum [24]
Mahāpadm-ântare [25] punaḥ [26] | Mahāpadm-ântaraṁ [27] ca yat [28]
antaraṁ tac [29] chatāny [30] aṣṭau ṣaṭ-triṁśat [31] tu [32] samās tathā [33]
tāvat [34] kāl-ântaram bhāvyam [35] Andhr-ânt-âdyāḥ prakīrtitāḥ [36]

[7] So Vā, Bḍ, *bcden*Mt. *ACfgjklm*Mt *evaṁ*.
[8] In *e*Vā *eva*.
[9] So Mt, *bdeh*Vā. Vā genly *kṛtsnaṁ*; *e*Mt *kṛtaḥ praśnaḥ*, cMt *kṣataḥ°*.
[10] So Mt genly; *cen*Mt *'yaṁ*: *e*Vā *vā*. Vā, Bḍ *vo*.
[11] Mt *mayā kramāt*.
[12] So *Cfgj*Mt, Vā, Bḍ, Vṣ. Mt genly reads the whole line in the nomin. sing., and *b*Mt the first half in locat. sing. Bh says—

ye 'tītā vartamānā ye bhaviṣyanti ca pārthivāḥ:

but *de*Bh *ye bhaviṣyanti pārthivāḥ* for the second half.
[13] In *fg*Mt *tu ye*. After this line Vṣ inserts this line—

ete vaṁśeṣu bhūpālāḥ kathitā muni-sattama.

Bh inserts this line—

te ta uddeśataḥ proktā vaṁśīyāḥ* Soma-Sūryayoḥ:

where **f*Bh *vaṁśayoḥ*, *adrs*Bh *vaṁśa-jāḥ*.
[14] This line is in Mt, Vā, Bḍ. So Mt. Bḍ *Mahānand-*, Vā *Mahādev-*, which both no doubt = *Mahāpadm-*; see l. 7.
[15] Bḍ *°ṣek-ântaṁ*.
[16] This line is in Vṣ, Bh. So Vṣ. Bh *ārabhya bhavato* equivalently.
[17] So Mt. Vā, Bḍ *janma yāvat*.
[18] So Mt, *e*Vā: *ln*Mt *ekaṁ*; *k*Vṣ *ete*: others *etad*.
[19] In *celn*Mt *eva*; *b*Mt *eka*.
[20] Bh *śatam*; *j*Bh *satam*.
[21] So Mt genly, Vā, Bḍ: *cej*Mt *°śat=ôttaram*, *b*Mt *°śato trayam*: *ln*Mt, *bl*Vṣ *pañca-śat-ôttaram*. But *e*Vā, Vṣ, Bh *pañcadaś-ôttaram*.
[22] This line is in Mt. So *fjm*Mt; *bcen*Mt *°te*; *g*Mt *Pulobhās tu*; *e*Vā also *Pulomā ca*. *ACdkl*Mt *Paulomās tu*. The correct reading would seem to be *Pulomāt tu*, referring to the last Andhra king.
[23] So *ACdklm*Mt; *b*Mt *°Ândhrās tu*; *fg*Mt *tato 'ndhrās tu*; *j*Mt *tath=Êndrās tu*; *n*Mt *tathā c=Ândhra*; cMt *†tathārv=Ândhrā*; *e*Mt *†tathārvākaḥ*. The correct reading seems to be *tath=Ândhrāt tu*.
[24] This line is in Vā, Bḍ. So $a^1a^3a^4$*dfghl*Vā, Bḍ; *m*Vā *°vaktu*; 3 MSS of *C*Vā *°vaktam* (= Pkt *vuttam*?); a^3*j*Vā, 3 MSS of *C*Vā *°c=ôktam*: *e*Vā (see note [22]) *tato vaktum*; *b*Vā *yathā vaktur*. *Vuttam* is most prob. the original Pkt word, and all these are attempts to Sanskritize it without infringing sandhi.
[35] In *b*Mt *-ôttare*.
[26] In *j*Mt *puraḥ*.
[27] So Vā. Bḍ *-ôttaraṁ*.
[28] In *e*Vā *yataḥ*.
[29] So Vā. Bḍ *°ca*. Mt genly *anantaraṁ*; *j*Mt *antare ṣaṭ*. This half line in *l*Mt is *nā[nā]ntaram pakṣatāny aṣṭau*; in *b*Mt *†anaṁtastaṣṭanāmatyau*.
[30] In *e*Mt *śatā*.
[31] So also *n*Mt *ṣaḍiṁśat* (= *ṣaṭ-triṁśat*); *d*Mt *śastr°*: *b*Mt, a^3*b*Vā *ṣaḍ-viṁśac*, *d*Vā *ṣad-v°*; *h*Vā *ṣatriṁśac* or *ṣadr°*.
[32] So Mt. Vā, Bḍ *ca*.
[33] So Mt. Vā, Bḍ *smṛtāḥ*.
[34] So Mt. Vā, Bḍ *etat*.
[35] So Mt, *efm*Vā, Bḍ; *c*Mt *bhāvya*. Vā genly *bhāvyā*.
[36] So a^2–^{4}*fghm*Vā, Bḍ; *bd*Vā *c=Ân°*. *Ca*^{1}*jl*Vā *Andhr-ântā ye* (*l* omits *ye*) *pra°*; *e*Vā *sandhān bhāvyaḥ pra°*. Mt genly *Ândhr-ântād ā-Parīkṣitaḥ*; *fg*Mt *Andhr°*, *cen*Mt *kṣatr°*: *b*Mt *†saṁbhrātrādāyarākṣināt*, *j*Mt *athādyā dīpitās tataḥ*. Mt reading is corrupt, because from Parīkṣit to the end of the Andhras comprises the two periods in

Bhaviṣye[37] te prasaṅkhyātāḥ[38] purāṇa-jñaiḥ śrutarṣibhiḥ[39]

<table>
<tr><td>saptarṣayas tadā[40] prāṁśu[41]
pradīpten⸗âgninā[43] samāḥ[44]
sapta[47]-viṁśati-bhāvyānām[48]
Āndhrāṇ⸗ânte[51] 'nvagāt[52] punaḥ[53]
saptarṣayas tu vartante[57]
yatra[60] nakṣatra-maṇḍale</td><td>saptarṣayas tadā prāhuḥ[42]
Pratīpe rājñi[45] vai śatam[46]
sapta-viṁśaiḥ śatair[49] bhāvyā[50]
Andhrāṇ⸗ânte[54] 'nvayāḥ[55] punaḥ[56]
sapta-viṁśati[58]-paryante[59]
kṛtsne nakṣatra-maṇḍale</td></tr>
</table>

ll. 5–8. The reckoning is from the end of the Andhras onwards into the future.

[37] So Mt: *c*Mt °*ṣyai*; *l*Mt omits. Vā, Bd *bhaviṣyais*; *b*Vā *na divyais*.

[38] So Mt genly: *celn*Mt °*samākhyātaḥ*; *j*Mt, *e*Vā *tat prasaṅkhyātam*. *Ca*[1]*a*[2]*a*[4]*j*Vā, Bd *tatra saṅkhyātāḥ*; *a*[3]Vā °*khyātam*; *bdfghlm*Vā °*khyānām*: *b*Mt *naṣṭa-saṅkhyā-nāḥ*.

[39] In *l*Mt [*śu*]*śrū*[*ṣa*]*tārṣibhiḥ*; *b*Mt *surarṣi-bhiḥ*; *j*Mt *maharṣibhiḥ*: *ce*Mt *purāṇe śruti-sarpibhiḥ*.

[40] In *bcdefgjn*Mt *tathā*.

[41] This line is in Mt. So *ACdkm*Mt: *e*Mt *pāṁśru* (or *yā*°); *c*Mt *pāśu*; *n*Mt *prāyuḥ* or *prāpuḥ*; *b*Mt *āyuḥ*; *fg*Mt *te syuḥ*; *j*Mt *vācyāḥ*. These readings and Vā, Bd readings appear to be crp. It seems necessary to the sense of this whole passage that some lunar constellation should be meant here, and the true reading may perhaps be *Puṣye*. Puṣya as the constellation in Pratīpa's time might tally with Maghā in Parīkṣit's time (see ll. 22, 24) about a century and a half later; see JRAS, 1910, p. 28.

[42] So Vā; *g*Vā *prāhu*. Bd *prāptāḥ*: *e*Vā [*ca*] *tathākhyāś ca*.

[43] So Mt genly: *d*Mt *pradīpen*°; *k*Mt *pratapten*°; *j*Mt *pradīptā c⸗âgni vai*. Mt appears to be crp.

[44] So *AClm*Mt: *cdefgkn*Mt *samam*; *b*Mt *śamam*; *j*Mt *śase*.

[45] So Vā genly; *h*Vā °*rojñi*; *e*Vā °*rājā*: *d*Vā *Pratīpaṁ rījñi*, altered to *Pratīpa-rājñi*. Bd *pitrye Pārīkṣite* (omitting *vai*).

[46] In *fj*Vā *viṁśatam*; *e*Vā *saṁsthite*. All the readings of this line in Mt, Vā, and Bd are no doubt attempts to Sanskritize an old Prakrit śloka, which was obscure. Perhaps the true reading should be, having regard to the forms of letters in the old scripts—

saptarṣayas tadā Puṣye Pratīpe rājñi vai samam:

cf. *samam* in l. 19; or *śatam*, see l. 22.

[47] This line is in Mt: *c*Mt *saptā*; *bn*Mt *aṣṭā*.

[48] So *ACk*Mt: *cdefgjmn*Mt *bhāvyena*; *b*Mt *bhāvena*.

[49] So Vā genly, Bd: *d*Vā °*viṁśati tair*; *bh*Vā °*viṁśatair* (short): *e*Vā *saptā-viṁśe śate*, prob. the true reading.

[50] In *e*Vā *bhāvye*.

[51] So *ACm*Mt for first 3 syll.: *d*Mt *Andh*° *fg*Mt *Adh*°: *bcen*Mt *astrāṇāṁ*; *jk*Mt *astre-ṇāṁ*. For last syll. *cefgjkn*Mt *te*; *ACbm*Mt *tu*; *d*Mt *tvaṁ*. The whole is clearly *Ān-dhrāṇ⸗ânte*, see note [54].

[52] In *k*Mt *'nvagā*, *ce*Mt °*gāt*, *n*Mt °*gat*: *f*Mt *'ndhakāt*; *g*Mt *dhakāt*; *j*Mt *'ṣṭakā*; *AC*Mt *yadā*; *bdm*Mt *tataḥ*. The correct word seems to be *'nvagāt* (aorist of *anugā*) or *'nugāḥ*, the former meaning '(the cycle) followed on again', and the latter '(the Seven Ṛṣis were) following on again'. The readings are thus equivalent, but the former seems preferable, because the *v* appears to be original, and was easily misread as *dh* in the Gupta script, while *yadā* and *tataḥ* are obvious emendations.

[53] In *j*Mt *sudhāḥ*.

[54] For first 3 syll. Vā, Bd *Andhrāṇāṁ*, *h*Vā °*ṇā*; *e*Vā *mantrāṇāṁ*. For fourth syll. Vā, Bd *te*. The whole is clearly *An-dhrāṇāṁte*, which means *Andhrāṇ⸗ânte*, Pkt for *Andhrāṇām ante*, as the sense shows. But *m*Vā reads this half line *Adhā saṅkhyayā smṛtam*, which belongs partly to l. 15.

[55] So *a*[3]*h*Vā, Bd; and *d*Vā (altered from *tvayāḥ*); *g*Vā *'nvayā*; *e*Vā *'nvayaḥ*. Vā genly *tvayā*.

[56] In *b*Vā *punat*; *g*Vā *yutaḥ*; *a*[3]Vā *śubhāḥ*.

[57] This line is in Mt. So *CGVa*[2]*a*[4]*m*Mt; *d*Mt °*pravartante*: *j*Mt *saptarṣay⸗êti par-yante*: *a*[1]*a*[3]*b*Mt *sapta-viṁśati-paryante*, *ce*Mt °*paryanta-h*, *k*Mt °*paryataḥ*, *fg*Mt °*parjanyo*.

[58] This line is in Vā, Bd: *e*Vā °*viṁś⸗êti* or *viṁśe 'ti*.

saptarṣayas tu tiṣṭhanti [61] paryāyeṇa [62] śataṁ śatam [63]
saptarṣīṇāṁ yugaṁ hy etad [64] divyayā saṅkhyayā smṛtam [65]
māsā [66] divyāḥ [67] smṛtāḥ [68] ṣaṭ ca [69] divy-âbdāni tu [70] sapta hi [71]
tebhyaḥ [72] pravartate kālo [73] divyaḥ saptarṣibhis [74] tu vai [75]
saptarṣīṇāṁ [76] tu [77] yau pūrvau [78] dṛśyete [79] uditau niśi [80]
tayor madhye tu nakṣatraṁ [81] dṛśyate yat [82] samaṁ divi [83]
tena saptarṣayo [84] yuktā jñeyā [85] vyomni śataṁ samāḥ [86]
nakṣatrāṇām ṛṣīṇāṁ ca [87] yogasy=aitan [88] nidarśanam

59 In *d*Vā *paryate*; *b*Vā *payate*.

60 In *bcdefgj*Mt *kṛtsne*.

61 In *b*Mt *bhidyanti*.

62 In *f*Mt *paryāye sā*.

63 In *f*Mt *sataṁ satam*; *d*Mt *śataḥ śatam*; $a^{1}a^{3}a^{4}$*dfgl*Vā *śatāc chatam*; *bj*Vā *śatān śatam*; *m*Vā *śatā śatam*: a^{1}*b*Mt *śataṁ samāḥ*.

64 So Vā; *e*Vā *hy ete*; Bḍ *tv etad*; *fg*Mt *yuge hy etad*, *k*Mt °*ete*: *bh*Vā *sugaṁ hy etad*. But *b*Mt *tu paryanta*, *cen*Mt °*paryāye*. Mt genly *upary etat*.

65 So Vā, Bḍ: *cen*Mt *tat smṛtaṁ divya-saṅkhyayā*: *k*Mt *smṛtaṁ vai divya-saṅkhyayā*, *AC*Mt °*sañjñayā*: *fg*Mt *smṛtaṁ divyaṁ tu saṅkhyayā*; *bm*Mt °*sañjñayā*, and *d*Mt crp.

66 So Bḍ. Vā genly *sā sā*; *j*Vā *sāṣa*; *m*Vā *sāpa*; *h*Vā *sayā*; *f*Vā *sā[sā]ya*. Mt *samā*; *n*Mt *samo*; *e*Mt *kṣado*; *c*Mt *tado*. Instead of this line *e*Vā has two other lines—

ṣaṣṭir daivata-yugānāṁ c=aika saptabhir epi ca
triṁśac c=ânyāni varṣāṇi smṛtaḥ saptarṣi-vatsaraḥ.

67 So Mt, Bḍ. Vā *divyā*: *n*Mt *ditās*; *ce*Mt *ditvāt*.

68 Vā *smṛtā*; *bcefgln*Mt *tathā*.

69 So Bḍ. Mt, Vā *ṣaṣṭir* erroneously.

70 So *ACjkl*Mt; *cn*Mt °*ca*; *e*Mt *divy-âṣṭāni ca*. Bḍ *divy-âbdāś c=aiva*. Vā *divy-âhnāś c=aiva*: *bdm*Mt °*âhāni tu* (*b*, *ca*), *fg*Mt °*âhāniś ca*.

71 So Bḍ: *cdefgn*Mt, *g*Vā *saptati-ḥ*; other Mt, Vā genly *saptabhiḥ*; *j*Vā *saptāmiḥ*: *bh*Vā *saptaṣaṇabhiḥ*, where in *b*Vā *ṇabhiḥ* represents *tebhyaḥ* in next line.

72 So Vā, Bḍ, *bcekln*Mt: *e*Vā *ebhyaḥ*; other Mt *ebhiḥ*: *d*Vā reads this half line *pravartate mahān kālo*.

73 In *k*Mt *pravartitaḥ*°, *d*Mt *pravartane*°; *b*Mt °*tite kāle*.

74 In *cen*Mt *saptarṣitas*.

75 So Mt, *e*Vā. Vā, Bḍ *taiḥ*.

76 In *fg*Mt *sapta-śīrṣaṁ*.

77 In *ACdkm*Mt, Vṣ genly, *a*Bh *ca*.

78 So *CGVa*^{4}*m*Mt, Bḍ, Vṣ, Bh; *ar*Bh *pūrvau yau*. Vā *ye pūrvā* (altered in *d*Vā to *yau pūrvau*), *ak*Vṣ °*pūrve*: a^{1-3}*bcdefgln*Mt, *e*Vā *yaḥ pūrvaṁ*, *k*Mt °*pūrva*, *j*Mt °*pūrve*. The dual is right as there are two stars, and see next line.

79 So *CGVa*^{4}*m*Mt, Bḍ, Vṣ, Bh, *d*Vā. Vā genly *dṛśyante*; *eh*Vā, *a*Vṣ *dṛśyate*. For this half line a^{1-3}*bcdejkln*Mt read *udyan* (*l*, *udyat*; *j*, *mudyan*; *k*, *sudhan*) *vai dṛśyate niśi* (*j*, *divi*; *k* omits): *fg*Mt *udyāte dṛśyate niśi*.

80 *CGVa*^{4}*m*Mt *hy uditau niśi*; *e*Vā *hy udito*°. Vṣ, Bh *uditau divi*; *a*Vṣ *'bhyuditau*°; *jk*Vṣ, *j*Bh *udito*°; *g*Bh *udite*°. Vā, Bḍ *uttarā-diśi*.

81 So Mt genly, Bḍ; *fg*Mt °*madhye 'ti*°; *e*Vā °*madhye ca* [*taṁ*]°; *b*Mt °*mādye tu rajataṁ*. Bh, *bl*Vṣ *tayos tu madhye nakṣatraṁ*; Vṣ °*madhya-nak*°; *k*Vṣ °*madhyamaṁ kṣatraṁ*. In a^{2}Vā *tato madhye ca nakṣatraṁ*; Vā genly °*madhyena ca kṣetraṁ*; *bdh*Vā °*cākṣetraṁ* (altered in *d* to *ca nakṣatraṁ*); *m*Vā crp.

82 In *n*Mt *yaḥ*; *e*Vā, *b*Vṣ, *dfkq*Bh *tat*; *ce*Mt *sa*; *b*Mt *ca*.

83 Vṣ, Bh *niśi*.

84 Bh *ten=aita ṛṣayo*; *aber*Bh *ten=aiva*°; *f*Bh *tena vai*°.

85 So Vā, Bḍ; *l*Vā °*yayā*. Mt genly *jñeyā yuktā*, *j*Mt °*muktā*, *bd*Mt °*bhuktā*; *l*Mt *devā yuktā*. Vṣ, Bh *yuktās tiṣṭhanty*, *a*Vṣ *muktās*°; *k*Vṣ *muktāsthityanty*; *f*Bh *yuktā bhavanty*.

86 In *b*Vā *śate*°. Vṣ, Bh *abda-śataṁ nṛṇām*; *h*Vṣ, *g*Bh *aṣṭa-ś*°; *k*Vṣ *aka-ś*°.

87 In *e*Vā *ca sarveṣāḥ*.

88 So Mt, Vā genly: *bdg*Vā *yogyasy*°. Bḍ

saptarṣayo Maghā-yuktāḥ [89] kāle Pārīkṣite [90] śatam [91]
Andhr-ânte [92] tu [93] catur-viṁśe [94] bhaviṣyanti [95] śataṁ samāḥ [96].

Viṣṇu.	*Bhāgavata.*
te tu Pārikṣite kāle Maghāsv āsan [97] dvijottama	te tvadīye dvijāḥ kāle adhunā c=âśritā [98] Maghāḥ yadā devarṣayaḥ sapta Maghāsu vicaranti hi

tadā pravṛttaś ca [99] Kalir dvādaś-âbda[1]-śat-âtmakaḥ

yad=aiva bhagavad-Viṣṇor aṁśo yāto [3] divaṁ dvija [4] Vasudeva-kul-ôdbhūtas tad=aiva Kalir āgataḥ [6]	Viṣṇor bhagavato [2] bhānuḥ Kṛṣṇ-âkhyo 'sau [5] divaṁ gataḥ tad=âviśat Kalir lokam pāpe yad ramate janaḥ [7]
yāvat sa pāda-padmābhyām pasparś=êmāṁ vasundharām tāvat pṛthvī-pariṣvaṅge samartho n=âbhavat Kaliḥ gate sanātanasy=âṁśe [10] Viṣṇos tatra bhuvo [11] divam [12] tatyāja s-ânujo rājyaṁ Dharma-putro Yudhiṣṭhiraḥ	yāvat sa pāda-padmābhyāṁ spṛśann āste [8] Ramā-patiḥ tāvat Kalir vai pṛthivīm parākrāntuṁ na c=âśakat [9]

bhogasy° : *h*Vā *yogyasya tan* ; *b*Mt *tu yogasy=êti* ; *n*Mt reads this half line *yāgasy=êti darśayan.*

[89] Bḍ *hy ath=âyuktāḥ* : *fg*Mt *mayā hy uktāḥ*, *d*Mt *may=âpy°* ; *e*Vā *mayā proktāḥ.*

[90] In *j*Mt this half line is *kālena paritoṣitāḥ*, *k*Mt *°tam.*

[91] In *n*Mt *śrutam* ; *b*Mt *kṣutan* ; *fg*Mt *same* ; *m*Mt *divi.*

[92] So *a¹a³a⁴gh*Vā ; *l*Vā *Andh-°*, *b*Vā *Adhm-°*, *d*Vā *Adhry-°* ; *e*Vā *Andhāṇ=ânte* (omitting *tu*) in Pkt form, see note [54]. *Ca²jm*Vā, Bḍ *Andhr-âṁśe*, *f*Vā *Adhr°*. Mt genly *brāhmaṇās* (= *saptarṣayaḥ* ?) ; *C*Mt *°ṇas* ; *fg*Mt *°ṇam.*

[93] So Mt genly ; *j*Mt *ca.* Vā genly, Bḍ *sa-*.

[94] *Cbfg*Mt *°śa* ; *j*Mt, *d*Vā *°śo* ; *n*Mt *°śad.*

[95] In *f*Mt, *d*Vā *°ṣyati.*

[96] So Mt, Bḍ ; *f*Mt *satam°* ; *d*Vā *sate°* (altered to *gate°*) : *jm*Mt, *f*Vā *sate mama*, *bh*Mt *°manā*, *g*Mt *°matā* : *e*Vā *śatan tadā* ; *l*Vā *same matā.* *A*Vā *mate mama.*

[97] In *b*Vṣ *Maghāś c=âsan* ; *k*Vṣ †*Maghādyāsan* ; *aj*Vṣ crp.

[98] In *q*Bh *hy āśritā.*

[99] So Vṣ. Bh *tu.*

[1] In *h*Vṣ, *g*Bh *âṣṭa* ; *l*Vṣ *âtma.*

[2] In *d*Bh *Viṣṇus tu bhagavān.*

[3] In *ab*Vṣ *jāto* ; *k*Vṣ *aṁśa-jāto.*

[4] In *k*Vṣ *dvijottama.*

[5] In *s*Bh *sa* : *d*Bh *Kṛṣṇo 'sau* ; *e*Bh †*Kṛṣṇaṣyotsau* apptly.

[6] In *bl*Vṣ *°aiv=âtr=âgataḥ Kaliḥ.*

[7] In *d*Bh *manaḥ.*

[8] In *f*Bh *āsīd.*

[9] In *f*Bh *v=âś°* ; *kqr*Bh *c=âśakṛt.*

[10] In *de*Vṣ *-ânte.*

[11] In *k*Vṣ *tvayo* ; *a*Vṣ *divo.*

[12] In *ah*Vṣ *divi.*

Viṣṇu.	*Bhāgavata.*
viparītāni dṛṣṭvā ca	
nimittāni sa Pāṇḍavaḥ	
yāte Kṛṣṇe cakār=âtha	
so 'bhiṣekam Parikṣitaḥ [13]	
prayāsyanti yadā c=aite	yadā Maghābhyo [14] yāsyanti
Pūrv-Âṣāḍhām maharṣayaḥ	Pūrv-Âṣāḍhām maharṣayaḥ

tadā Nandāt [15] prabhṛty [16] eṣa [17] Kalir vṛddhiṁ gamiṣyati [18].

---

yasmin Kṛṣṇo divaṁ yātas [19] tasminn eva tad=âhani [20]
pratipannaṁ Kali-yugaṁ [21] tasya saṅkhyāṁ nibodhata [22]

catuḥ-śata[23]-sahasraṁ tu	sahasrāṇāṁ śatān=îha
varṣāṇāṁ[24] vai[25] smṛtam budhaiḥ[26]	trīṇi mānuṣa-saṅkhyayā [27]
ṣaṣṭi-varṣa[28]-sahasrāṇi	ṣaṣṭiṁ c=aiva sahasrāṇi
saṅkhyātam [29] mānuṣeṇa tu [30]	varṣāṇāṁ t=ûcyate [31] Kaliḥ [32]

[13] So all Vṣ, but *C*Vṣ °*kṣite*.

[14] In *b*Bh °*bhyāṁ*; *d*Bh *Maghāto*.

[15] In *j*Vṣ °*Nanda*, *e*Bh °*Naṁtāt*; *d*Bh *tadā tadā*: *r*Bh *tato Nandāt*.

[16] In *de*Vṣ *prabhūm*.

[17] In *bjk*Vṣ, *e*Bh *eva*.

[18] In *c*Bh *kariṣyati*.

[19] In *e*Vā *divā jāta*: *j*Mt reads—
yadā Kṛṣṇaś chavi yātaḥ śuklo Nārāyaṇas
tathā.

[20] So Mt, *e*Vā, Vṣ, Bh. Vā, Bḍ *tadā dine*, altered in *d*Vā to *tad-âditaḥ*.

[21] So Mt, *e*Vā, Vṣ, Bh. Vā, Bḍ °*pannaḥ* °*yugaḥ*.

[22] So Vā, Bḍ. Vṣ °*nibodha me*. Mt *pramāṇaṁ tasya me śṛṇu*; *l*Mt *prapannaṁ*°. Bh *iti prāhuḥ purā-vidaḥ*; *d*Bh *iti-r-āhuḥ*°, see Appendix I, § ii.

[23] So Mt; *j*Mt *śatā*; *e*Mt *śatī*: a^{2}Mt *ṣaṣṭi*; *dm*Mt *ṣaṭ* (one syll. short).

[24] In *b*Mt *varṇāṇi*: *e*Mt reads this half line *tadā sandhyā pravartate*.

[25] In *c*Mt *yat*; *fgjk*Mt *tat*; *d*Mt *tu*; *b*Mt *na* (for *nu*?).

[26] In *j*Mt *tathā*.

[27] So Vā, Bḍ.

[28] So *bjkln*Mt; a^{1-3}*dm*Mt *ṣaṣṭir*°; *cfg*Mt *ṣaṣṭiṁ*. *AC*Mt *catvāry aṣṭa-*.

[29] In *bfgn*Mt °*khyātā*; *d*Mt °*khyāte*.

[30] In *j*Mt *tat*.

[31] So Bḍ, *f*Vā; *g*Vā *tyūc*°; *b*Vā *tuc*°; *d*Vā *tucyāta*, altered to *tu smṛtaḥ*; *m*Vā *rūvyate* (for *r-ucyate*?), see Appendix I, § ii. Vā genly *ucyate*.

[32] Instead of this and the preceding line Vṣ has these lines—
trīṇi lakṣāṇi varṣāṇāṁ* dvija mānuṣa†-
saṅkhyayā
ṣaṣṭiṁ c=aiva sahasrāṇi bhaviṣyaty eṣa vai
Kaliḥ:
where * *hl*Vṣ *varṣāṇi*; † *l*Vṣ *varṣāṇān dvija*. Bh omits this statement.

[33] In *g*Mt *divya-*. *C*Vā *divye*.

[34] So $a^{3}a^{4}$*cfgklmn*Mt: *CGV*$a^{1}a^{2}$*bd*Mt °*saṅkhyā*°; *j*Mt *tathā sandhy=âpav*°, unless it = °*sandhyā prav*°.

[35] So Vā genly: *fm*Vā °*âṁsaṁ hi kīrtite*, Bḍ °*âṁśe*°; *j*Vā °*sandhyā sihā kīrtite*. But *gl*Vā °*sandhy-âṁsa hi kīrtyate*, $a^{1}a^{3}$Vā °*sandhyā sā hi*°, *bh*Vā °*sandhyā sā hi* [*tā*]°: *d*Vā for this half line (with clerical errors uncancelled) *saṁdvedhiś ca iti tathā saṁdhyā saṁdhy-âṁśa sahita kīrtyate*: *e*Vā *sa-sandhy-âṁsam udāhṛtam*. For this line Vṣ reads—
śatāni tāni divyāni sapta pañca ca
saṅkhyayā *:
where * *h*Vṣ *divyayā*; but *sandhyayā* appears to be the correct word since 1200

divyaṁ varṣa-sahasraṁ tu	divyaṁ [33] varṣa-sahasraṁ tu
tadā sandhyā pravartate [34]	tat-sandhy-âṁśam prakīrtitam [35]

nihśeṣe tu [36] tadā [37] tasmin [38] Kṛtaṁ vai pratipatsyate [39].

divine years include the two sandhyās. Bh says—

divy-âbdānāṁ * sahasr-ânte caturthe tu †
punaḥ Kṛtam :

where * *gkp*Bh *aṣṭānāṁ* ; † *e*Bh *caturthena*.

[36] This line is in Mt, Vā, Bd, Vṣ. So Mt, *e*Vā. Vā, Bd °*ca*; *d*Vā *naiḥśeṣe ca*. Vṣ *niḥśeṣeṇa*, *j*Vṣ °*śeṣanaṁ*.

[37] Vṣ *tatas*.

[38] In *j*Mt *tasya*.

[39] So Mt, Vā, Bḍ. Vṣ *bhaviṣyati punaḥ* (*a*Vṣ *tadā*) *Kṛtam*. Bh adds—

bhaviṣyati yadā * nṛṇām mana ātma-
prakāśakam † :

where * *adqr*Bh and v. r. in *G*Bh *tadā* ; † *c*Bh *ātm-âp*°.

TRANSLATION

This translation is close to the original though not absolutely literal, and generally combines the various versions where they supplement one another. Words in italics are not expressed in the original but are supplied to complete the meaning. The notes deal only with the salient points, and for the rest reference must be made to the notes to the original text.

Preface.

Listen as I narrate all future *events*, as Vyāsa, unwearied in work, proclaimed to me formerly, both the future Kali age and the manvantaras also. Thus I will first declare now the kings who are to be, both those descended from Aila [1] and the Ikṣvākus and also the kings descended from Sudyumna [2], among whom the splendid kṣatriya stock of the families of Aila and Ikṣvāku is brought to an end. I will proclaim all those kings *as* mentioned in the Bhaviṣya *Purāṇa*. Moreover *there will be* other kings besides them, who shall arise, kṣatriyas, pāraśavas [3], śūdras, and others who will be foreigners; Andhras, Śakas and Pulindas, Cūlikas and Yavanas, Kaivartas, Ābhīras and Śavaras, and others who will be of Mleccha origin; Pauravas, Vītihotras, Vaidiśas, five [4] Kosalas, Mekalas, Kośalas [5], Pauṇḍras, Gaunardas, and Svasphrakas, Sunidharmas, Śakas, Nīpas and others who will be of Mleccha race. I will declare those kings according to the total of their years [6] and by name.

Pauravas.

Abhimanyu's son by Virāṭa's daughter Uttarā was Parīkṣit. Parīkṣit's son was king Janamejaya who was very righteous. From Janamejaya was born valiant Śatānīka. Śatānīka's son was valiant Aśvamedhadatta.

From Aśvamedhadatta was born a victorious son, righteous Adhisīmakṛṣṇa [7], who now *reigns* great in fame.

Adhisīmakṛṣṇa's son will be king Nicakṣu [8]. When the city Hastināpura is carried away by the Ganges, Nicakṣu will abandon it and will dwell in Kauśāmbī.

[1] That is the Pauravas.

[2] See p. 2, note [13].

[3] A mixed caste said to be descended from a brahman father and śūdra mother.

[4] This would seem to be meant for Pañcālas.

[5] The people of Mahākosala apptly.

[6] Or Mt, 'according to their succession'.

[7] Or *Asīmakṛṣṇa*.

[8] Or *Virakṣu*. Vā *Nirvaktra*. Bh *Nemicakra*.

He will have eight sons of great might and valour. His eldest son *will be* Uṣṇa[1]; after Uṣṇa Citraratha is remembered; after Citraratha Śucidratha[2]; and after Śucidratha Vṛṣṇimat[3]; and after Vṛṣṇimat Suṣeṇa will be a pure king. After Suṣeṇa Sunītha[4] will be king; after Sunītha will be Ruca[5]; after him will be Nṛcakṣus[6]. Nṛcakṣus' heir will be Sukhībala[7]; and Sukhībala's son will be king Pariplava[8]; and Pariplava's son will be king Sunaya[9]. His heir Medhāvin will be king; and Medhāvin's son will be Nṛpañjaya. Durva[10] *will be* his son; and Tigmātman his son. After Tigma will be Bṛhadratha; after Bṛhadratha Vasudāna[11]; after Vasudāna Śatānīka; after him will be Udayana[12]; and after Udayana will be the warrior king Vahīnara[13]; and Vahīnara's son will be Daṇḍapāṇi[14]. After Daṇḍapāṇi Nirāmitra[15]; and after Nirāmitra Kṣemaka.

These 25 kings will exist born of Pūru's race. In this connexion this genealogical verse was sung by ancient brahmans—'The race honoured by gods and rishis, from which sprang brahmans and kṣatriyas, will verily on reaching Kṣemaka reach its end in the Kali age.' Thus has been correctly proclaimed this Paurava race, *the offspring* of Pāṇḍu's wise son, high-souled Arjuna.

Aikṣvākus.

Next I will declare *the race* of the high-souled Ikṣvākus. Bṛhadbala's heir was the warrior king Bṛhatkṣaya[16]. His son was Urukṣaya[16]; after Urukṣaya was Vatsavyūha[17]; after Vatsavyūha Prativyoma[18].

His son is Divākara[19] who now rules the city Ayodhyā in Madhyadeśa.

Divākara's *successor* will be famous Sahadeva. Sahadeva's heir *will be* high-minded Bṛhadaśva[20]; his *successor* will be Bhānuratha[21]; and his son will be Pratītāśva[22]; and Pratītāśva's son will be Supratīka[23]. His son *will be* Marudeva[24], and his son Sunakṣatra. After Sunakṣatra will be victorious Kinnarāśva[25]; and Antarikṣa will be Kinnarāśva's great son. After Antarikṣa *will be* Suparṇa[26]; and

[1] Mt *Bhūri.*
[2] Bh *Kaviratha* and *Kuv°.*
[3] Or *Vṛṣṭimat.* Vā *Dhṛtimat.*
[4] Vā *Sutīrtha.*
[5] Vṣ *Ṛca.*
[6] Vā *Tricakṣa.*
[7] Vṣ *Sukhābala.* Bh *Sukhīnala.*
[8] Or *Paripluta* or *Pariṣṇava.*
[9] Mt *Sutapas.*
[10] Mt *Urva.* Vṣ *Mṛdu.* Gr *Hari.*
[11] Mt *Vasudāman.* Gr *Sudānaka.* Bh *Sudāsa.*
[12] Gr *Udāna.* Bh *Durdamana.*
[13] Or *Mahīnara.* Vṣ *Ahīnara.*
[14] Vṣ *Khaṇḍapāṇi.*
[15] Vṣ *Naramitra.* Bh *Nimi.*
[16] For the variations in these names see p. 9.
[17] Mt *Vatsadroha.* Bh *Vatsavṛddha.* Vṣ inserts a king *Vatsa* before him.
[18] Vā *Prativyūha.*
[19] Bh *Bhānu Divārka.*
[20] Mt *Dhruvāśva.*
[21] Bh *Bhānumat.* Mt crp.
[22] Mt *Pratīpāśva.* Bh *Pratīkāśva.* Gr *Pratīvya.*
[23] Mt *Supratīpa.* Vā *Supratīta.* Gr *Pratītaka.*
[24] Vā *Sahadeva.*
[25] Or *Kinnara.* Bh *Puṣkara.*
[26] Mt *Suṣeṇa.* Vṣ *Suvarṇa.* Bh *Sutapas.*

after Suparṇa Amitrajit [1]. His son *will be* Bṛhadbhrāja [2]. Dharmin [3] is remembered as his son. Dharmin's son will be Kṛtañjaya. Kṛtañjaya's son will be wise Raṇañjaya [4]; and after Raṇañjaya will be Sañjaya, a warrior king. Sañjaya's son *will be* Śākya. After Śākya *will be* king Śuddhodana [5]. Śuddhodana's *son* will be Siddhārtha; Rāhula [6] *will be his* son. After him will be Prasenajit [7]. After him will be Kṣudraka. After Kṣudraka will be Kulaka [8]. After Kulaka Suratha is remembered; and Suratha's *son* Sumitra will be the last king.

These Aikṣvākus have been declared, who will exist in the Kali age; born in Bṛhadbala's lineage they will enhance their family, being warriors and learned, true to their word, self-restrained. *These* kings who were ancient have been all declared. In this connexion this genealogical verse was sung by ancient brahmans—'This race of the Ikṣvākus will terminate with Sumitra; on reaching king Sumitra it will indeed reach its end in the Kali age.' Thus has been declared the kṣatriya stock descended from Manu, and that descended from Aila.

Bārhadrathas.

Next I will declare the Bārhadrathas of Magadha, who are kings in Sahadeva's lineage in Jarāsandha's race, those past, those existing and also those who will exist. I will declare them according to their prominence: listen as I speak.

When the Bhārata battle took place and Sahadeva was slain, his heir Somādhi [9] became king in Girivraja; he reigned 58 years. In his lineage Śrutaśravas was 64 years [10]. Ayutāyus reigned 26 years [11]. His *successor* Niramitra enjoyed the earth 40 years [12] and went to heaven. Sukṣatra [13] obtained the earth 56 years. Bṛhatkarman [14] reigned 23 years.

Senājit [15] is now enjoying the earth the same number of years [16].

Śrutañjaya will be for 40 years, great in strength, large of arm, great in mind and prowess. Vibhu will obtain the earth 28 years [17]; and Śuci will stand in the kingdom 58 years. King Kṣema will enjoy the earth 28 years. Valiant Suvrata [18] will obtain the kingdom 64 years. Sunetra will enjoy the earth 35 years [19] *(or*

[1] Mt calls him *Sumitra* also.
[2] Mt, Vṣ, Bh *Bṛhadrāja*. Vā *Bharadvāja*.
[3] Mt crp.
[4] Gr *Dhanastraya*. Vā aptly inserts a king *Vrāta* before him.
[5] Vṣ *Kruddhodana*.
[6] Vṣ *Rātula*. Gr *Bāhula*. Bh *Lāṅgala*. Mt *Puṣkala*.
[7] Gr *Senajit*.
[8] Vā *Kṣulika*. Vṣ *Kuṇḍaka*. Gr *Kuḍava*. Bh *Raṇaka*.
[9] Bd, some Vṣ, Gr *Somāpi*. Vṣ genly *Somāmi*. Bh *Mārjāri*.
[10] Vṣ *Śrutavat*. Bd, many Vā, 67 years.
[11] Mt *Apratīpin*. Mt, some Vā, 36 years.
[12] Vā, Bd, 100 years.
[13] Vā *Sukṛtta*. Mt *Surakṣa*. Bh *Sunakṣatra*.
[14] Bh *Bṛhatsena*. Gr *Bahukarmaka*.
[15] Bh *Karmajit*.
[16] That is, 23 years. Mt, 50.
[17] Vṣ, Bh *Vipra*. Vā, Bd merely *nṛpa*, and say 35 years.
[18] Vā genly *Bhuvata*. Mt *Anuvrata*.
[19] Some Mt, 25 years.

Dharmanetra[1] will be 5 full years). And Nirvṛti[2] will enjoy this *earth* 58 years. Trinetra will next enjoy the kingdom 28 years (*or* Suśrama's[3] sovereignty will last 38 years). Dṛḍhasena will be 48 years[4]. Mahīnetra[5] will be resplendent 33 years (*or* Sumati will next obtain *the kingdom* 33 years). Sucala will be king 32 years[6]. King Sunetra[7] will next enjoy *the kingdom* 40 years. King Satyajit will enjoy the earth 83 years[8]. And Viśvajit will obtain this earth and be 25 years[9]. Ripuñjaya[10] will obtain the earth 50 years.

These 16 kings are to be known as the future Bṛhadrathas; and their kingdom will last 723 years[11]. And these 32 kings are the future Bṛhadrathas; their kingdom will last full 1000 years indeed.

Pradyotas.

When the Bṛhadrathas, Vītihotras and Avantis have passed away, Pulika[12] will kill his master and anoint his own son Pradyota, by force[13] in the very sight of the kṣatriyas. He (Pradyota) will indeed have the neighbouring kings subject to him and be destitute of good policy[14]. He, an excellent man[15], will be king 23 years. Pālaka will then be king 24 years[16]. Viśākhayūpa will be king 50 years[17]. Ajaka[18] will have the kingdom 21 years[19]. His son Nandivardhana will be 20 years[20].

Those 5 kings after enjoying the earth 52 years perished[21].

Those 5 sons, the Prādyotas, will endure 138 years[22].

Śiśunāgas.

Śiśunāga will destroy all their prestige and will be *king*. Placing his son in Benares he will make Girivraja his own abode[23]. Śiśunāga will reign 40 years. His son Kākavarṇa will obtain the earth 36 years[24]. Kṣemadharman will be king next 20 years[25]. Kṣatraujas will obtain the earth 40 years[26]. Vimbisāra will be

[1] Bh *Dharmasūtra*. Vṣ, Gr *Dharma*.
[2] Vā, Bḍ, merely *nṛpati*.
[3] Bh *Śama*. Vā *Suvrata*.
[4] Mt *Dyumatsena*. Vā, Bḍ, 58 years, crp.
[5] Some Mt, merely *Netra*.
[6] Mt *Acala*. Vṣ, Bh, Gr *Subala*. Vā, 22 years; Bḍ, 40.
[7] Vṣ *Sunīta*. Bh *Sunītha*. Gr *Nīta*.
[8] Mt, 80 years.
[9] Vā *Vīrajit*, 35 years.
[10] Vā, Bḍ *Ariñjaya*. Gr *Iṣuñjaya*.
[11] See p. 17, note [89].
[12] Vā *Munika*. Vṣ *Sunika*. Bḍ, Bh *Śunaka*.
[13] Or 'Pulika's offspring'. Mt has the name *Bālaka* for Pradyota.
[14] Or (some copies) '*will* not *act* righteously'.
[15] Or (some copies) 'sickly in mind'.
[16] Mt, 28 years.
[17] Mt, 53 years.
[18] Bh *Rājaka*. Vṣ *Janaka*. Mt *Sūryaka*.
[19] Vā, 31 years.
[20] Vā *Vartivardhana*. Mt, 30 years.
[21] So Mt; some copies, 152 years.
[22] So Vā, Bḍ, Vṣ, Bh.
[23] So Mt. Vā, Bḍ seem to mean the same.
[24] Vā *Śakavarṇa*. Mt, 26 years.
[25] Mt, 36 years.
[26] Bh *Kṣetrajña*. Mt *Kṣemajit*, 24 years.

king 28 years[1]. Ajātaśatru will be king 25 years[2]. Darśaka will be king 25 years[3]. After him Udayin[4] will be king 33 years. That king will make as his capital on the earth Kusumapura on the south bank of the Ganges in his fourth year[5]. Nandivardhana will be king 40 years[6]. Mahānandin[7] will be 43 years.

These will be the 10 Śaiśunāga kings[8]. The Śiśunāgas will endure 360 (*or better*, 163[9]) years, being kings with kṣatriya kinsfolk.

Early Contemporary Dynasties.

Contemporaneous with these *aforesaid* kings there will be other kings; all these *following* kings will endure an equal time: *namely*, 24 Aikṣvākus[10], 27 Pañcālas[11], 24 kings of Kāśi, 28 Haihayas[12], 32 Kaliṅgas, 25 Aśmakas, 36 Kurus[13], 28 Maithilas, 23 Śūrasenas, and 20 Vītihotras. All these kings will endure the same time.

Nandas.

As son of Mahānandin by a śūdra woman will be born a king[14], Mahāpadma (Nanda[15]), who will exterminate all kṣatriyas. Thereafter kings will be of śūdra origin. Mahāpadma will be sole monarch, bringing all under his sole sway[16]. He will be 88 years on the earth[17]. He will uproot all kṣatriyas[18], being urged on by prospective fortune[19]. He will have 8 sons, of whom Sukalpa[20] will be the first; and they will be kings in succession to Mahāpadma for 12 years.

A brahman Kauṭilya will uproot them all; and, after they have enjoyed the earth 100 years, it will pass to the Mauryas.

[1] All vary in this name. Bḍ 38 years. After him Mt erroneously inserts the first two Kāṇvāyana kings: see *Kāṇvāyanas, infra*.

[2] Mt, 27 years.

[3] Bḍ, Vṣ, Bh *Darbhaka*. Mt *Vaṁśaka*, 24 years.

[4] Vṣ *Udayāśva*. Mt *Udāsin*. Bh *Ajaya*.

[5] This statement is in Vā, Bḍ.

[6] Vā, 42 years.

[7] Bḍ *Sahānandi*.

[8] Many copies of Mt say 12, because of the mistake mentioned in note[1].

[9] So Mt according to its real meaning apptly: corrupted by Bḍ and Bh to 360; by Vā and Vṣ to 362.

[10] For their list, see p. 65.

[11] Vā, Bḍ, 25.

[12] Vā, Bḍ, 24.

[13] For their list, see p. 64, prob.

[14] Mt says apptly, he will be 'born as a portion of Kali'. Vā and Bḍ say, he will be 'enveloped by Fate'.

[15] So Vṣ and Bh.

[16] Vṣ, Bh, 'his rule will be untransgressed'.

[17] Vā, Bḍ, 'he will protect the earth 88 (or some copies, 28) years'.

[18] Vṣ, Bh, 'like a second Paraśu-Rāma'.

[19] Vā, Bḍ, 'urged on by predestination', apptly.

[20] Or *Sahalya*. Vṣ *Sumātya*. Bh *Sumālya*.

Mauryas.

Kauṭilya will anoint Candragupta as king in the realm. Candragupta will be king 24 years[1]. Vindusāra will be king 25 years[2]. Aśoka will be king 36 years. His son Kunāla will reign 8 years[3].

Mt and eVā.

Kunāla's son Bandhupālita will enjoy *the kingdom* 8 *years*[1]. Their grandson Daśona will reign 7 years[4]. His son Daśaratha will be king 8 *years*. His son Samprati will reign 9 years. Śāliśūka will be king 13 years[5]. Devadharman will be king 7 years[5]. His son Śatadhanvan will be king 8 *years*[6]. Bṛhadratha will reign 70 years[8].

These are the 10 Mauryas[9] who will enjoy the earth full 137 *years*. After them it will go to the Śuṅgas[10].

Vā genly and Bḍ.

Kuṇāla's son Bandhupālita will enjoy *the kingdom* 8 *years*. Bandhupālita's heir Indrapālita will reign 10 *years*.

Devavarman will be king 7 years. His son Śatadhanus will be king 8 years. Bṛhadratha will be king 7 years[7].

These 9 Mauryas will enjoy the earth full 137 *years*. After them will go the Śuṅga[11].

Śuṅgas.

Puṣyamitra the commander-in-chief will uproot Bṛhadratha and will rule the kingdom as king 36 years[12]. *His* son Agnimitra will be king 8 years. Vasujyeṣṭha[13] will be king 7 years. *His* son Vasumitra will be king 10 years. Then his son Andhraka[14] will reign 2 years. Pulindaka will then reign 3 years. *His* son Ghoṣa[15] will be king 3 years. Next Vajramitra will be king 9 years[16]. Bhāgavata[17] will be king 32 years. His son Devabhūmi[18] will reign 10 years.

These 10 Śuṅga kings will enjoy this earth full 112 years. From them the earth will pass to the Kaṇvas.

1 Mt wants this statement.

2 Mt omits. All except Vṣ vary this name.

3 Mt omits. Vṣ, Bh mention *Suyaśas* instead.

4 Mt, 'his (*i.e.* Aśoka's) grandson', but the text is crp.

5 Mt wants this statement.

6 So also Vṣ, Bh: eVā *Śataṁdhanus*. Mt, 6 years.

7 Vā *Vṛhadaśva*, but *Vṛhadratha* at beginning of next dynasty.

8 So Mt genly; eVā, 87.

9 So also Vṣ, Bh: eVā, 9.

10 But eVā, 'after them will be the Śuṅga'.

11 Or, 'the earth will go to the Śuṅgas'.

12 Vā, Bḍ, 60 years.

13 Vā, Bḍ, Vṣ, Bh *Sujyeṣṭha*.

14 Mt *Antaka*. Bḍ, Bh *Bhadra-ka*. Vṣ *Ārdraka*.

15 Vṣ *Ghoṣavasu*. Mt crp *Yomegha*.

16 Bḍ, 7 years. Vā no term.

17 Mt *Samābhāga* apptly, but text crp.

18 Vā *Kṣemabhūmi* here, but *Devabhūmi* in next dynasty.

Kāṇvāyanas (Śuṅgabhṛtyas).

The minister Vasudeva, forcibly overthrowing the dissolute king Devabhūmi because of his youth, will become king among the Śuṅgas[1]. He, the Kāṇvāyana, will be king 9 years[2]. His son Bhūmimitra will reign 14 years[3]. His son Nārāyaṇa will reign 12 years. His son Suśarman will reign 10 years[4].

These are remembered as the Śuṅgabhṛtya Kāṇvāyana kings. These 4 Kaṇva brahmans will enjoy the earth; for 45 years they will enjoy this earth. They will have the neighbouring kings in subjection and will be righteous. In succession to them the earth will pass to the Andhras.

Andhras.

The Andhra Simuka[5] with his fellow tribesmen, the servants of Suśarman, will assail the Kāṇvāyanas and him (Suśarman), and destroy the remains of the Śuṅgas' power and will obtain this earth. Simuka will be king 23 years. His younger brother Kṛṣṇa will next reign 10 years[6]. His son Śrī-Śātakarṇi will reign 10 years[7]. Then Pūrṇotsaṅga will be king 18 years[8]. Skandhastambhi will be king 18 years[8]. Śātakarṇi will reign 56 years; his son Lambodara 18 years[8]. His son Āpīlaka[9] will reign 12 *years*. Meghasvāti will reign 18 years[8]. Svāti will be king 18 years[10]. Skandasvāti will be king 7 years[8]. Mṛgendra Svātikarṇa will reign 3 years[8]. Kuntala Svātikarṇa will be king 8 years[8]. Svātivarṇa will be king one year[8]. Pulomāvi will reign 36 years[11]. Ariṣṭakarṇa[12] will reign 25 years. Then Hāla will be king 5 years[13]. Mantalaka[14] will be a powerful king 5 *years*. Purikaṣeṇa will reign 21 years[15]. Sundara Śātakarṇi will reign one year. Cakora Śātakarṇi will reign 6 months. Śivasvāti will reign 28 years. King Gautamīputra *will be* king next 21 years. His son Pulomā[16] will reign 28 *years*[8]. [Śātakarṇi will be king 29 years[17].] Śivaśrī Pulomā[18] will be king 7 *years*[8]. His son Śivaskandha Śātakarṇi will be king *three*[19] years[8]. Yajñaśrī Śātakarṇika will reign 29 years[20].

1 Mt, 'will become the Śauṅga king'.
2 Bḍ, 5 years.
3 Vā, Bḍ, 24 years.
4 Bḍ, 4 years.
5 This is the name emended. Mt *Śiśuka*. Vā, Bḍ *Sindhuka*. Vṣ *Śipraka*.
6 Mt, 18 years.
7 Vā, Bḍ, no number.
8 This sentence is not in Vā genly nor Bḍ.
9 Much variation in this name.
10 Or *Āti*, 12 years. Not in Vā, Bḍ.
11 Vā, Bḍ, 24 years. Much variation in this name.
12 Much variation in this name.
13 Vā, Bḍ, one year.
14 Or *Pattalaka*. Bh *Talaka*. Vā *Saptaka*.
15 Mt *Purīndrasena*, but no number.
16 Properly *Pulomāvi*.
17 A doubtful line found only in *e*Vā.
18 Or 'after Puloma Śivaśrī'.
19 Conjectural emendation; no number mentioned.
20 Vā, Bḍ, 19 years.

After him Vijaya will be king 6 years. His son Caṇḍaśrī Sātakarṇi will reign 10 years [1]. Another [2] of them Pulomāvi will reign 7 years.

These 30 Andhra kings [3] will enjoy the earth 460 years [4].

Various Local Dynasties.

When the kingdom of the Andhras has come to an end *there will be* kings belonging to the lineage of their servants: 7 Āndhras [5], and 10 Ābhīra kings; also 7 Gardabhins [6], 18 Śakas [7]. There will be 8 Yavanas, 14 Tuṣāras [8], 13 Muruṇḍas [9], 11 Maunas [10].

The Śrīparvatīya Āndhras will endure 52 years [11]; the 10 Ābhīra kings 67 years; the 7 Gardabhins will enjoy the earth 72 years [12]; the 18 Śakas [13] 183 years. The 8 Yavanas [13] will enjoy this earth 87 years [14]. The earth is remembered as belonging to the Tuṣāras 7000 years [15]. The 13 future Muruṇḍas [16] along with low caste men, *all* of Mleccha origin, will enjoy it half 400 years [17]. The 11 Maunas will enjoy it 103 years [18]. When they are overthrown by Time there will be Kilakila kings [19].

Then after the Kilakilas Vindhyaśakti [20] will reign. He will enter upon the earth after it has known *those kings* 96 years [21].

Dynasties of Vidiśā, &c.

Hear also the future kings of Vidiśā. Bhogin, son of the Nāga king Seṣa, will be king, conqueror of his enemies' cities [22], a king who will exalt the Nāga family. Sadācandra [23], and Candrāṁśa *who will be* a second Nakhavant [24], then Dhanadharman [25],

[1] Vā, Bḍ *Daṇḍaśrī*, 3 years.

[2] Or 'the last'.

[3] Mt, 19.

[4] Bḍ, 456; Vā crp, but apptly the same.

[5] Bh and Vṣ *Andhra-bhṛtyas.*

[6] Or *Gardabhilas.*

[7] Vā, Bḍ, 10. Bh, Vṣ, 16. Bh calls them *Kaṅkas.*

[8] Or *Tukhāras* or *Tuṣkaras.*

[9] Mt, Bḍ, Bh *Guruṇḍas.* Vṣ *Muṇḍas* (for *Muruṇḍas*).

[10] Vā genly, 18. Mt, 19 *Hūṇas.*

[11] Or possibly 'twice 50'. Vā, Bḍ crp but probably 112 or 102.

[12] Mt *Gardabhilas*, but no term.

[13] Vā and Bḍ no number.

[14] Vā and Bḍ, 82.

[15] Vā, Bḍ, 500; but prob 107 and 105 are meant respectively.

[16] See note [9].

[17] That is, 200 years; Vṣ, Bh say 199. Vā, Bḍ erroneously, 350.

[18] Mt *Hūṇas.*

[19] Vṣ says they were Yavanas.

[20] Vṣ says he was a Kilakila.

[21] This seems to be the meaning; but literally, 'he after having known 96 years will enter upon the earth'. But perhaps *sameṣyati* may mean 'he will come to an end' (= *saṁsthāsyati*, see p. 8, note [85]), for, though *sam-i* does not have that meaning, yet *samaya* has it. The sentence would then be, 'After having known the earth 96 years he will come to his end.'

[22] Vṣ treats the word *purañjaya* as his name.

[23] Vṣ *Rāmacandra.*

[24] Or 'Nakhapāna's offspring' in *e*Vā.

[25] Vṣ *Dharma.*

and Vaṅgara [1] is remembered as the fourth. Then Bhūtinanda will reign in the Vaidiśa *kingdom*.

When the family of the Śuṅgas [2] ends, Śiśunandi [3] will reign. His younger brother was named Nandiyaśas [4]. In his lineage there will be 3 kings. *His* daughter's son named Śiśuka was king in Purikā.

Vindhyaśakti's valiant son, named Pravīra, will enjoy the city Kāñcanakā 60 years, and will sacrifice with vājapeya sacrifices replete with choice largesse. His 4 sons will be kings.

Dynasties of the Third Century, A.D.

When the family of the Vindhyakas has passed away, there will be 3 Bāhlika kings. Supratīka and Nabhīra [5] will enjoy *the earth* 30 years. Śakyamāna [6] was king of the Mahiṣis. There will be 13 Puṣyamitras [7] *and* Paṭumitras [8]. In Mekalā 7 kings [9] will reign 70 years. In Kosalā there will be 9 very powerful and wise kings celebrated as 'Meghas'. All the kings of Niṣadha [10], born in the family of Nala, valiant and very powerful, will exist till the termination of the Manus [11]

Of the Māgadhas the king will be very valiant Viśvasphāṇi [12]. Overthrowing all kings he will make other castes *kings, namely*, Kaivartas, Pañcakas [13], Pulindas, and brahmans. He will establish those persons as kings in various countries. Viśvasphāṇi the magnificent *will be* mighty, Viṣṇu's peer in battle [14]. King Viśvasphāṇi is called eunuch-like in appearance. Overthrowing the kṣatriya caste he will create another kṣatriya caste. After gratifying the gods, the pitṛs and brahmans once *and* again, he will resort to the bank of the Ganges and subdue his body; after resigning his body he will go to Indra's world.

Contemporary Dynasties of the Early Fourth Century.

Nine Nāka [15] kings will enjoy the city Campāvatī; and 7 Nāgas will enjoy the charming city Mathurā. *Kings* born of the Gupta race will enjoy all these territories, *namely*, along the Ganges, Prayāga, Sāketa, and the Magadhas. *Kings* born from Maṇidhānya [16] will enjoy all these territories, *namely*, the Naiṣadhas, Yadukas, Śaiśītas [17], and Kālatoyakas. The Devarakṣitas will enjoy the Kośalas, Andhras [18],

[1] Bh *Vaṅgiri*. Vṣ *Varāṅga*. Vā *Viṁśaja*. Bḍ, 'born in the race'.
[2] Many Vā *Aṅgas*.
[3] Vṣ genly *Suṣinandi*. Vā *Madhun°*.
[4] Bh *Yaśonandi*.
[5] Bḍ *Gabhīra*.
[6] Bḍ *Śaṅkamāna*.
[7] Or *Puṣpamitras*. Bh names one of them as *Durmitra*.
[8] Vṣ adds *Padmamitras*.
[9] Bh says *Andhras*.
[10] Bh calls them 'lords of Vaidūra' also.
[11] Or perhaps, 'as long as Manu's race'.
[12] Bh *Viśvasphūrji*. Vṣ *Viśvasphaṭika*.
[13] Bḍ *Madrakas*. Vṣ *Yadus*. Bh both.
[14] Bh says his city will be Padmavatī.
[15] So Vā; but Bḍ, Vṣ *Nāgas*.
[16] Vṣ *Maṇidhāra*.
[17] Or *Śaiśījas* or *Śaiśikas*. Vṣ *Naimiṣikas*.
[18] Vṣ *Odras*.

and Pauṇḍras, the Tāmraliptas and coast-folk and the charming city Campā [1]. Guha will protect all these territories, *namely*, the Kaliṅgas, Mahiṣas, and the inhabitants of the Mahendra mountains. He who is named Kanaka will enjoy Strīrāṣṭra [2] and the Bhokṣyakas [3]. The Saurāṣṭras, Āvantyas and Ābhīras, the Śūdras [4], Arbudas and Mālavas [5], *there* the kings will be outcaste dvijas and non-dvijas, mostly śūdras. Śūdras, outcaste dvijas and others, and Mlecchas destitute of Vedic holiness will enjoy the Sindhu's bank, the Candrabhāgā, Kauntī [6] and the Kāśmīra realm.

All these kings will be contemporaneous, niggards in graciousness, untruthful, very irascible and unrighteous.

Evils of the Kali Age.

There will be Yavanas here by reason of religious feeling *or* ambition *or* plunder; they will not be kings solemnly anointed, but will follow evil customs by reason of the corruption of the age. Massacring women and children [7] and killing one another, kings will enjoy the earth at the end of the Kali age. Kings of continual upstart races, falling as soon as they arise, will exist in succession through Fate. They will be destitute of righteousness, affection, *and* wealth. Mingled with them *will be* Ārya and Mleccha folk everywhere [8]: they prevail in turn; the population will perish.

Chronological and Astronomical Particulars.

All the Purāṇas.

When the moon and the sun and the constellation Tiṣya and Bṛhaspati shall come together in the same zodiacal sign, then may the Kṛta age be.

This is the entire series of genealogies which has been declared in due order—the kings who have passed away, and those who exist *now*, and those who are future.

Now from Mahāpadma's [9] inauguration to Parikṣit's birth, this *interval* is indeed known as 1050 years [10]. Moreover in the interval which *elapsed* from the *last* Andhra *king* Pulomāvi to Mahāpadma—that interval *was* 836 years. An equal space of time *is still* future; subsequent *kings* beginning from the end of the

[1] Vṣ *Samudrataṭa-purī*.
[2] Or *Strīrājya*.
[3] Bḍ *Bhojakas*. Vṣ *Mūṣikas*.
[4] Or *Śūras*.
[5] Vṣ *Marubhūmi*.
[6] Vṣ *Dārvikorvī* in various forms.
[7] Bh adds 'cattle and brahmans'; and says 'they will ravish other people's wives and riches'. Vṣ similarly.
[8] Vṣ adds 'they will be audacious through royal support'.
[9] Bḍ *Mahānandī*. Vṣ, Bh *Nanda*. Vā *Mahādeva*.
[10] Vṣ, Bh, 1015 years.

Andhras are declared *therein*. They have been enumerated in the Bhaviṣya *Purāṇa* by śrutarṣis who knew the ancient stories.

The Great Bear [1] *was situated* equally with regard to *the lunar constellation* Puṣya [2] while Pratīpa [3] was king. At the end of the Andhras, who will be in the 27th century *afterwards*, the cycle repeats *itself* [4]. In the circle of the lunar constellations, wherein the Great Bear revolves [5], and which contains 27 *constellations* in its circumference [6], the Great Bear remains 100 years in (*i.e.* conjoined with) each in turn. This is the Cycle of the Great Bear, *and is* remembered *as being*, according to divine reckoning, 6 divine months and 7 divine years. According to those *constellations* divine time proceeds by means of the Great Bear. The two front stars of the Great Bear, which are seen when risen at night [7], the lunar constellation which is seen *situated* equally between them in the sky [8], the Great Bear is to be known as conjoined with that constellation 100 years in the sky. This is the exposition of the conjunction of the lunar constellations and the Great Bear. The Great Bear was conjoined with the Maghās in Parīkṣit's time 100 years. It will be in (*i.e.* conjoined with) the 24th constellation [9] 100 years at the termination of the Andhras.

Viṣṇu and Bhāgavata.

The Great Bear was in (*i.e.* conjoined with) the Maghās in Parīkṣit's time; then began the Kali age comprising 1200 *divine* years [10]. When the portion of the lord Viṣṇu, which was born in Vasudeva's family and named Kṛṣṇa, went to heaven, then the Kali age set in. As long as he touched the earth with his lotus-feet, so long the Kali age could not encompass the earth. When that portion of the eternal Viṣṇu had departed from earth to heaven, Dharma's son Yudhiṣṭhira with his younger brothers relinquished his kingdom. That Pāṇḍava, beholding the adverse omens when Kṛṣṇa had departed, performed Parīkṣit's inauguration. When the Great Bear will pass from the Maghās to Pūrvā Āṣāḍhā, then, starting from Nanda [11], this Kali age will attain its magnitude.

1 Called the 'Seven Rishis'.

2 Or 'was in (i.e. conjoined with) Puṣya 100 years'. These readings are emendations, see p. 59, note 46.

3 Ancestor of Parīkṣit in the seventh degree, see JRAS, 1910, p. 28.

4 This statement read with the preceding statements would imply that some 814 years are allowed for the interval between Pratīpa and Parīkṣit: thus Pratīpa to Parīkṣit 814 years, Parīkṣit to Mahāpadma Nanda 1050 years, Mahāpadma to the last Andhra king 836 years—total 2700 years. Thus the period from Pratīpa to the end of the Andhras comprised a complete cycle of the Great Bear, and then the cycle began again.

5 So Mt: explained in subsequent statements.

6 So Vā, Bḍ.

7 Or 'in the sky'; or 'in the northern region'.

8 That is, according to the commentators, 'the constellation which is situated equally on a line drawn south and north between the two front stars (the two Pointers) of the Great Bear'.

9 Apptly, either no. 24 in the order of reckoning the lunar constellations, or the 24th after the Maghās.

10 Including the twilights.

11 That is, the Great Bear was conjoined with Pūrvā Āṣāḍhā in Mahāpadma Nanda's time.

All the Purāṇas.

On the very day, on which Kṛṣṇa departed to heaven, the Kali age arrived. Hear its reckoning. It is remembered by the wise, as computed according to human reckoning, to be 360,000 years [1] or 1000 divine years. Then the twilight sets in. When that is completely finished, the Kṛta age will then arrive.

[1] Mt, 460,000 years.

APPENDIX I

The Account was originally in Prakrit.

Proof is offered here of the statement made in the Introduction, § 15, that the Sanskrit account as it stands in the Matsya, Vāyu, and Brahmāṇḍa is a Sanskritized version of older Prakrit ślokas, as indicated by these peculiarities: *first*, certain passages violate the śloka metre, whereas in Prakrit form they would satisfy the metre; *secondly*, certain Prakrit forms actually occur, especially where they are required by the metre, which the corresponding Sanskrit forms would violate; *thirdly*, Sanskrit words occur at times in defiance of syntax, whereas the corresponding Prakrit forms would make the construction correct; *fourthly*, mistaken Sanskritization of names and words; *fifthly*, the copious use of expletive particles; *sixthly*, irregular sandhi. Those three Purāṇas will be dealt with first, and along with them such portions also of the Bhāgavata and Viṣṇu as have preserved the old ślokas uncondensed; but the main portions of these two Purāṇas consist almost entirely of a condensed redaction, and their character will be considered afterwards.

i. As an illustration of the first peculiarity, the Mt and Vā [1], when naming the last Paurava king, end the line thus (p. 7)—*Nirāmitrāt tu* (or *ca*) *Kṣemakaḥ*, 'after Nirāmitra was Kṣemaka'; where the *tu* or *ca* in the fifth syllable should be short but is long by position before *kṣ*. No one composing in Skt could end a śloka line with *Kṣemaka*, but its Pkt form *Khemaka* satisfies the metre perfectly. There can be no doubt therefore that this line was composed in Pkt originally, and that the Skt redactor restored the Pkt name to its Skt form and in so doing overlooked the fact that the change violated the metre. The fault was however noticed afterwards, because *e*Vā corrects it by altering the half line to *bhavitā Kṣemakas tathā* (p. 7, note [71]). Precisely similar is the mistake in the line that ends with *samā bhokṣyanti triṁśatim* [2], where no difficulty would occur in Pkt since *triṁśati* would drop its *r* there [3].

Again the Mt reads at the end of a śloka line, *aṣṭāviṁśatir Haihayāḥ* [4], where the fifth syllable is long by position contrary to rule; and here the literary Pkt form *visati* without a termination would fit the metre. The Vā and Bḍ read instead *caturviṁśat* (or *-viṁśas*) *tu Haihayāḥ* and avoid the irregularity by reducing *viṁśati*

[1] The Bḍ has lost this line in a large lacuna.

[2] P. 50 (*Dynasties of the 3rd Cent.*), l. 2; the differences of reading there do not affect this point.

[3] The phrase *ā-Manu-kṣayāt* in the Vā and Bḍ at the end of a line (p. 51, l. 8) does not militate against this view, because the *kṣ* in the middle of this expression would have been *kkh* in Pkt.

[4] P. 23, l. 4: *b*Mt avoids the fault by reading *aṣṭāviṁśati*, keeping as near to Pkt as possible.

to *viṁśat* or *viṁśa* and replacing the lost syllable by a superfluous *tu*, which is the nearest approach to it. This expedient is very common as will be seen in the notes.

Next may be cited cases where a half line has a syllable too much, which would disappear in Pkt, and the significance of these cases lies in the fact that the superfluity was unnecessary since good Skt equivalents were available, if the verse had been composed directly in Skt. Thus the Bh has a śloka prophesying Viṣṇu's incarnation as Kalki thus—

dharma-trāṇāya sattvena Bhagavān avatariṣyati [1].

The second half line has a syllable too much, but the Pkt verb *otarissati* would exactly suit the metre and was no doubt the word used originally, as *d*Bh (an old MS of 1407) shows by reading *Bhagavān vatariṣyati*, where *n* and *va* are separate letters. Many two-syllabled equivalents for *bhagavān* were available to suit the metre. Again *e*Vā has for the first half of a line, *sapta varṇaṇi Devadharmā* [2], where *varṇaṇi* is obviously a misreading of *varṣāṇi*, and there is a syllable too much; but the Pkt form *varṣā* or *vassā* satisfies the metre. To one composing in Skt *samāḥ* would have avoided all difficulty. Similarly *b*Mt has the first half of a line, *aṣṭāvimśati tathā varṣā* with a syllable too much [3], but the Pkt *aṭṭhāvīsaṁ* would rectify the metre; whereas one composing in Skt could have written simply *aṣṭāviṁśati-varṣāṇi*, which is indeed the general reading of the Mt now. This instance may give us an insight into the process of Sanskritization, if, as the *b*Mt reading suggests, the original Pkt was *aṭṭhāvīsaṁ tathā vassā*.

ii. Actual Pkt forms occur rather often. First may be cited the Vā and Bḍ line [4]—

sthāpayiṣyati rājāno nānā-deśeṣu te janā:

where *rājāno* and *te janā* are Pkt accusatives after the verb. They were misunderstood as nominatives, and the verb was altered to the plural in all copies of the Vā except *e*Vā, and in the Bḍ. Similarly the Bh introduces the Bārhadratha dynasty with the old line [5]—

atha Māgadha-rājāno bhavitāro vadāmi te.

Here *rājāno* and *bhavitāro* are accusatives, hence the line is not Skt but is actually good Pali. *Br*Bh correct the faults by altering *bhavitāro* to *bhāvino ye*. Again the Mt has a half line *prasahya hy avanīṁ nṛpaḥ* in many copies, and *prasahya vyasanī nṛpam* in some copies, while the corresponding reading of the Vā and Bḍ is *bālyād vyasaninaṁ nṛpam* [6]. The Mt reading should evidently be *prasahya vyasanīṁ nṛpam*, and points to a Pkt original something like *pasajjha* (or *pasayha*) *vasanīṁ* [7] *napam*; but this when Sanskritized became *prasahya vyasaninaṁ nṛpam* with a syllable too much, and so was adjusted in two ways, (1) the half-Pkt form *vyasanīṁ* was used as an accus. in many copies and became corrupted to *hy avanīṁ*; or (2) the half line was emended to *prasahya vyasanāturam* in some copies. The Vā and Bḍ may have substituted *bālyād* (or *balād* ?) for *prasahya* to rectify the metre.

Next may be cited a number of actual Pkt or half-Pkt words. All such forms cannot be deemed original, because the copyists, who were not always sufficiently literate, did write Pkt forms sometimes instead of Skt forms, but such deviations are

[1] Bh xii, *2*, 16; omitted from p. 57.
[2] P. 29, l. 11, and note [38].
[3] P. 19, note [28].
[4] P. 52, l. 13 and notes.
[5] P. 14, note [1].
[6] P. 33, note [2].
[7] This would be the correct accus. in Pkt, see Pischel's Prakrit Grammar, § 405.

trivial and obvious mistakes [1]. It is different however when the Pkt forms violate grammar or sandhi, or suit the metre, and such are these—*uccādayitvā* (p. 53, note [52]), *mahāyaśāḥ* as a nomin. plural [2] (p. 51, note [25]) and *varṣā* (see p. 78). There are also instances of the Pkt genit. plural in °*āna* (p. 35, note [41]), and of its blending with *ante* into °*ān*:*ânte*, namely *kulānânte* (p. 50, note [2]) and *Andhrāṇânte* (p. 59, notes [51, 54]; p. 61, note [92]). Other words appear to be Pkt survivals and not copyists' errors, such as *aṭṭitriṁśat* (p. 19, note [41]), *athôchādya* (p. 34, note [3]), *teṣûcchanneṣu* (p. 48, note [82]), *samā* for *samās* before *tasmāt* in Vā genly (p. 34, note [18]), and *Aśakāḥ* in Vā and Bḍ (p. 24, note [15]). In an old verse *l*Bh has *papannān uhariṣyati* (p. 26, note [36]), which seems more than a mere clerical error. Mistakes precisely like these are found in Buddhist Skt.

The Bhāgavata has an old verse—

> yasmin Kṛṣṇo divaṁ yātas tasminn eva tadâhani
> pratipannaṁ Kaliyugaṁ iti prāhuḥ purāvidaḥ.

The Mt, Vā, Bḍ, and Vṣ all have this verse, but read the last half line *tasya saṅkhyāṁ nibodhata* or in equivalent words [3]. The Bh reading appears to be the oldest version, because its verse is complete in itself and is obviously an old saying, whereas the last half line in the other authorities was evidently substituted to connect this statement with the following verse when this collective account was drawn up: the reverse is hardly credible. Further, one old Bh MS (*d*Bh, dated 1407) reads *iti-r-āhuḥ purāvidaḥ*, and this with its euphonic Pkt *r* is no doubt the original form, which in the process of Sanskritization was amended to *iti prāhuḥ* as in all the other Bh copies; here also the reverse is hardly credible. *Iti-r-āhuḥ* is the Pkt *iti-r-āhu* [4]. There are one or two other instances of an *r* inserted, which seems to be euphonic [5]; and it may possibly be that the final *r* in the nominatives of numerals is sometimes as much a euphonic Pkt *r* as a Skt *r* by sandhi [6].

Similarly no doubt are to be explained the Bḍ reading of p. 62, l. 40 and the Vā readings in note [31] thereto. The reading in literary Pkt would have been something like *vassāna uccate Kali* or rather *vassāna-r-uccate Kali*. Turned into Skt, *varṣāṇām ucyate Kaliḥ* was good and sufficient, yet notwithstanding, the desire for an expedient to prevent the hiatus persisted in the Sanskritization, for *m*Vā has preserved the euphonic *r*, and *bdfg*Vā inserted *tu* instead. These were no doubt the original forms of the Sanskritizations, but it was perceived that no such expedient was wanted, hence most copies of the Vā dropped it. The reverse is not credible.

Most common is the use of numerals with the Pkt freedom from case-terminations, as well as only half Sanskritized, such as—*aṣṭāśīti* and *aṣṭāsiti* [7], and *viṁśati* often both in the text and in the notes. Some of these instances might be due to the carelessness of copyists in omitting visarga or anusvāra, but that does not account for all such peculiarities, since they are found in carefully written MSS and are sometimes obligatory for the sake of the metre. Thus the Vā and Bḍ read as the last half line of a śloka, *aṣṭāviṁśati Maithilāḥ* [8], and this was no doubt the

[1] *E.g.* see p. 2, note [16]; p. 43, note [27]: and these are found even in Bh MSS, see p. 46, note [27].

[2] This is possible only in Pkt and does actually occur, see Pischel, *op. cit.* § 409.

[3] P. 62, ll. 37, 38 and notes.

[4] See Pischel's Prakrit Grammar, §§ 353, 518.

[5] See *hatva-r* in p. 38, note [2].

[6] As in p. 43, l. 36, where the accusative would be proper.

[7] P. 25, l. 5 and note [17].

[8] P. 24, l. 6.

original reading because *fg*Mt have it also; but the Mt has generally altered *viṁśati* to *viṁśās* (or °*śat* or °*śa*) *tu*. The Skt form *viṁśatir* would violate the metre, and the Mt has avoided the difficulty of Sanskritization by substituting *tu* for the final syllable. This is the converse of the first irregularity noticed above (p. 78), and many similar instances of *tu* substituted for a final *ti* will be found in the notes.

iii. Of the third class of peculiarities the following are instances. As the last half line of a śloka the Vā and Bḍ have in one place *varṣāṇi bhavitā trayaḥ* [1], and in another *tasya putraḥ samās trayaḥ* [2]; and the Mt has in another place *bhaviṣyati samās trayaḥ* [3]. In all these passages grammatical concord is violated, because (1) these are accus. expressions denoting duration of time, and (2) *varṣāṇi* is neuter, *samās* feminine, and *trayaḥ* masculine and nomin.; but, if the Pkt *tao* be substituted for *trayaḥ*, concord is established, because *tao* is both nomin. and accus. in all three genders [4], and the metre also is satisfied. Such expressions could not have been composed in Skt originally. There can be no doubt that they were originally in Pkt and that, when the verses were Sanskritized, the exigencies of metre induced the redactor to convert *tao* into *trayaḥ*, because the correct equivalents *trīṇi* and *tisraḥ* would not suit the metre [5].

The same fault occurs in places where metre was not at stake. Thus all three Purāṇas read *catvāriṁśat trayaś caiva* as the first half of a line [6], where *samās* or *varṣāṇī* is implied and *trayas* is wrong as regards both gender and case. *C*Vā attempts to rectify the discord by reading *trayam*. Similarly in another passage the Mt has *samās trīṇy evaṁ*, while the Vā and Bḍ read *samās tisra eva* [7]. It is impossible to suppose that these wrong expressions were composed originally in Skt, and they are intelligible as perfunctory Sanskritizations of Pkt expressions containing the numeral *tao*, or *tiṇṇi* which also is of all three genders [8]. Similarly we find the phrase *ṣaṣṭy-uttara-śata-trayam* used with *varṣāṇi* in the Bḍ and with *samāḥ* in the Bh [9]. Other instances are *saptaṣaṣṭis tu varṣāṇi* [10], and *aṣṭāśitis tu varṣāṇi* [11], where the case is wrong; *ye cānye Mleccha-jātayaḥ* [12] which *e*Vā has corrected to *yāś cānyā*°; and perhaps *divyābdāni* [13] where the correct *divyābdās* was as easy as in the Bḍ.

iv. Some forms of names look strange as Skt but are readily intelligible if they are mistaken Sanskritizations of Pkt forms. Thus the name *Śiśunāga* as found in the Bḍ, Vṣ, and Bh appears as *Śiśunāka* in the Mt and Vā [14]. *Śiśunāga* as Pkt might naturally be Sanskritized as *Śiśunāka*, because a Pkt *g* often represents a Skt *k*: otherwise it is difficult to see how the form *Śiśunāka* could have arisen. Similarly *e*Vā has *Śuṅka* and *Śaṅka* for *Śuṅga* [15]; *eka-kṣatro* appears instead of *eka-cchatro*, and *eka-kṣatrām* instead of *eka-cchattrām* [16].

[1] P. 32, l. 8. The Mt reads correctly *trīṇi varṣāṇi*.

[2] P. 43, l. 32. The Mt reads differently, *samā daśa*.

[3] P. 40, l. 15. The Vā and Bḍ omit this, except *e*Vā which alters it to *samā-trayam*.

[4] Pischel's Prakrit Grammar, § 438.

[5] Unless he recast the line, which was obviously not attempted, except by Mt in the first instance, see note [1].

[6] P. 22, l. 14 and notes.

[7] P. 32, l. 7; but *dfgjm*Mt alter it to *tisro vai*.

[8] Pischel's Prakrit Grammar, § 438.

[9] P. 22, note [46].

[10] P. 46, l. 7.

[11] P. 25, note [17].

[12] P. 3, l. 11 and note [37].

[13] P. 60, l. 16 and note [70].

[14] P. 21, ll. 1, 3; p. 22, ll. 15, 17; and notes thereto.

[15] P. 30, note [50]; p. 32, note [47]; p. 49, note [17].

[16] P. 25, l. 4 and notes [14, 15].

In this class may be mentioned certain incorrect forms: thus the Vā generally reads *caturas* instead of *catvāras* in p. 34, l. 7 (note [20]), where the Pkt *caüro* may have been used as a nomin. though it is strictly accus.[1] So the Mt generally has *catvāriṁśad* instead of *catvāraś ca* (or *tu*), which would be an intelligible mistake if the Pkt was *cattāri ca*, for *cattāri* though neuter was often used as masculine [2]. The plural verb *bhokṣyanti* instead of the dual in p. 50 (*Dynasties of the 3rd Cent.*), l. 2, would be correct in Pkt but not in Skt.

Vernacular names had to be Sanskritized and so developed strange forms; compare for instance *Śimuka* in p. 38, note [17], and other Andhra names.

Attention may also be drawn to p. 59, l. 11, where all the divergent readings are obviously attempts to Sanskritize one and the same original Pkt statement that was puzzling.

v. The fifth class of peculiarities is a very noticeable feature of these texts, namely, the copious use of particles as mere expletives, such as *tu*, *hi*, *ca*, *vai*, &c., and especially *tu*. The lines in which two such particles occur are too numerous to be mentioned, but three and even four are sometimes found in a single line, and the following lines are cited as most illustrative:—

bhavitā câpi Sujyeṣṭhaḥ sapta varṣāṇi vai tataḥ [3]
Svātiś ca bhavitā rājā samās tv aṣṭādaśaiva tu [4]
Śivaśrīr vai Pulomā tu saptaiva bhavitā nṛpaḥ [5]
sapta Gardabhinaś câpi tato 'tha daśa vai Śakāḥ [6]
trayodaśa Muruṇḍāś ca Maunā hy ekādaśaiva tu [7]
saptaṣaṣtis tu varṣāṇi daś-Âbhīrās tathaiva ca [8]
śatāni trīṇy aśītiṁ ca Śakā hy aṣṭādaśaiva tu [9]
Pulomās tu tath-Ândhrās tu Mahāpadmântare punaḥ [10].

One cannot imagine that these verses were composed originally either in Skt or in Pkt with so many expletives, when the authors could easily have improved their verses by employing appropriate words denoting 'reign' or 'exist' or 'relationship'. No one composing in Skt would mar his verse and proclaim his literary poverty by such shifts; but these blemishes are readily intelligible, if the verses were originally in Pkt as chronicles of the past and were converted into Skt prophecies. Future tenses are longer than past tenses, and if they could not be fitted into the place of the past tenses, it would have been natural to substitute expletives. Thus it may be conjectured that the second, fifth, sixth, and seventh lines ended originally with a past verb corresponding to *abhavat* or *abhavan*. Again, Pkt forms are sometimes longer than their Skt equivalents, and the substitution of the latter would have been compensated for by adding an expletive; thus in the third line *Śivaśrīr vai* no doubt stands for the Pkt *Sivasiri*, and in the eighth line *Pulomās tu tath-Ândhrās tu* probably mean the ablat. case and stood originally something like *Pulomādo tath-Ândhrādo*, or *Pulomamhā tath-Ândhramhā*.

It has been noticed above (pp. 78, 80) that the particle *tu* is used sometimes to compensate for the loss of the final syllable of *viṁśati* and *triṁśati*. When the full forms of these words vitiated the metre, they were reduced sometimes to *viṁśat*

[1] Pischel's Prakrit Grammar, § 439.
[2] P. 35, note [22]. Pischel, § 439.
[3] P. 31, l. 4, Vā and Bd.
[4] P. 40, l. 13, Mt.
[5] P. 42, l. 29, Mt and *e*Vā.
[6] P. 45, note [11], Vā and Bd.
[7] P. 46, l. 5, Vā and Bd.
[8] P. 46, l. 7, Mt.
[9] P. 46, l. 9, Mt.
[10] P. 58, l. 7, Mt.

or *viṁśa*, and *triṁśat* or *triṁśa* and the lost syllable was replaced by an expletive *tu*. This expedient is very common and many instances of it will be found in the notes. Indeed it is hardly too much to say that the occurrence of *tu* throughout the account, if not required by euphony (see next para.), almost certainly indicates a lost syllable, and in many cases *tu* in the Mt and *e*Vā has been altered to *ca* in the Vā and Bḍ as an improvement. Other instances of compensatory expletives may be surmised in the notes, such as these—*Suṣeṇaś c-Ântarikṣāc ca* (p. 10, l. 13) is hardly explainable unless the second *ca* has replaced the lost syllable of the Pkt ablative; and *Dharminaḥ sa* (p. 11, l. 15) no doubt stands instead of the Pkt genitive *Dharminassa*.

The use of expletives was however carried beyond necessary requirements, and they are often inserted merely to prevent two vowels from coming together, as *tv* in the second of the above-cited lines, and *hy* in the fifth and seventh lines. Skt sandhi did not require this device, but it is intelligible in Pkt. This superfluity is found in the Bh also, where it has not condensed the older ślokas, as in *śūdra-prāyās tv adhārmikāḥ* (p. 25, l. 3).

vi. The instances of irregular sandhi may be divided into two classes; *first*, those in which the form it takes resembles Pkt sandhi and is unnecessary, because regular Skt sandhi would have been proper and sufficient; and *secondly*, those in which it consists of double sandhi in order to contract the words for the metre.

Of the first class may be cited *varṣāṇi 'kārayat* instead of *varṣāṇy akārayat* (p. 15, note [29]); *trīṇi 'śītiś* for *trīṇy aśītiś* (p. 46, note [48]); *Daśarathâṣṭau* instead of *Daśaratho 'ṣṭau* (p. 28, note [5]); and *Agnimitrâṣṭau* for *Agnimitro 'ṣṭau* (p. 31, note [10]). Such sandhi can be explained through Pkt, and it is difficult to understand how any one composing in Skt could have adopted it; nor is it probable as a copyist's error.

The second class is commoner, and we find—*bhaviṣyâṣṭau* for *bhaviṣyāḥ aṣṭau* (p. 5, l. 10); *bhaviṣyôdayanas* for *bhaviṣyaḥ Udayanas* (p. 7, l. 23); *Yavanâṣṭau* for *Yavanāḥ aṣṭau* (p. 45, l. 4; p. 47, l. 10); and *bhāvyânyāḥ* for *bhāvyāḥ anyāḥ* (p. 47, l. 13). Here ordinary sandhi would have given a superfluous syllable, and the double sandhi rectifies the metre; but the significance of it is that it was easily avoidable in Skt, because the first two phrases might have been written *bhāvino 'ṣṭau* and *bhavit-Ôdayanas*. The simplest explanation seems to be, that the conversion of the Pkt past tense into the Skt future was made perfunctorily, and overloaded the verse with a superfluous syllable which was adjusted by the double sandhi. The third phrase would have been *Yonā aṭṭha* in Pkt, and the Sanskritization of *Yonā* into *Yavanāḥ* produced the difficulty of the extra syllable. Attempts at improvement were made; see p. 45, note [16]. There are many similar instances, such as *tatôtsādya* and *tatôtpāṭya* (p. 34, notes [3, 5]); *atôddhṛtya* and *tatôdhṛtya* (p. 38, note [4]).

Crasis of this kind is ordinarily explained as *ārṣa-sandhi*, but this explanation is manifestly untenable here [1]. All these irregularities are readily intelligible on the two suppositions, that Pkt words were converted into their Skt equivalents, and that past tenses were changed to futures, with the metrical difficulties that naturally ensued.

vii. All these peculiarities are found in the Mt, Vā, and Bḍ throughout, and show that their version must have been composed originally in Pkt ślokas and that the ślokas were Sanskritized for incorporation in the Bhaviṣya, from which the Mt

[1] In the Purāṇas what is called *ārṣa-sandhi* is really Prakrit sandhi; see p. 20, note [2].

and Vā confessedly, and the Bḍ impliedly, borrowed their accounts (see Introdn. § 7). The Prakritisms which have been cited are not mere casual variations, for such might be due to the ignorance or carelessness of copyists, but have an important *raison d'être* in the verse in many cases. The same conclusion holds good for the Vṣ and Bh in the passages where they have preserved the old śloka form.

viii. The main part of the Viṣṇu account is in prose and, not being affected by the exigencies of metre, runs in ordinary Skt, and displays no verbal peculiarities. It contains the same matter found in the Vā and Bḍ but in a condensed shape, and closes its account where they end, so that it must have been composed directly in Skt from them or their original, the revised version in the Bhaviṣya, for it is not probable that its account was a new and independent compilation, when the compilations in those Purāṇas were available. A difference may be noticed in its account to this extent that the dynastic matter is generally narrated in curt sentences, often without regard for sandhi [1], and that the subsequent matter of the evils of the Kali age is in ordinary good prose Skt with a predilection for compound phrases. Hence it would seem that the dynastic portion was an earlier and somewhat crude condensation, and that the latter portion was an addition made with regard to the canons of good prose.

ix. The Bhāgavata account, which is mainly a condensation, is evidently a later redaction. Peculiarities of the kinds noticed above do not appear therein, but it is in good Sanskrit, and phrases occur in it which indicate that it must have been composed directly in Skt. Two are especially significant. A śloka line ends with the words *ekādaśa kṣitim* (p. 48, note [77]), where the *śa* is long by position before *kṣ* as it should be, but would not have been long in Pkt in which *kṣ* would have become *kh*; so that this line must have been composed in Skt and not in Pkt. Similarly another line ends *iti śrutaḥ* (p. 32, note [45]), where the second *i* is long by position in Skt but would not have been so in Pkt.

x. The Garuḍa has no Prakritisms except in some of the names, and these are too uncertain a basis on which to argue, for those Prakritisms might be original or might be due to the carelessness of copyists, yet one name certainly seems somewhat suggestive [2]. All that is clear is that its account is the last and concisest redaction, that it was probably composed afresh in Skt, and that it makes frequent use of the termination *ka* for the sake of the metre. Its treatment of the name Adhisīmakṛṣṇa suggests that it was composed from a bare list of kings, for it divides the name into two, *Adhiśīma + ka* (ending one line) and *Kṛṣṇa* (beginning the next line) [3]—which seems inexplicable unless it had only a prose list and chopped the names up into groups for each line.

[1] As in p. 18, note [7]; p. 30, note [46]; and in these curt sentences *tasyâpi Aśoka-vardhanaḥ, tataś ca Ariṣṭakarmā*, and *tasmāt Yajñaśrīḥ*.

[2] *Dṛḍhasenaka* appears as *Daṭhasenaka* in *ab*Gr, which may be a faulty Sanskritization of the Pkt *Daḍhasena + ka*, though it might also be the form of that name in one kind of Pkt; see p. 16, note [75].

[3] See p. 4, note [10].

APPENDIX II

The Oldest Scripts used in the Account.

Mistakes are found in the MSS, which can, it seems, be only explained satisfactorily by supposing that they arose out of misreadings of the ancient scripts (see Introdn. § 26). Some mistakes are obviously mere clerical blunders, but others cannot be accounted for naturally in that way. Kharoṣṭhī being the oldest Indian script that we know of, mistakes that could be traced to misreadings of its letters would be most significant. Such instances may singly be open to some distrust, but collectively they would have cumulative force; and without pronouncing a positive opinion, it does yet seem to me that certain misreadings do point to Kharoṣṭhī as their source. Such mistakes may prevail in many MSS, if they passed undetected from the beginning; otherwise they may only occur in single MSS, having been corrected in all the others.

i. First may be cited an instance from the Vṣ, because it affords the best illustration of a misreading that seems significant, though the Vṣ does not contain the oldest version. It calls Aśoka generally Aśokavardhana, but *k*Vṣ has *Ayośoka-vardhana* (p. 28, note [28]). Here *yo* is obviously a misreading of *śo*; the copyist read the *śo* as *yo* and wrote *yo*, then he (or some one else) perceived the mistake and wrote or inserted *śo* in the copy, but the *yo* was not cancelled and the erroneous name *Ayośoka* remained and was repeated till it appears in *k*Vṣ. Now *śo* could not be mistakenly read as *yo* in any Indian script except Kharoṣṭhī, and in that *śo* and *yo* were often written so much alike, that it is very difficult at times to say merely from the shape which letter was meant. Hence it seems reasonably certain that this passage in the Viṣṇu must have been originally taken from a Kharoṣṭhī MS. Had this mistake occurred in verse, the extra syllable would probably have been detected and the error corrected, but there was no such check in the prose of the Vṣ, and the mistake might have been followed in one copy (from which was descended *k*Vṣ) though rectified in others.

Other misreadings of *ś* and *y* occur, namely—*Ayoda* for *Aśoka* in *l*Mt [1], where the second misreading of *k* as *d* might have arisen later in the Gupta script [2]; *Māgadhéśo* in *j*Mt [3] where the more general readings are *Māgadhā ye*, *Māgadho yo* or *Māgadheya*; *Koyāla* in *cg*Vṣ [4] for *Kośala*, where *yā* might easily be read for *śa* because Kharoṣṭhī often did not distinguish between long and short vowels; and *Śāliyūka* in *e*Vā for *Śāliśūka* [5]; *Mauryā dayo daśa* in *l*Vṣ [6], where *daśa* was probably first misread and written as *daya*, which was afterwards amended so as to read *Maury-ádayo* incorrectly.

ii. Some similar variations seem to point to the same conclusion. The Mt

[1] P. 27, note [3].

[2] See Bühler's Ind. Palaeog., Table IV, cols. xxi, xxiii, and Table V, cols. viii, ix.

[3] P. 14, note [1].

[4] P. 54, note [20]. Koyāla is an error in writing, different from *Koj'ala* which was a variation of *Kauśalya* in pronunciation; see Actes du XIVe Congrès International des Orientalistes, Alger, 1905, p. 217.

[5] P. 29, note [37].

[6] P. 30, note [46].

reading, *Kāśeyās*, appears in *dj*Mt as *Kāleyās*; and the mistake of *l* for *ś* seems best explainable by their similarity in Kharoṣṭhī. The Vā and Bḍ read *Kālakās*, which is probably a similar misreading of the equivalent name *Kāśakās*[1].

iii. Two other letters which might be confused in Kharoṣṭhī but not in any other script are *k* and *bh*, and there are some variations which seem to have so originated. The Vā generally, and the Mt sometimes, have *Tuṅga* instead of *Śuṅga*[2], a misreading the cause of which is not clear[3], but the name *Śuṅgabhṛtya* is generally corrupted to *Tuṅgakṛtya* in the Vā, while *e*Vā alone among the Vā MSS has preserved it nearly right as *Śuṅgavṛtya*[4]. Here it seems certain that *bh* was misread as *k* in a Kharoṣṭhī MS. The converse appears to be the cause of the faulty Mt reading in p. 41, line 22, where *saumyo bhaviṣyati*, with no mention of the length of the reign, seems to be a misreading of the Vā and Bḍ reading *so 'py eka-viṁśatiṁ*, for, while *saumyo* might be a later mistake and emendation for *sopye*, *bhaviṣyati* could be a misreading of *ka-viṁśati* in Kharoṣṭhī only. The two forms would be *bhavissati* and *ka-vīsati* in Pali and probably also in literary Pkt, and these two would be almost identical in Kharoṣṭhī which generally wrote long and short vowels alike and doubled letters as single.

iv. As regards Brāhmī, I have not found any variations of importance which can be assigned definitely to misreadings of it, and there is not the same scope for detecting such errors, because there is more resemblance between Brāhmī and Gupta letters than between them and Kharoṣṭhī. All the mistakes that I have detected, which might be attributed to misreadings of Brāhmī letters, might equally well, or even better, be attributed to misreadings of Gupta letters. Hence it seems to me, speaking with diffidence, that no light is thrown by Brāhmī on the age of the account or the MSS, and that, so far as the negative argument is of weight, Brāhmī writing played no part in the early MSS of these dynastic accounts. If this be so, the accounts passed from Kharoṣṭhī into the Gupta script.

v. If these explanations of these variations be reasonable and not fanciful, it appears that the Mt, Vā, and Vṣ all betray the fact that their accounts were originally copied from MSS written in Kharoṣṭhī. This script was in use till A.D. 300, or perhaps even half a century later[5]. This conclusion would, as regards the Mt and Vā, agree with the period assigned to them[6]. There is no further indication regarding the date of the Vṣ, and as Kharoṣṭhī MSS would have lasted some centuries, the Vṣ account might well be later and yet have been extracted from such a MS. There has been no opportunity of testing the Bḍ account in this way, because I have not been able to collate any MS of it; and the printed edition betrays no misreadings of this kind; but it is so closely like the Vā that the same conclusion probably holds good for it.

vi. Nor have I found any variations in the Bhāgavata which point to misreadings of Kharoṣṭhī or even of Brāhmī. I have noticed only two peculiarities which may perhaps be significant.

In the list of Andhra kings Hāla was succeeded by a king whose name consisted of four syllables, the best supported forms of which are Mantalaka or

[1] P. 23, note [9].

[2] P. 32, note [47]; p. 33, note [52].

[3] Perhaps through the Pkt form *Suṅga*; *s* carelessly made might be read as *t* in Kharoṣṭhī. The mistake is ancient as it is found so widely.

[4] P. 34, note [25]; *vṛtya* might be a modern misreading of *kṛtya*.

[5] JRAS, 1907, pp. 184-5.

[6] See Introdn. §§ 21-24.

Pattalaka[1]. The Bh calls them *Hāleya* and *Talaka* respectively, Hāleya ending the first half of a line and Talaka beginning the second half, thus:—

Aniṣṭakarmā Hāleyas Talakas tasya câtmajaḥ.

These two names seem to be mistakes for Hāla and Pattalaka, the *pa* being misread as *ya*. If so, the wrong division of these two names in the middle of a line seems only explicable on the supposition that the Bh prepared this verse from a bare prose list of kings and divided the letters of the two names incorrectly. If this suggestion has any validity, it would appear that the Bh could not have been composed till after the time when *y* approximated to *p* in shape, that is, after the 7th century A.D.

The other instance is the name of the Andhra king Āpīlaka, which appears in the Bh generally as *Civilaka*. The probable genesis of the changes in the name is suggested in p. 39, note [45], and the fact that seems significant here is that the compiler of the Bh account apparently drew his information from a Vṣ account in which he misread the initial *d* as *c*. This mistake could arise only in the Gupta script and not very well before the 7th century A.D.[2]

APPENDIX III

Janamejaya's Dispute with the Brahmans.

The dispute between the Paurava king Janamejaya[3] and Vaiśampāyana and other brahmans is narrated in *A*Mt *50*, 57[b]–65 and *A*Vā *99*, 250–256 and gives us an instance of how the text was revised[4]. The Mt version, which is the oldest, says the king made a successful stand against them for some time, but afterwards gave in and, making his son king, departed to the forest (according to custom); but the Vā version has abridged the inconvenient verses, and says he perished and the brahmans made his son king. This alteration may have been made (1) either in the Bhaviṣya when it was revised, and so passed into the Vāyu[5], or (2) in the Vāyu itself; but it is impossible to decide this point, because *e*Vā and the Bḍ, which would have thrown much light on it, have unfortunately lost this passage in lacunae. What is clear is that a story of royal opposition to brahmanic claims was modified early in the 4th century A.D. to maintain brahmanic prestige.

As regards MSS, *bdhp*Mt omit l. 6, read l. 9 instead of it and omit l. 9 from its place; *cefgjn*Mt omit l. 9; *k*Mt ll. 9, 20; *l*Mt ll. 6–9; *m*Mt reads l. 9 instead of l. 6, as well as in its proper place; *a*[1]*dh*Vā omit ll. 11–13; *b*Vā ll. 11–13, 18–20; *k*Vā ll. 14, 15; *l*Vā ll. 16, 17; and *efjm*Vā want the whole.

[1] P. 41, l. 2.
[2] See Bühler's Ind. Pal., Table IV.
[3] See p. 4, l. 2.
[4] See Introdn. §§ 24, 30.
[5] See Introdn. § 23.

Matsya.

Janamejayaḥ Parīkṣitaḥ
putraḥ parama-dhārmikaḥ [1]
brahmāṇaṁ [2] kalpayāmāsa
sa vai [3] vājasaneyakam [4]
sa [6] Vaiśampāyanenaiva [7]
śaptaḥ [9] kila [10] maharṣiṇā
na sthāsyatîha [12] durbuddhe [13]
tavaitad vacanam bhuvi
yāvat sthāsyasi tvaṁ loke [14]
tāvad eva [15] prapatsyati [16]
kṣatrasya vijayaṁ jñātvā [19]
tataḥ prabhṛti sarvaśaḥ
abhigamya sthitāś [20] caiva [21]
nṛpaṁ ca Janamejayam
tataḥ prabhṛti śāpena
kṣatriyasya tu yājinaḥ [25]
utsannā [26] yājino [27] yajñe [28]
tataḥ prabhṛti sarvaśaḥ
kṣatrasya [29] yājinaḥ [30] kecic [31]
chāpāt [32] tasya mahātmanaḥ

Vāyu.

Parikṣitas tu dāyādo
rājâsīj Janamejayaḥ [1]
brāhmaṇān kalpayāmāsa
sa vai vājasaneyikān [5]
aśapat taṁ [8] tadâmarṣād
Vaiśampāyana [11] eva tu
na sthāsyatîha durbuddhe
tavaitad vacanam bhuvi
yāvat sthāsyāmy ahaṁ loke
tāvan naitat [17] praśasyate [18]

abhitaḥ [22] saṁsthitaś [23] câpi
tataḥ sa [24] Janamejayaḥ

[1] This is l. 2 on p. 4.
[2] In *fh*Mt *brāhmaṇaṁ*, *j*Mt *brah°*.
[3] In *cn*Mt *makhe*; *j*Mt *makhaṁ*; *e*Mt *makha*.
[4] In *cfg*Mt *°yikam*; *k*Mt *°yake*.
[5] In a^3a^4dhklVā *°yakān*.
[6] In *h*Mt *taṁ*.
[7] In *cejn*Mt *°yane caiva*.
[8] So $a^1a^3a^4bdghl$Vā. Ca^2kVā *asapatnaṁ*.
[9] In *ben*Mt *saptaḥ*; *h*Mt *śaptaṁ*; *l*Mt *śapuḥ*.
[10] In *e*Mt *kali*.
[11] So Ca^2lVā: but $a^1a^3a^4bdghk$Vā *°yanam*.
[12] In *bd*Mt *°îti*.
[13] In *j*Mt *durbuddheḥ*.
[14] So $CGVa^2a^4$Mt: *l*Mt *vai loke*; *en*Mt *loke tvaṁ*; a^1a^3kMt *loke 'smin*; *c*Mt *lokeṣu*. But *bdfghmp*Mt *sthāsyāmy ahaṁ loke*, and *j*Mt crply.
[15] In *h*Mt *etat*.
[16] So $CGVa^2a^4$Mt; *mp*Mt *°paśyati*; *e*Mt *°yaśyati*; *d*Mt *°śatsyati*; *jk*Mt *°vatsyati*; a^1a^3cfghMt *°vartsyati*; *n*Mt *°raśyati*; *l*Mt *°vatsyasi*.
[17] In a^3Vā *naiva*.
[18] So Ca^1a^2lVā: but a^3a^4gVā *prapatsyati*; *bdhk*Vā *°paśyati*.
[19] In *fgj*Mt *jñātuṁ*: *bdhmp*Mt substitute l. 9 for this line; see note [26].
[20] In *bcdefgj*Mt *sthitaś*.
[21] *Caivaṁ* in *cen*Mt.
[22] In *bh*Vā †*pravi[ti]taḥ*; *d*Vā †*pracittitaḥ*.
[23] In *dh*Vā *sa sthitaś*.
[24] In *h*Vā †*taka sa*; *b*Vā †*takasaj*; *d*Vā †*tak sa*.
[25] In *cn*Mt *yāyinaḥ*; *bdfgjmp*Mt *vājinaḥ*; *h*Mt *rājinaḥ*.
[26] So *AC*Mt: *bdhp*Mt omit this line, see note [19], but *m*Mt has it here also. In *bd*Mt *uchannā*; *m*Mt *trasyannā* above, *utsannā* here; *h*Mt *utkalasya*.
[27] In *bdmp*Mt *vājino*; *h*Mt *rāj°*.
[28] In *dhmp*Mt *jajñe*.
[29] In *l*Mt *kṣatra[ya]sya*.
[30] In *l*Mt *yājinā*, *fg*Mt *vāj°*: *bdjmp*Mt *vājinaḥ*, *h*Mt *rāj°*.
[31] In *cen*Mt *kaścit*.
[32] In *dj*Mt *chāpāṁ*.

Matsya.

paurṇamāsena[33] haviṣā
iṣṭvā tasmin[34] prajāpatim
sa[35] Vaiśampāyanenaiva
praviśan[37] vāritas[38] tataḥ[39]
Parīksitaḥ suto 'sau vai[42]
Pauravo Janamejayaḥ
dvir aśvamedham āhṛtya[43]
mahā-vājasaneyakam[44]
pravartayitvā taṁ sarvam[46]
ṛṣir[47] vājasaneyakam[48]

vivāde[55] brāhmaṇaiḥ sārdham
abhiśapto vanaṁ yayau
Janamejayāc Chatānīkas
tasmāj jajñe sa vīryavān[58]
Janamejayaḥ[59] Śatānīkam
putraṁ rājye 'bhiṣiktavān[61].

Vāyu.

paurṇamāsyena haviṣā
devam iṣṭvā prajāpatim
vijñāya saṁsthito 'paśyat[36]
tadvadhiṣṭāṁ[40] vibhor makhe[41]
Parikṣit-tanayaś câpi
Pauravo Janamejayaḥ
dvir aśvamedham āhṛtya
tato vājasaneyakam[45]
pravartayitvā tad brahma
trikharvī[49] Janamejayaḥ
kharvam[50] Aśvaka[51]-mukhyānāṁ
kharvam[52] Aṅga-nivāsinām
kharvaṁ[53] ca Madhyadeśānāṁ
trikharvī[54] Janamejayaḥ
viṣādād[56] brāhmaṇaiḥ sārdham
abhiśastaḥ[57] kṣayaṁ yayau
tasya putraḥ Śatāniko
balavān satya-vikramaḥ
tataḥ sutaṁ[60] Śatānīkaṁ
viprās tam abhyaṣecayan[62].

33 In *d*Mt *pūrṇa*°.

34 In *f*Mt *dṛṣṭvā*°; *e*Mt *iṣṭvā te 'smin*; *d*Mt *i tasmin*; *n*Mt *iti 'smin*.

35 In a^2a^3*cekn*Mt *taṁ*; *j*Mt *te*; *h*Mt *tad*; *l*Mt *tad*[*e*].

36 In *g*Vā °*taḥ paśye* (for *paśyet*?).

37 In *f*Mt °*viśat*; *c*Mt °*viśen*; *d*Mt °*viśaṁ*.

38 In *h*Mt *nāvitas*.

39 In *mp*Mt *tutaḥ*.

40 Sic: read *tadvad dhiṣṭaṁ*?

41 In a^3a^4*g*Vā *mukhe*.

42 In *Cbdfp*Mt *so vai*, *cen*Mt *yo*°: *h*Mt *tataḥ śāpāt*.

43 In *j*Mt *ākṛtya*; *p*Mt *āruhya*.

44 So *Cbdhjlmp*Mt; *Aefgkn*Mt °*yakaḥ*, *c*Mt °*yikaḥ*.

45 In *g*Vā °*yikam*.

46 In *chj*Mt *tat*°; *fg*Mt *tān sarvān*.

47 So *bcdefgklnp*Mt: *ACm*Mt *ṛṣiṁ*; *j*Mt *ṛṣer*: *h*Mt reads this half line *svavarcā* (for *kharvaś ca*?) *Janamejayaḥ*.

48 In *c*Mt °*yikam*; *efgjkl*Mt °*yakaḥ*.

49 So *C*a^2a^4*bg*Vā; a^1Vā °*khārvī*: with dialectic variation of *kh* and *ṣ*, *gl*Vā °*ṣarvī*, a^3Vā °*ṣairvī*; *d*Vā °*svarcā*; *h*Vā °*svacī*.

50 In *gh*Vā *sarvam*.

51 In *g*Vā and one MS of *C*Vā *Aśmaka*.

52 In *g*Vā *sarvam*.

53 In *gh*Vā *sarvaṁ*.

54 In *d*Vā °*kharvā*; *h*Vā °*khabī*; *g*Vā °*ṣarvī*; *k*Vā °*ṣadyī*.

55 In *bdp*Mt °*dam*; *j*Mt °*do*.

56 In a^3*k*Vā *viṣādo*.

57 In *h*Vā °*śataḥ*.

58 In *j*Mt *su-v*°; after this line *j*Mt inserts Mt l. 6 on p. 4.

59 In *n*Mt °*jayā*; *h*Mt *tatas te tu*.

60 In *d*Vā *taṁ tu*.

61 In *h*Mt *viprā rāj*°, altered to *putraṁ tasyâbhyaṣecayat*.

62 In *dgh*Vā *tasyâbhy*°. *C*Vā *tam abhyaṣecayat*.

INDEX

This Index contains all the names mentioned in this work, except those that are obviously erroneous or untrustworthy. The following abbreviations are added to distinguish the names; and all names that are not so distinguished are the names of kings or princes :—

b = brahman.	*p* = people.
c = country.	*pat* = patronymic.
d = dynasty.	*q* = queen.
f = family.	*r* = river.
k = king *or* prince.	*t* = town.
mt = mountain.	